Eat-Em Up Frank and Diamond Tooth Gertie, Swift Water Bill and The Oregon Mare: These and hundreds of others pioneered the North for excitement, good times and gold.

They were men of swift action, courage and humor. They had to judge quickly and correctly. Their dogs could save a man's life in the pathless wilderness, or fall in a pack on his child. Indians were jovial comrades, skilled in survival, or treacherous murderers in the brush. Some of the women were dauntless as men, and others grew hardened and sophisticated in the parlor houses in town.

They were men qualified for their task, in a land that measured each at his worth. Most were over six feet tall. Few struck it rich. But there was a dangerous majesty in the North, where floating crystals of ice formed prisms in the cool sun, and froze a man's lungs in his chest, and nights were rent with the explosion of breaking ice or curtained in the silent splendor of the Northern Lights. They stayed for that, and for a way of life that was golden, where their most valuable asset was their fellow man, and their struggles were against the furious wild.

SOURDOUGH SAGAS

Edited by

Herbert L. Heller

Foreword by
Senator Ernest Gruening

BALLANTINE BOOKS • NEW YORK

© 1967 by Herbert L. Heller

Library of Congress Catalog Card Number: 66-25883

SBN 345-22620-8-125

First Printing: May 1972
Second Printing: December 1973

Printed in the United States of America

BALLANTINE BOOKS, INC.
210 East 50th Street, New York, N.Y. 10022

Contents

Foreword

THE LAST CENTURY has seen the greatest changes on earth recorded in the history of man. Man's inventions have annihilated distance, reducing weeks of travel to hours and reducing communication time from weeks to instantaneousness. In no other country has the transformation been as great as in the United States, and among these states none has witnessed greater change in the span of a lifetime than has Alaska.

Herbert Heller has gathered first-hand and hitherto unpublished accounts of life in Alaska that make these striking yet self-evident facts clear and fascinating. The Alaska of the 1880's was a remote, unexplored and unknown wilderness. It was truly "the last frontier," as it still is lovingly called by Alaskans. It was a stern and savage country, one that exacted its toll of life and limb from those hardy and adventurous spirits who sought to penetrate its vast and forbidding fastness. These adventurers represented in Alaska the final advance guard in the great American epic—the westward questing for greater freedom and greater opportunity. Alaska was indeed for America the last frontier in both time and space, its last great geographical and political discovery, its outermost reaches, its farthest west and farthest north. What is intriguing is that some few still living can recall those days, and that many more have heard these tales of adventure and hardship from the lips of those who lived them.

These narrators bring to life those of their fellow-pioneers who made the still largely unwritten history of those early days: "Jack" McQuesten (whose full name was Leroy Napoleon McQuesten) and his associates in the great Yukon River country, Al Mayo and Arthur Harper; Gordon Bettles, John Bremner, Frank Densmore, George Carmack, John Hughes, Joe Ladue, Captain James Carroll—traders, prospectors, miners, riverboatmen, mushers, trappers, explorers—in short, frontiersmen who had to do whatever was needed to survive; and the first missionaries, Bishop Bompas, Bishop Charles J. Seghers, Bishop Peter Trimble Rowe, and the Reverend John W. Chapman; as well as others whose names Alaskan "old-timers" will recall; and finally, a host of lesser characters, some of whom we know only by the picturesque semi-anonymous appellations of the frontier: Missouri Frank, Arkansas Jim, Buckskin Miller, Three-finger Jake, Dutch John, Calamity Bill, Caribou Jim, French Charley, and Indian Joe.

These men courageously trespassed upon the unknown. They battled elements more perilous than they had ever before known. They lived off the country, subsisting in no small measure on its abundant wildlife. They struggled, they drank, they gambled—both literally and figuratively—and not a few lost their gamble and perished.

Sourdough Sagas is a valuable contribution to the larger saga of America. It will appeal to countless Americans not wholly reconciled to the benefits of civilization—those who, while enjoying civilization's creature comforts, still hold a nostalgic longing for a vanished era in which men pitted themselves against nature's hazards and still yearn for the risks and challenges of an unspoiled wilderness. *Sourdough Sagas* is truth that vies with fiction—describing, as it does, the coarse, robust reality that inspired Jack London's immortal stories and Robert Service's poems—and is appropriately available as Alaska—changed, but retaining all of its scenic beauty and many of its frontier characteristics—celebrates the centennial of its purchase from Russia by the United States.

Ernest Gruening
United States Senator
for Alaska

Sourdough
Sagas

The Alaska Sourdoughs

Herbert L. Heller

As Yankees, Rebels, Hoosiers, Buckeyes, Pukes and others with similar nicknames ventured to the Far North, they underwent a change of name. Many of these men and women in Alaska became known as Sourdoughs.

"Sourdough" is a dough made of flour and water fermented without yeast for baking bread, cakes and flapjacks. The practice of keeping a "sourdough pot," or starter, going was widespread in pioneer Alaska, and is still prevalent in the Alaska of today. It is an economical and convenient way to prepare a meal, for the pots can be kept going indefinitely, and food can be prepared without much labor simply by adding water to the dough and then cooking. Some say the sourdough pot was introduced to the Alaskan miners by those who came from Ireland or perhaps it was carried into the Territory by the prospectors of earlier days in California. The sourdough pot was just as important to the old-timer as his sled and team of dogs; a diet of beans alone would soon have become unbearable. When a sourdough pot was lost, the owner could only hope he would soon meet a generous friend with an extra pot.

Just how the name Sourdough became attached to the gold rush pioneer is not known. When the vast horde of gold-seekers came into the Territory in the rush of '98, they found men who already lived in frontier camps and who already were veteran prospectors. These men, who had come north during the fifteen years prior to the big rush, were simply called "old-timers," and were respected and revered for their earlier adventures into the unknown land. But as Alaskan communities along the Yukon River became crowded with the newly arrived prospectors, it did not take long for a distinction to be drawn between these men and women and those already living in the Territory.

Today the title is not gained as easily as in former years. Although the distinction between old-timers and newcomers

1

was at first based simply on the date of arrival in the Territory, it was not long before the name Sourdough was given to anyone who remained in Alaska long enough to see the Yukon River or one of its tributaries freeze in the fall and thaw in the spring. As Alaskan winters are unusually long, this confined the honor to those who held promise of remaining and of truly becoming Alaskan residents.

As the year passed after the rush of '98, the requirements for becoming a Sourdough became more extensive. During the 1920's the name was given only to those who had met the above-mentioned requirement with the added stipulations of having bathed in an ice-covered Alaskan river or lake and of having kicked an Alaskan bear.

By the same token there was established a custom of calling all newcomers to Alaska by the name "Cheechako," an Indian word meaning "newly arrived" and pronounced "Chee-chaw-ko."

In the earliest camps justice was determined by meetings of all men. They generally elected a judge or presiding official, and after the stories of the plaintiff and defendant were heard, decisions were rendered by vote of the mass group. In general, the legal codes were unwritten, and when a party was found guilty, sentence was also passed by the group. In severe cases, the sentence was banishment from the camp and from Alaska. There is evidence that the miners readily gave way to law-enforcement officers, for the justice of the miners' meetings in some instances became warped by the influence of the vocal minority or by the indifference of the majority. In time this caused some miners to question the adequacy or fairness of such trials.

It has been said that lodges were formed in the gold camps because the need for miners' meetings was lessened by the presence of law-enforcement officers in the Territory, but this does not seem too plausible. Life in every gold camp included many social activities such as parties, dances and dramatics. The men spent hours sitting around their cabins swapping tales of daring and adventure based on their earlier experiences in the Far North. It seems likely that the organization of lodges appealed to them, for the social and recreational activities of these groups included the same kind of entertainment that the old-timers had carried on individually and informally.

Before the Pioneers of Alaska was organized, in 1902, other similar fraternal and social groups had been formed in some Alaskan and Yukon communities. The earliest lodge was the Sons of the Northwest, first organized at Sitka in 1887, but not in existence today. The oldest active organization is the Yukon Order of Pioneers, which was started at Forty Mile in 1894. The Arctic Brotherhood was formed aboard the steamer City of Seattle, en route to Alaska in 1899. Later-formed groups include the Order of Alaska Moose at Valdez; the Alaska Pioneers at Kodiak; and the '87 Pioneers Association at Juneau, started in 1908. Elks lodges also existed in many Alaskan mining camps in early days. These lodges seem to have been composed exclusively of Alaskan pioneers—unlike the ones earlier formed whose membership also included men from Canadian communities.

Today, those who qualify for membership in the Pioneers of Alaska Lodge include men and women who were in Alaska prior to 1930. This fraternal, intellectual and social order was first organized in Nome. Its chapters are called igloos and are established in most Alaskan communities.

The vastness of the land—the topography of the country, with the virtually impenetrable mountain ranges dividing the southern Alaskan coast from the valleys of the interior— gives one an impression of being *in* Alaska. The interior, with the spacious valley of the Yukon and its many tributaries, is an area isolated from the oceans and other parts of the world. To reach and leave the valleys of gold the original pioneers climbed rock-strewn mountain passes. Thus it was not long before the expression "outside" was used to designate the world beyond Alaskan borders.

Living in solitude and isolation, constantly alert to the dangers of the Arctic climate, many of the pioneers developed provincial traits. Strange as it may seem, the Golden Rule provided the Sourdoughs with guidance in most of their relationships with their fellow men in this land of gold. This principle played a great part in and immeasurably influenced the life of the people in Alaska for more than half a century. Its observance was not entirely a matter of necessity, as might be assumed from the dangers of living in a vast and unpopulated wilderness. Most pioneers were sincerely concerned for the welfare of their fellow men and were interested in looking out for them—knowing that they in turn might need the same attention some day.

For some of the older pioneers the passing of years brought confusion of memory, shyness born of living alone too long, a high degree of nostalgia, feelings of intense loyalty to

Alaska, and an attitude that would not tolerate challenge as they told their cherished stories of past days.

Almost all Sourdoughs were highly individualistic in their ways of living and in their ideas, and these were fixed and cemented by years of living alone in remote places. Several characteristics typified the early Sourdoughs. Exceptional sentiment was one. This is seen in the unusual amount of poetry written by these men in moments of reflection as they tried to express their feelings about the North. Another was ingenuity. Living without ready access to stores, they did not possess many niceties of life, and this led to numerous instances of ingenious improvisation. One oft-told tale reveals an incident of this kind. This story has been repeated for over fifty years in Alaska, with each story-teller adding to and embellishing the tale to suit his fancy and imagination, but the basic facts remain unaltered:

> Old Paddy Meehan—or it might have been old man Smith—was living some distance from Fairbanks, working his claim throughout the winter, when without warning his teeth began to go bad. This imposed a real problem, for he was too far away to easily make the trip to town by dog team—even if he had been willing to take the time. After the situation became grave with the loss of his last teeth, he came upon an ingenious solution—that of making a set of false teeth out of the gold nuggets which he had saved. After careful filing and fashioning, he was able to complete a set of gold teeth which he fastened on homemade plates of soft tin, made from kitchen utensils. This made a workable set which lasted for many months but unfortunately became useless as the gold wore down. As it was plainly too expensive to fashion another set of gold teeth, he looked for yet another solution.
>
> Paddy had enjoyed a variety of wild game meat during the winter—everything from rabbits to mountain sheep—and shortly after facing his second dilemma he was lucky enough to kill a bear near his cabin. After dressing the bear and placing the meat in his cache, he thought of another idea to provide himself with teeth. Taking some teeth from the skull of a mountain sheep, he fastened them on the dental plates and then placed the bear's teeth on the plates as molars. It is said he then ate the bear with its own teeth.

Other versions of this tale explain that this unusual set of teeth was later recovered by a visiting dentist from New York

City, who took them back with him and put them on display in a metropolitan museum.

Storytelling was an evening pastime with the Sourdoughs. Confined to their small, overheated cabins during the long winter nights, there was little else for them to do except to play cards. Many of these men became famous for their ability to relate the unique stories of early Alaskan life. One of their favorites was that of three miners working a claim north of Fairbanks who stayed out a little too long one fall only to be caught in the first snowfall and cold snap:

> Knowing that they were not supplied for a winter on their claim, the three men hastily loaded up their sleds with a few tools and possessions and took off by dog team for town. Having delayed their departure until afternoon, they were soon caught by nightfall and lost their way in the blinding snowstorm. As is often the case, the end of the falling snow saw a severe drop in the temperature, and it was not long until one of the men froze to death from exposure. Not wanting to delay their trip, the two others put his body on the sled and continued their wanderings, but very shortly the second Sourdough also succumbed to the subzero temperature and froze to death.
>
> The third miner, knowing he was in a tragic situation and that he could not take long to dispose of the bodies of his two companions without endangering his own life, pondered the matter. He could not break the hard-frozen ground, and he did not want to put the bodies in snow graves because they would thaw in the spring and be exposed to ravenous animals. For the same reason, he considered it impractical to place the bodies in trees; although safe from animals, when thawed in the spring they would drop to the ground. As his situation became increasingly critical, he reached a plan born of desperation. Clearing snow from a small piece of ground, he stood his frozen friends on their heads, sharpened them with an axe and drove them into the ground like stakes, ingeniously and effectively giving them a comfortable burial.

Following the purchase of Alaska from Russia in 1867, very little was known about the new possession. A few government publications contained geographical, geological and anthropological data; and a few books were written by men who had traveled the inhabited part of the Territory. Most of these accounts, however, were not available to the public.

In spite of this, interest ran high and newspapers carried articles from time to time about Alaska. In 1885, B. K. Cowles, who was the Commissioner for Alaska to the American Exposition in New Orleans, published a small pamphlet of "interesting and reliable information" on Alaska. It also contained the provisions of the Organic Act of the Territory, passed in 1884, which provided Alaska with its first civil government. This pamphlet was his method of replying to the "thousands of questions and dozens of letters" which he received asking for information about the new acquisition of the United States. In this pamphlet he tried to answer the question "Where is Alaska?" as well as to describe the means of transportation and routes to the North. He said:

> We will suppose your starting point to be east of the Rocky Mountains. You will go to Portland, Oregon, undoubtedly by the Northern Pacific Railroad. That line offers the inducements of through trains from St. Paul with a deservedly popular Dining Car service. The ride from St. Paul to the Pacific Coast on the N.P.R.R. is replete with interest and speed. At Portland you can take the steamer between the first and third day of each month, direct to all points in Alaska.

After describing the trip north to Sitka, he concluded with the following information:

> There is a paucity of domestic animals in Alaska, as yet, five mules, two horses, and not to exceed a dozen cows constitute the entire outfit in that line, in the southeastern portion of the Territory. At Sitka there are a few chickens that sell for $1 each; eggs bring 75 cents per dozen and milk 80 cents a gallon. There is good grazing on islands in the Sitka Harbor and a remunerative industry might be worked up raising vegetables, milk and poultry for the Sitka and Juneau markets.

TABLE OF RATES

St. Paul to Sitka	$153.50
St. Paul to Portland	93.50
St. Paul to Portland, Emigrant	53.50
Sleeping car fare, one berth from St. Paul to Portland	15.00
Meals on Dining Car, each	.75
Portland to Tacoma by rail	7.00
Tacoma to Port Townsend by boat	3.75

Tacoma to Victoria by boat	4.75
Meals on boat on Puget Sound, each	.50
Portland to Port Townsend by steamer	10.00
Portland to Victoria by steamer	10.00
Portland to any point in Alaska	60.00
Port Townsend or Victoria to any point in Alaska	50.00

The fare on the Alaska steamer includes stateroom and meals.

N.B.: The N.P.R.R. furnish free of charge sleeping accommodations to the purchasers of emigrant tickets, the purchaser furnishing his own bedding.

The Northern Pacific Railroad had been extended westward to Portland only slightly more than a year before this information was provided for the public, and it was not until 1887 that its lines were further extended to Seattle. Some pioneers traveled west on the Canadian Pacific Railroad, which had its western terminus at Port Moody near Vancouver.

The search for gold in Alaska was not confined to men of any race, color or creed nor to those of any particular walk of life. Some men came endowed with wealth, others without sufficient funds to pay for their way into the Territory. Many came with skills for making a living—trades, professions, and experience at common labor. When gold was not readily found, many of these men fell back on these skills for survival.

Most gold-seekers came with excessive supplies—more than they could carry or afford to have packed into the interior. It is said this worked to the benefit of the inhabitants of the river towns in which the newcomers disposed of food and baggage they did not need. Very few men traveled alone on the gold rush trails. Though they may have left Seattle without company, they soon attached themselves to others making the same trek. Some came as agents of private financiers from their hometown or state, and others came as a part of organized companies supported by monied interests seeking to gain wealth in Alaska. Others were just wilderness wanderers attracted by the prospect of ready wealth.

The later gold rush pioneers of 1898 had more travel information available. Several books were written by men who had already been to Alaska, reporting what they had seen and giving advice on how to prepare for the country and climate —as well as how to mine for gold.

The government explorations of the 1890's were reported in documents and books, and in national magazines such as *The Century* and *Harper's*. Lieutenant Schwatka's accounts of his trips along the Yukon River were published in book form for popular reading. It is doubtful that many of those men going north benefited greatly from these publications, for this was a time of changing prices and conditions of living. In Seattle, pocket-size maps and pamphlets were available in the stores. In addition, West Coast newspapers as well as those in Chicago and New York printed Klondike editions with information helpful to the gold-seeker. The Klondike edition of the *Chicago Daily Tribune* gave extensive information gained from a party of reporters sent to the gold rush regions in the summer of 1897. Practically all of the material available on Alaska was written in an optimistic vein and said little to discourage men from venturing north.

The Alaska trading companies did their part to encourage men and women to come north. In 1898 the North American Transportation and Trading Company published a booklet titled *Alaska and the Gold Fields of the Yukon, Koyukuk, Tanana-Klondike and Their Tributaries.* This contained highly useful information for the inexperienced prospectors. One section dealt with ideas for blazing trails and making camps in the wilderness and contained the following:

Hints for Trail and Camp

The following bits of suggestion were based on the experience of the Klondike pioneers and will apply at least in part to all Alaskan goldseekers:

On the road to the gold diggings, don't waste a single ounce of anything, even if you don't like it. Put it away, and it will come in handy when you do like it.

If it is ever necessary to cache a load of provisions, put all articles next to the ground which would be most affected by heat, providing at the same time dampness will not affect their food properties to any great extent. After piling your stuff, load it over carefully with heavy rocks. Take your compass bearings, and also note in your pocketbook some landmarks nearby, and also the direction in which they look from your cache—i.e., make your cache, if possible, come between exactly north and south of two given prominent marks. In this way, even though covered by snow, you can locate "your existence." Don't forget that it is so.

Shoot a dog, if you have to, behind the base of the skull, a horse between the ears, ranging downward. Press the trigger of your rifle; don't pull it; don't catch hold of the barrel when thirty degrees below is registered. Watch out for getting snow in your barrel. If you do, don't shoot it out.

A little dry grass or hay in the inside of your mitts, next your hands, will promote great heat, especially when it gets damp from the moisture of your hands. After the mitts are removed from the hands, remove the hay from the mitts and dry it. Failing that, throw it away.

If by any chance you are traveling across a plain (no trail) and a fog comes up, or a blinding snowstorm, either of which will prevent your taking your bearings, camp and don't move for anyone until all is clear again.

Keep all your drawstrings on clothing in good repair. Don't forget to use your goggles when the sun is bright on snow. A fellow is often tempted to leave them off. Don't you do it.

If you build a sledge for extreme cold, don't use steel runners. Use wooden and freeze water on same before starting out. Repeat the process, if it begins to drag and screech.

If you cannot finish your rations for one day, don't put back any part, but put into your personal canvas outfit bag; you will need it later on.

Take plenty of tow for packing possible cracks in your boat; also two pounds of good putty, some canvas, and if possible, a small can of tar or white lead.

Establish camp rules, especially regarding the food. Allot rations; those while idle should be less than when at work, and also pro rata during heat and cold.

Keep your furs in good repair. One little slit may cause you untold agony during a march in a heavy storm. You cannot tell when such will be the case.

Travel as much on clear ice towards your goal as possible in the spring. Don't try to pull sledges over snow, especially if soft or crusty.

Be sure, during the winter, to watch your foot gear carefully. Change wet stockings before they freeze, or you may lose a toe or foot.

In building a sledge use lashing entirely. Bolts and screws rack a sledge to pieces in rough going, while lashing will "give."

Keep the hood of your kooletah back from your head, if not too cold, and allow the moisture from your body to escape that way.

When your nose is bitterly cold, catch hold of it and pull and squeeze it.

Don't try to carry more than forty pounds of stuff the first day.

If your furs get wet, dry them in a medium temperature. Don't hold them near the fire.

No man can continuously drag more than his own weight. Remember that this is a fact.

In cases of extreme cold at toes and heel, wrap a piece of fur over each extremity.

Keep your sleeping bag clean. If it becomes inhabited, freeze the inhabitants out.

Remember success follows economy and persistency on an expedition like yours.

White snow over a crevasse if hard, is safe. Yellow or dirt color, never.

Don't eat snow or ice. Go thirsty until you can melt it.

Shoot a deer behind the shoulder or in the head.
Choose your bunk as far from tent door as possible.
Keep a fire-hole open near your camp.

These suggestions were born of experiences of the Sourdoughs, most of whom were in no way hesitant to advise any Cheechako. In general, the Sourdoughs were inclined to be highly intolerant of those who did not listen and heed. When a newcomer got into difficulty, he often found the experienced Sourdoughs more critical of his ignorance than sympathetic with his dilemma.

All these hints were good advice, but the writer failed to suggest ways to carry on the incessant warfare with the Alaskan mosquitoes and flies. A reporter for the *Chicago Daily Tribune* had the following to say regarding Alaskan insects:

> The cold in winter is not the only climatic drawback. In summer the people are beset by flies and mosquitoes. The torture inflicted by these pests is something no one can do justice to in a descriptive way. Strong men have been known to lie down and cry like babies as a result of the bites. There is seldom a breath of air during the summer and to wear even a piece of cheesecloth as a protection against the flies and mosquitoes is unbearable on account of the heat.
>
> The Arctic mosquito is said to take the prize of all the mosquitoes in the world. He is filled with a ferocity which almost surpasses belief. He is big, active, and does not know what cowardice means. He will attack you alone or in company with friends. He travels in such numbers at times that the heavy sky is said to be darkened. There is no relief from him on the land and even out in the middle of the streams he pursues his daring quest for blood. It is even related that these bloodthirsty insects have attacked bears and stung them to blindness. Many a poor bruin is said to have fallen by the wayside from an encounter with this pest, starving to death after the sight has been lost. One miner in describing the mosquito said: "He is not large enough to fry and therefore utterly useless." The average hungry miner looks at the Arctic mosquito with tender eye from a food standpoint until he finds his legs are not large enough to furnish a stew.

Robert Sheldon, who is famous for having made and driven the first automobile in Alaska, has entertained countless visitors by telling the following experiences of the first gold prospectors in the Kantishna River area. The first of these men to enter this region northwest of Mt. McKinley found it impossible to work because of the mosquitoes, which unrestrainedly penetrated both the headnets and bednets. Forced to abandon their prospecting, they returned to Fairbanks determined to solve the problem. The following summer a committee of men again entered the area to study the life of the mosquitoes in that part of Alaska. Returning to town after a couple of months, they reported that the mosquitoes were traveling in swarms or groups of five. When encountering a man they would land on the netting, four would seize the separate side of the webbing and extend it so the fifth could enter and get a bite. After discussion with other prospectors, the committee decided the best solution was to order mosquito netting with five-sided webbing. This was done and their prospecting efforts in the Kantishna continued without difficulty. Years later a research study by scientists from the state university confirmed the fact that the mosquitoes from this region were unusual in that they traveled in groups.

Although the severity of the Alaskan winters was dreaded, most Sourdoughs found the coming of the cold weather a blessed relief from the vicious and never-ending attacks of mosquitoes and flies. The flies were called "no-see-ums" by the Indians as they were of a variety so small that a person was unaware of their presence until bitten, and their bite left a persistent and annoying itch.

The life of the early settlers in Alaska has long been considered one of lawlessness and crime, struggle and hardship. *Sourdough Sagas* has been compiled to show that this was not entirely true. Most of the bona fide pioneers were basically hard-working, honest, decent middleclass men and women—albeit somewhat disillusioned or naive regarding their chances for finding and retaining fortunes in gold.

Relatively few of these gold rush prospectors took time to keep diaries; however, in their later years some were prompted to write of their experiences. Others wrote home to their families or to hometown newspapers; thus the records of their experiences were stored away in family attics or published.

The stories in *Sourdough Sagas* were kept alive through the foresight of one man who saw the importance to future generations of the written records of the earliest pioneers. This man was Lynn Smith, who came to Alaska as a gold-seeker in the late 1890's and remained to become U. S. Marshal in the Fourth Judicial District of Alaska some 30 years later. Before his death, in 1933, he collected manuscripts from the few remaining Sourdoughs of the earlier gold rush period. Some sent him handwritten manuscripts; others related their life stories to him, which he then wrote into the form of a journal or diary.

Life in the interior of Alaska in that early day was comparatively simple. Since the few major disasters, unusual happenings or deviations from the law stood out in the minds of the Sourdoughs, such events are described in more than one account in this book.

Neither names of people or places nor dates have been changed in these stories. Occasional editing was necessary to help the reader better understand some of the pioneers' expressions that resulted from lack of literacy.

Although nothing is known of the background of D. A. Murphy, Jim Bender, and Gordon Bettles, they are mentioned in most of the histories of Alaska as men who were trading and prospecting throughout the interior during the 1880's and 1890's.

Frank Buteau tells of his origin in his account. His whereabouts in Alaska during the first part of the twentieth century is unknown, but he resided in Fairbanks during the 1920's with a daughter who died sometime during these years. Buteau died in the 1930's.

Henry Davis was born in Rose Bud, Montana, located just west of Billings, on the Northern Pacific Railroad. Lynn Smith considered him a typical pioneer and said:

> So few people have had the privilege of knowing and talking with one of the old-timers, men who were adventurers, generally speaking, and who did not have a care, who lived from day to day with full assurance that they could combat any emergency that might arise. We offer the life of Henry Davis as told to Lynn Smith, United States Marshal. The first few years of this account are taken from the Davis diary, and the balance from his memory.
>
> We suggest in following him you refer to a map of Alaska; possibly you can imagine the hardships and hard work, for these events were lived in days when snowshoes and dog teams in winter, poling boats in the

summertime were about the only modes of transportation with the exception of an occasional steamer on the Yukon River. The names and other references in this narrative are true names, well-known characters who have crossed their last divide.

It is no blot on the memory of Henry Davis that Lynn Smith said he might not be remembered by the name Henry, "as he had worked so hard he was very stooped and was always spoken of as Broken Assed Davis."

John A. Clark was born on April 26, 1879, in Stockton, California. After completing his schooling there, he attended and graduated from a Chicago law school and for two or three years practiced law in his hometown. Clark went to Alaska in 1906, but returned to marry his Stockton sweetheart, Jeanette Rugh Drury, whom he then took north to live in Fairbanks. Two sons were born to them—John Drury Clark and Warren H. Clark, both of whom are living today. John A. Clark died in 1931, after spending twenty-five years in Fairbanks, where he was a much-respected lawyer, and prominent in the civic and social life of the community. Of the Sourdoughs whose stories are related here, Mr. Clark was the only one who had an education beyond that of the public schools.

As is evident from his stories of life in Fairbanks in 1906, Mr. Clark was shrewd and humorous and, like a great number of the early Alaskans, held in disdain many of the conventionalities of life.

Robert Lynn Smith was born in 1871, on St. Patrick's Day, the son of Robert Barclay Smith and Catherine Taylor Smith of New Castle, Indiana. As a youth he was apprenticed to a local jeweler. Having mastered the trade, he accepted an offer of a position in Rockville, Indiana, for one year and then moved to a better position in this work in Anderson, a community nearer his hometown and friends. While living in Anderson, he first heard of the gold strike in Alaska. A friend showed him a letter that had been written from there, reporting that gold was found at the roots of the grass and that the writer had taken a fabulous fortune out of the ground in one summer of work. All of this information was accepted without question, and soon he and three others went to the gold fields.

Lynn Smith's departure from Anderson was quite a social

affair. The night before his train left he was surprised by a dance given in his honor by the Columbia Club. The program consisted of twenty-six numbers by the Van Riper and Vance Mandolin Club, and the dancing lasted until one o'clock in the morning.

The following day the *Anderson Bulletin* reported the auspicious departure:

> The sound of fife and drum, the scene of young men marching south and one shouldering an old musket this morning led a stranger to remark that a company of volunteers was leaving to quiet the Spaniards around Havana. For such service every mother's son in that procession would respond if necessary, but the company halted at the Big Four station. The Columbia Club was escorting a member, Lynn Smith, to the train. He was headed for Alaska.
>
> Lynn is 25 years old, unmarried, and has a great big heart, and as one of his girl friends said, "It was just too bad," that Lynn was leaving alone for the land of horrors and gold for a test of fate vs. fortune. But Lynn was determined. He used to read what Horace Greeley said and he had decided that this venture should be a chapter in his life, and he left as game as any young man could, when he reviewed home and friends and affairs of heart.
>
> The 10:30 train carried him away.
>
> The club boys gave Lynn a send-off that ought to comfort him when he finally leaves earth for the Klondike. As the train approached, the drum corps set in on "The Girl I Left Behind Me." John Rust, as military escort, with gun in hand, accompanied Lynn to a seat in the car, and then there were cheers and exchanges of well wishes. A big card placed on the car vestibule read, "Off for the Klondike."
>
> Among the many friends at the station were some of Lynn's young lady friends, whose feelings were expressed in crystal tears, and Lynn's heart got out of place and clogged articulation for a time. . . .

The incident related in the last paragraph of this report became one of Lynn Smith's favorite stories in his later years.

The train carried him to Chicago, where he changed to the Chicago and St. Paul, which he rode across the western plains and mountains to Seattle. With him were Jasper Rozelle, J. H. Padgett and O. S. Judd. Judd, an older man, assumed the task of purchasing supplies for one year. This task delayed him, and he did not depart with the others; in fact, he never reached Alaska, although he did start north on a boat. On reaching Vancouver, B. C., Judd decided the trip was too strenuous for a man of his age and turned back, leaving on the boat the supplies to be delivered to St. Michael for transshipment up the Yukon River to Rampart, the ultimate destination of the younger men.

Crowded conditions in the Dawson gold fields, as well as glowing reports of the Rampart region described in a booklet of the North American Transportation and Trading Company, led the three men to proceed downriver to this community. In Rampart Smith joined two newcomers from New York state, Harlan Belden and Volney Richmond, in constructing and selling log cabins. Years later Richmond became president of the influential Northern Commercial Company, whose trading posts furnished food, clothing and supplies to the populace of interior Alaskan towns for several decades.

Lynn Smith's life in Alaska took him to the scene of many gold strikes. For a short time in 1900 he was at Nome, but missed the major discovery of gold by a few months. In 1907 he moved to the Fairbanks area and settled in Chena, where he was elected the first mayor of the town—only to find that it involved no pay and that council meetings were held infrequently and ineffectively. This was his only stab at local politics.

After several fruitless years of labor, he moved to the Hot Springs strike where he stayed until 1912. He then joined the rush to Ruby, where he began a business in his jeweler's trade. Here he stayed until 1920, alternately mining and plying his trade. In 1922 he was appointed deputy U. S. Marshal at Flat, and in 1926 was commissioned the U. S. Marshal at Fairbanks—a position he held until his death, in 1933.

In every community where he lived Lynn Smith was a respected citizen. In those outposts of civilization he was always actively engaged in parties, dances, dramatics and bridge playing—as well as church and lodge activities. In 1916 he had a piano shipped to Ruby from the Krell-French Piano Company in his hometown in Indiana. Although he was unable to play a piano, this instrument served as a means of adding gaiety to many parties and music for many church services.

Throughout his life he was a member of the Presbyterian Church, and his letters tell of frequent attendance at the services of the Presbyterian missionaries in the gold camps. Where he resided at any length, he was a faithful member of the small church choirs.

Lynn Smith never married. The following story explains part of his reason for remaining single:

> The men in the north have been and now and always have been pickins for the women, and it was the custom for them when leaving to get some present from almost everybody.
>
> This happened to a friend. He promised the lady a nugget and asked me if he could get one from my collection, and I brought out the poke and picked out about twenty of them and said, "I will take her these and let her take her choice."
>
> He dolled up and about two o'clock left for her home. About four-thirty he came back and walked straight for the office. When six o'clock came, I said, "Are you ready for supper?" and he replied, "No. Go ahead and don't wait for me." Nothing said. He showed up about eleven o'clock the next morning and went straight for the office, where I could notice him walking back and forth with his eyes on the floor—in a deep study. He finally walked out and stopped in front of me and turned and said, "Smith, tell me what is the matter with me, anyway?" I asked him what he meant and he said, "What makes me so easy with these women?" and followed this up with, "You know those nuggets I took yesterday? Well, she was to have her choice and I went down to see her. She gave me the glad hand, took my coat and hat, hung them up, and we chatted for about a half hour and I thought the time was ripe for the presentation so took the paper out and began to open it. I said, 'I brought your nugget down, Mrs. N.' and she just beamed with delight and said, 'Oh, are these for me, Mr. Maker? Oh thank you, thank you, THANK YOU.' And I just said in a weak voice, 'Yes, those are for you,' and she took the whole works. I'll pay you for them." He did—over $100 worth. Many is the time since then it would have looked big to him, for it has been coffee and doughnuts many times for him when he had a $10 appetite. Oh the North country is a hard country.

At a few times in his life, Lynn Smith acquired fairly large sums of money but was never able to retain them nor to invest them successfully. His exceptional generosity to friends in need made him a much-loved Alaskan Sourdough. The failure to strike riches never concerned him other than to cause a feeling of disappointment, for as he often said in later years, he was never without food and shelter or a means of obtaining them.

The last eight years of his life were spent in Fairbanks as the U. S. Marshal of the Fourth Judicial District of Alaska. This was a vast region—larger than most existing states. Alaska had enacted a dry law in 1917, and most of the duties of Marshal Smith were connected with stopping the manufacture and sale of illegal liquor. His successful efforts filled the jails and detention houses to overflowing. Although this did not make him popular among a certain set of men, he was respected for his efforts and recognized as doing his duty impartially. Two weeks before Lynn Smith died, in 1933, Herbert Hoover wrote to him:

> Before leaving this office, I wish to express to you the appreciation I have for the devoted public service you have given these past years. That service has, and deserves to have, the gratitude of your community. And I want you to know of my gratitude for the friendship you have extended to me.

After his death, many of Lynn Smith's friends and acquaintances paid tribute to his character and personality. Sam Kincaid, a deputy marshal at Flat and close associate, gave insight into his regard for his fellow men and his fondness for children when he wrote:

> Lynn Smith had no enemies, the children always called him Lynn and he was one of them. They would climb on his spacious lap, put their arms around his neck and they never went away empty handed. People who were in distress or trouble came and told him their troubles, he comforted them and often went down in his pocket to help them. . . . Many a pioneer who has grown too old to work and is broke will miss Lynn for he had many pensioners. Alaska has sustained an irreparable loss—Lynn lived like a man and he died like a man, leaving a reputation in Alaska that will stand as a living monument to the state of Indiana from whence he came. . . .

New Castle, Indiana, his hometown, was always a fond memory to Lynn Smith. He spent much time and money on trips back to see his parents, sister and brothers. A boyhood friend, later an editor of a hometown newspaper, expressed in an editorial how his New Castle friends regarded him:

> . . . We knew Lynn Smith: knew him in our boyhood; knew him in our mature years; loved him. He was our hero in those youthful days of dreams of adventure because he dared do what every red-blooded boy dreamed of doing. . . . Up through the years he has been to all of us, who knew him, New Castle's son of the great far north.

The warmth, understanding, honesty, and integrity praised by these writers may not be revealed in Lynn Smith's accounts of his experiences. However, one characteristic—the one best remembered by all who met and knew him—is much in evidence: a keen, vigorous and earthy sense of humor.

Frontier Incidents at Juneau

D. A. Murphy

I CAME UP on the Steamer Idaho with Captain Carroll Master and landed in Juneau on July 10, 1883. At that time there was only a monthly steamer. Silver Bowl Basin was the placer mining center, and on the Silver Bowl Basin trail about two miles from Juneau on Gold Creek there was a man who had a saloon.

There was no civil law in Alaska, as it was a district and we governed ourselves by miners' meetings. At the head of each meeting we had what was called an executive committee. I can only remember the names of two of the committee of the meeting at that time. One was N. A. Fuller, who was well-known here, and the other was Carl Kohler, the head of the Northwest Trading Company at that time in Juneau.

It developed that three Indians who had been drinking had gone up to this saloon on Gold Creek and demanded liquor, which was refused them. They then beat out the brains of the saloonkeeper with a bung starter. The alarm was sounded and the Indians captured, and they admitted to killing this man and were placed in jail, with an old man in charge as jailer.

He had confidence in the Indians and, before they could be brought to trial, in doing something around the jail he laid down his Colt 45 pistol and one of the Indians took the pistol and shot him. Another old-timer who had been drinking heard the shot and rushed up there as the Indians came out of the jail and they shot and killed him also. The Indians then took to the woods and we started out to hunt them.

We found one Indian and he was brought to trial before the miners' meeting. An attorney for the prosecution was appointed and one for the defense. A jury of twelve men was named. A night session of the court was held and the Indian admitted everything and was of course convicted and sentenced to be hung. The next day the scaffold was erected on the beach.

It just so happened that just as we hung this Indian the monthly steamer came in and tied up to the wharf and of course the people on it could see what happened. There were quite a number of tourists aboard and between sixty and seventy white men in Juneau at that time. So that we would all assume equal responsibility for hanging the Indian we all pulled on the rope.

The search continued for the other two Indians. Three white men searching together suddenly came upon the Indian who had the revolver. He attempted to get the gun in action but a 44 Winchester bullet struck him between the eyes. Later on that same afternoon the third Indian was taken. We then decided that as long as they had pleaded guilty it was useless to hold another meeting, so we hung the last Indian on the same scaffold on the beach. It so happened as we hung him the steamer left the wharf, and upon the return of the next steamer we had clippings from all over the world saying that we were hanging Indians just for fun.

This was in 1883. Some bogus gold dust was in circulation and a man named Charlie Forrest, a machinist, was accused of making this and circulating it. The gold dust was brass filings and chippings. A miners' meeting was called and they tried him for circulating it. Several ounces were produced as evidence and placed in a glass. Acid was poured in on it and the result was a dense cloud of black smoke arising out of the glass.

The meeting was held in the dance hall and was packed with miners and as it was summer the door was open. I went in with my dog which was quite a fighting dog and met another dog. The result was a real dog fight. It was so good that the miners forgot their meeting and went out and bet on which dog would win. After the dog fight, the meeting resumed and Forrest was acquitted.

In 1885 there was lots of work at the mine digging the glory hole and the local Indians wanted this work but a great many Chinese had been employed by the company and there was trouble between the natives and the Chinese over this matter. A citizens' committee held a meeting and decided they would ship the Chinese out of the country and it was a beautiful sight and one of the few days when the channel was smooth the day it was done.

There were at least fifty large Indian canoes or war boats

propelled by the Indians with paddles and they were loaded with the entire Chinese population, with the exception of one. The exception was China Joe, who was a baker in Juneau and who had at one time saved the miners in the Cassiar district from starvation. When he later died he had the largest funeral of anyone ever buried in Juneau. The Chinese upon being landed in Juneau were placed aboard a schooner and deported to Puget Sound. Incidentally, in connection with the removal of the Chinese there was no rioting.

APPROXIMATE DISTANCES
To Dawson via St. Michael's and the Yukon River by the Water Route

	Miles
Seattle to St. Michael's	2,500
St. Michael's to Klondike (Dawson)	1,700
Total	4,200

Via Dyea and Chilkoot Pass

Seattle to Dyea	1,000
Dyea to Dawson (Klondike)	550
Total	1,550

Via Stikeen River

Seattle to Wrangel	750
Wrangel to Telegraph Creek	150
Telegraph Creek to Teslin Lake	150
Teslin Lake to Klondike	550
Total	1,600

Distances of the Yukon

From Dyea to the Summit	18
Lake Lindeman	9
Foot of Lindeman	12
One-Mile River	1
Foot of Bennett	25
Three-Mile River	8
Tagish Lake	20
Four-Mile River	4

Foot of Marsh Lake	19
Canon Head	26
Head of Rapids	2
Takhena River	10
Lake Le Barge	15
Foot of Lake Le Barge	44
Hootalinqua River	32
Big Salmon	33
Little Salmon	36
Five Fingers	69
Rink Rapids	6
Pelly River	58
White River	96
Stuart River	10
Sixty-Mile Post	20
Indian Creek	18
Klondike	43
Fort Reliance	6
Forty-Mile Post	34
Circle City	270

From Dyea to Circle City   931

FROM: The *Chicago Daily Tribune*—Tribune Extra Klondike
      Edition, 1898.

Recollections

Henry Davis

ON MAY 14, 1884, I arrived in Alaska on the Steamer Idaho at Juneau. It was a very small boat and ran close to the mountains where we landed at a small wharf. My partner and I went uptown. It was a rough place, mud and stumps and no sidewalks, and not many people living here. It didn't look very bright, but you can't tell a mining camp at the first look.

We got back to the boat and got our things ashore to look for a place to stop. There were no hotels, but we rented a cabin from Pete Bolger, the blacksmith, on the water front. We couldn't find a bakeshop so bought some eggs, bacon, canned milk, tea and coffee at Brady's Store. We then looked around some more for work, as we were not well supplied with money. After resting up, we went over to Douglas Island to see about getting a job—hiring an Indian to take us across the channel.

We walked to the mill, saw the boss and got a job working around the mill on night shift. We worked at this until August, then the miners went on strike because the mining company hired Chinamen, so we had to stop work and went back over to Juneau to stay until the trouble was settled. We stayed around two weeks, but there was no sign of settlement so we went to work for Frank Starr in the woods until November, but we had to stop work as there was too much rain.

After stopping this work, we saw Joe Woods, who had some ground on Montana Creek about sixteen miles up the coast. Then we hired an Indian and went with him in a canoe and packed grub to the Creek. The sluice boxes were already on the ground ready to put up. Having packed over to the claim, we started cleaning out the drain and putting up the boxes. We shoveled a week's digging and cleaned it up. It did not look like very much to us, but Woods seemed to think it was all right. He took it to camp, dried it and blew

24

out the black sand, and then weighed it and found he had
five ounces worth $90, which was not so bad for our first
mining.

After that it was not so good, as we worked three more
weeks and got sixteen and a half ounces, so we quit work
and went back to Juneau. It was still raining hard and as we
happened on an Indian we gave him $5 to take the three of
us back.

It was then Christmas week and the trouble was all over
in the mines so, thinking we might get our jobs back, tried
to see the mill boss but were unable to do so. I then went to
Brady's Store for some things. He asked me where I was
working and I said, "Nowhere." He said, "Well, my boy,
will you work for me?" So I worked in the store and kept
goods until April 12, 1885. At that time, my pardner got
homesick and pulled out for California, his home, but he
never got there as he was lost at sea someplace. His name
was Thomas Slater.

When I saw Frank Densmore, he told me all about the
Yukon and the bar where he worked last summer and that
got me interested, so I got a job with Frank Starr again in
the logging camp and worked until he closed down. Then I
tried the Treadway mine, but there was no work except in
the glory hole. This was not for me as it was too dangerous
and men were getting hurt and killed there everyday. Here
I met French Joe and as we were both bent on going to the
Yukon, we made up as pardners.

Joe was short of money so we went hunting to kill time
until New Year's Day, 1886. Then we got a job from Treadwell cutting piling for a wharf. We cut two hundred piles
and made a boom which he sent a tug after. However, it
broke the line and we lost all of them. All went out to sea.
When I saw Treadwell he said he would pay us for half of
the pilings but no more. For these he paid us $200 and called
the grub bill square. That incident was a little bad luck.

We then fooled around until spring, catching lots of fish
and clams, and lived on them because we wanted our money
for an outfit to go to the Yukon in the spring. Joe and I got
a job working on the jail at $2.50 a day and made $15 each
and this helped out. I then worked for Brady in the store, as
his clerk had gone to Hoonah Hot Springs. Brady had a fine
daughter (half-breed) and we went to a dance in the courthouse—a small place. We closed the store at nine o'clock
every night as no Indians were allowed in town after that.

All the town was there, and we did a big business while Mr. Brady was away. When he returned, he was surprised at so much fur and I told him to praise his daughter as she could talk to the Indians.

We then got ready for a start for the Yukon. We didn't get much, for we had no money to pay for a pack over the summit. French Joe got his outfit and left May 6, 1886. We hired an Indian to take us to Dieka (Dyea) and reached Haines Mission May 9 and then waited for high tide to go up Dixon Straits. We camped here with French Pete. We had a big canoe with three Indians with squaw and five kids. Although this was a big load, we made Dixon Straits about 5 P.M.

Here the officers from the gunboat Pinto came and looked over our outfit, so I asked one man if I could go over to their boat to see if I could buy or trade for a rifle. He laughed and said, "Yes, you see the Captain." I went about a mile and a half to the ship when a guard stopped us, saying, "What do you want, don't come any nearer." He got the Captain and when I said I wanted a rifle to take to the Yukon country, he said to come aboard. He then loaned me a 45.90 rifle and said send it back sometime with Brady's Store in Juneau. They also gave me 200 rounds of ammunition. The Captain then said, "You had better turn back as there was lots of trouble with the Indians last week," but I said I couldn't go back.

May 8, 1886—We started for Dyea early on the high tide, with a fair wind all the way up from Haines Mission. I was very tired from sitting in the boat. There was a trader there but I forget his name. He said the Indians were on the trail between Dyea and the summit and to keep our eyes open. We fixed our packs for the morning so that we had three packs each (100 lbs.). We thought it was fourteen miles to the summit. My, what a pack! We could only go to the glacier crossing and had to camp there until it froze that night. Everybody was tired out. The current in the stream was very strong, and the stream was about two feet deep and two hundred feet across. We had to put out a line from bank to bank to hold onto and had to go back for the axe we had forgotten. We met three Englishmen straight from England and were glad as they would be company. They had to rest for two days while we packed one load to Sheep Camp and the next day had it all on top. We were glad for that. This was the 13th of May and a bad night on the summit and I was very tired. We went off again the next day with it clear and nice but harder to go downhill than up as lots of spills came from stepping between rocks in soft snow. We went down about four miles and camped at timber line. French Joe came back and said the Indians were fishing on the lake, so we packed to the lake and Joe stayed to make camp for us.

We now had to find Frank Densmore and John Hughes someplace in camp. We did find a ripsaw, hand saw, and lots of trees for making a boat. We cut three and made a saw pit, and after sharpening one saw, put one log up and Joe and Jack first tried to cut it but cut it too crooked. I baked bread, so I dug in the ground and made a hot fire, fixed the bread and let it rise between gold pans.

I then went to watch the boys sawing. They could not keep the saw in the line and each blamed the other, so I took a hand with Joe on top and myself on the underside. My, how it would pull and would not run straight but twisted and pulled, so we went to dinner to cool off. I then put the bread in a hole and covered it up with hot ashes and coals and let it bake for another hour.

Then we greased the saw and it went better and Joe and Jack made four cuts twenty-eight feet long. I got back and took out the loaf of bread and it was fine. After we were in bed, the three Englishmen came in with big packs—all tired out, so we cooked and fed them, then talked a lot. They said the Indians had held them up at Sheep Camp and that they had paid them five dollars to let them cross Chilkat summit. They stayed all night and then went back to the summit to bring down another pack, and I went on sawing with Jack, and Joe went fishing. He caught Lotsee and one of them was twenty inches long, spotted all over its body.

May 18, 1886—We finished sawing and were ready for building the boat. Jack and I worked on the boat, and Joe went over on the other side of the lake to get pitch off the spruce trees, as there were all pine trees on this side. We put the bottom and two sides on the boat and the next day ran out of nails, but we found an old box marked:

U. S. Army Swatka $\frac{\text{Sur}}{\text{Y}}$ 1881.

Some Indians showed up who called themselves Stick Indians. We asked them about the river ahead and they said, "lots Skookum water," meaning swift water and strong current. As they talked Chinnook, I could talk to some of them. They said about four days down the lake there was plenty of strong water. The boat when finished looked rough. It was pointed on both ends and was twenty-two feet long with a four and a half foot beam. We put the boat into the river and the next day, May 20, loaded the boat and were just ready to start when two of the Englishmen came and said that one man had drowned crossing the glacier stream. His brother said he slipped on a rock with a pack on his back which pulled him under.

They said they could not find him. So the next morning we went to look and took two Indians along. We found the body about three miles downstream. I can't remember the brothers' names, but the other man was named Clarke. The pack was still on the man's back, poor fellow.

May 23, 1886—We then put our stuff in the boat and went down Lake Bennett about ten miles, but the wind got too strong so we had to camp. We kept on going and stopped at Canyon City and the water really looked bad, so we packed our stuff around the canyon and did not sleep much that night.

The next morning Joe and I took the boat, Joe in the bow and me in the stern, and Jack packed the balance of our outfit over. Away we went like a "bat out of Hell." I kept the boat on the comb of the swell but we took water all the time, sometimes with the water all over us, but we got through to opposite the big rock where we had our outfit. There we emptied the water out of the boat and loaded up again and away we went, still headed God knows where.

The next river was full of rocks and very bad. We packed our outfit around White Horse Rapids and caught the boat in the big eddy below, just as everybody did in 1898. We then went on about twelve miles and camped. We saw three Indians and they wanted to go with us. Joe said, "All right," but I said, "No, they don't look right to me and you can't tell what an Indian will do anytime"—so they went away. Thinking we would fool them, we went across the river and went to bed. Pretty soon French Joe kicked me and I jumped up trembling and he said there were lots of Indians on the other side of the river. We hurried and made fire, cooked coffee and ate some beans and pulled out. We came to the

Indian camp about three miles below, but there were no canoes so they could not follow us. We finally reached a big lake called LeBarge and camped on a small island of rocks, grass and small trees. Here we got lots of gull and duck eggs —so fared well. That day we killed a swan and goose. I have lost track of the date, but Jack thinks it was June.

Our boat leaked so much we had to bail water all the time, so we finally dragged it out on a bar. Here we saw Chris Sonnichson and French Charley working nearby. We turned the boat upside down to dry and the next day calked it and then tried panning for gold. It looked good, so Joe went to work making a rocker. He split boards from a spruce tree. We had only a few nails so we traded with French Charley in return for some fresh meat. We also got a rocker iron from him. We had a fine rocker five feet long and worked all day and that evening and saw gold on the blanket of the rocker. I then cut up our meat and hung it on poles in smoke to dry. We worked here three weeks, then the river got too high so we had to quit.

Our grub was getting short so we went hunting for more, and Joe and I got two porkies and a cub bear that day. When we washed the rocker blanket, there was so much black sand we couldn't clean up the gold until we got quicksilver. We slept all the next day and then saw a boat coming down river. They stopped and it was Frank Densmore, John Hughes and T. Boswell, whom we had known in Juneau. We had lots to say to each other. They told us they buried the Englishman at Haines Mission and that his brother had gone back to England. When they asked how the bar turned out, we said we didn't know as we had no quicksilver. So Frank and John then cleaned up for us, as they couldn't prospect in the high water. They worked off and on for three days. Frank had gold scales (little ones), and the next day they were ready to weigh. I kept track on a piece of birch bark. We had 123 ounces, quicksilver and all. That looked grand and was a big surprise to us all.

I asked Frank how he was fixed for grub and he said he was long on flour, so we bought flour, tea and about ten pounds of sugar. We paid him six ounces for cleaning the dust and the grub so everything was lovely. The river was still rising, with water all over the bar and driftwood coming down river. Joe and Chris went hunting and killed a small moose about two miles from camp. The next day we all packed it in and had meat for a few days.

We then moved down to Big Salmon River to prospect through July and August and then to pole out up river to go to Juneau for our winter's grub. We saw a camp at the mouth of Big Salmon River and found Mark Russell, Arkansas Jim, Missouri Frank and Bill Eagle. Bill had broken his leg by falling from a saw pit and Mark was the doctor. We turned up Big Salmon River but could not go far as the water current was too strong, so we camped on high ground.

The next day John Hughes and I went hunting and killed a big bull moose, fine and fat. We all packed the meat to camp, and Frank Densmore took the tallow and made a big plum duff. Somebody dug up two bottles of Hudson Bay Rum for the sauce for the duff. My, what a feed. We told yarns, smoked and went to bed. The next day we split up and some went to Stewart River to try and find a paying bar. Joe, Jack and I went to Salmon fork and Densmore, Hughes and Boswell went to the north fork of Salmon.

We saw Indians forking with round nets for King Salmon. They had a fish trap all across the river but we got by all right. They wanted to trade fish for flour but we could not spare grub. They had some fine furs—bear and marten. One man talked a little English and told us that a long time ago white men had taken out gold about two sleeps up river. We went on for two days and tried for a few days, then found a small creek and moved up it and tried between two boulders and found coarse gold about three feet down. Frank found the first nugget worth $2.75 and that put new life in all of us. The boulders were too big to move, so we moved upstream about 500 yards and tried again, but it was no use at all for there were all big boulders and clay and we had no tools.

As our grub was getting shy, we decided that Joe and I would start out for Juneau. At the mouth of the river we camped with Barney Hill, Mark Russell and Hank Summers. They had a fine poling boat so all five went along. Two were on the oars and two on the poles and one steered with the sweep. There was so much brush we could not keep close to the bank but we made about twelve miles that first day and were all tired out, hands blistered. The only lively one was Barney Hill, everybody else was crabby and sore.

We finally got to the Hootalinka River, and when we got to Thirty Mile River three of us got on two-line and the going was better. We camped about ten miles from Lake LeBarge. When we got to the lake, we made a sail from blankets. My, how we did go for awhile, then it blew so hard we had to make camp. All went hunting except Barney, and Joe got lost and stayed out all night. We got bear, one beaver, and had fresh meat again. The next night we camped at the head of the lake and met two men coming down—Tom Evans and Fred Hines. We got sugar and tea from them and there was lots of talk that night. They told us about the Chilkat Indians shooting at them at Sheep Camp, and said there were two more men coming down.

It was a man's job to tow the boat up White Horse Rapids but we made it and the next day came to the canyon (Miles). We were stuck because the water was too swift and there were high banks on either side. We could not take the boat around on the bank, and then somebody said, "Why not wheel her around?" "Yes, but where are the wheels?" Then Hank said, "I'll make the wheels." We found a great big tree and sawed out the wheels, but it took a long time to cut a hole in the center for an axle—using knives. We then loaded the boat on the wheels and were ready to move the next day. We got started and my, what a hill! When about halfway over, one wheel came off and rolled into the river, but we found it in an eddy below and fished it out and finally got the boat over the hill O.K. It was good going on level ground and we finally came to Mud Lake and hoped to get on to Windy Arm as it was a bad place for storms.

We were off again the next morning, rowing and paddling, and were coming close to the lake. There was a fair wind, so we put up a sail and got to an Indian camp. George Carmack was there with his squaw wife, but we didn't stay long and sailed all that afternoon until we reached the portage. We packed the boat over and slept sound that night, as we were on our last lap, thank goodness. We put the boat up on high ground and rolled our blankets and after a hard walk reached timber line that night. The summit looked awful high and didn't look like the same hill we came over when we came in, as there were just black rocks instead of snow. It was a hard climb and we had to rest often. Barney Hill got stuck between two rocks and we had to help him up as he hurt his foot. We slept at Sheep Camp that night and started down for salt water in the morning. We arrived at Dyea just in time to hear the whistle blow all aboard.

Five new men here wanted to know all about the inside camps, but we were too much in a hurry to talk. There were no accommodations or place to sleep on the boat, but we reached Juneau the next night. We went right over to Douglas Island to sell our gold. Captain Morgan gave us $17.50 an ounce for it, which was pretty good.

The Captain of the Sea Lion said he was going back in three days, so we bought an outfit and packed up in packs of 100 pounds each. French Joe said this was the fourth of September, which was pretty late to start back, but we had to get there. He was having a good time drinking and dancing with the squaws, but not for me, I only wanted to sleep and rest up for the big climb with pack going back.

There were nine of us on the Sea Lion and we landed on high tide at about 4 P.M. and this was a good thing, for we landed everything without a lighter. There were lots of Indians milling about, mostly Hoonahs and Chilkats. We soon found out that the Chilkat Indians did not want the Hoonah Indians to pack for the white men over the pass. We were stuck here for all day and finally sent for the storekeeper and he sent for some government help from Haines Mission. Nobody knew about it until the U. S. Government boat Pinto came into the bay. Ten men and two officers came ashore, fixed for business and not fooling. They sent for the head man from the Hoonahs and the Chilkat Indians and went in the store to talk with Healey, the storekeeper. After two hours, they came out. The Indians had had a big pow-wow and then made peace, saying they were all ready to pack.

My pardner and I hired ten Indians at $12.50 per one hundred pounds and got it all up to the pass in one trip. We got to Sheep Camp that night by my taking my rifle and blankets in the lead and my pardner coming in the rear. It was fine and clear the next morning, with the wind blowing hard, and we paid the Indians and they went back that night.

We made good progress going down to Lake Bennett although we struck the rocks many times and had to unload and calk and pitch the boat. We got George Carmack and two Indians to help us pack around the canyon and took three packs around that night. Here we met Frank Densmore and John Hughes coming out for grub. Frank helped me through the canyon with my outfit. He rode the bow of the boat and I was in the stern and away we went like a "bat out of Hell," dancing on the comb of the swells, and got through all right but with the boat full of water. After emptying the boat, we pulled the cork from a bottle and both had a good stiff drink.

We could not land at White Horse Rapids, and before we knew it we were headed down. We held the boat straight and took the jump-off with the boat full of water but swung into the big eddy O.K.

The trip was uneventful until we reached Lake LeBarge where we went down the right side of the lake. Finally reaching the big rock point, we found a little bay and camped. The bedding and some of the flour and sugar were wet. We found five men were asleep here who had not heard us land because the wind blew so hard.

I made a camp fire and cooked breakfast and hollered, "All hands to the grub pile." Everybody jumped out and washed themselves at the river and we passed the bottle around. There was plenty of talk now. There was Jack Tremley, Bill Cummings, John Riley, . . . Hines and Charley Prescott who said they were all coming back in the spring. We started for Salmon River, but the head winds prevented and we had to camp to fix the boat again and dry our blankets.

It was awfully cold in the boat and we stopped at a creek, found a hole and caught some greyling which tasted fine. We made fish hooks by wrapping tin foil from tobacco cans around hooks baited with bacon and made a sinker from shot.

We were hoping to see Charley Christianson at his bar but only saw Charles Dotery who was camped here waiting for freeze-up. He was planning to walk and pull his sled out and he would have a hard trip.

Near the Hootalinka River a young moose swam the river and I shot it in the water and had a hard time landing it on a bar. We cut it into four quarters and away we went with the big load in the boat. We then came to where Chris was still rocking on the bar and doing well, as the water was very low. We cooked a lot of moose meat and that night did some hard thinking of what we should do as winter was almost here. We decided to stay here all winter, so found a fine stand of timber two miles down river and the next day started to build my cabin. I built a fine cabin fourteen by sixteen feet in size; since we had no stove, we put up two logs for ridge poles to support the roof. These were four feet apart and we left an opening for a chimney like I had seen in Montana. We then went up and borrowed a whipsaw to start making a rocker. This we made by sawing out four boards, making the rocker and a wash tub. However, we lost our nails, but got a pound of nails from the other boys and made them do. We had brought silver plate and lots of quicksilver. We started rocking and changed off packing dirt to the edge of the river to the rocker, which was slow work as we could only wash about 300 pans a day.

Two boats came downriver today. In one of them was the storekeeper from Juneau by the name of Stitts, who was going to the Stewart River. He had too much of a load, so he wanted to leave 500 pounds of flour with us which could not be sold to anybody. Both Neil and I said we would take care of it, but wouldn't be responsible for any loss. He also left some more that belonged to Tom Jones, Lee Higgins and T. Conners who had Frank Densmore's boat.

It is awful cold at night as this is the 11th of October. We can only rock about four hours a day and have to pack the rocker up to the house to thaw out and clean the plate and blanket.

One more boat came downriver today and was full of priests, all from Italy, I believe. Only one spoke English, Father Tobin was his name. They had lost one man on Lake Bennett, but did not know what had happened to him—if he had gone back or been lost. They said Father Tobin was a fine man, but they had trouble with the crew. They had had one fight already and one priest had a black eye. It is no wonder, for they had a big scow with two logs tied on sides and had about five days yet to the Stewart River. They had better hurry up.

Chris came down here in a canoe, as the bar was not paying. He and Charles Dotery are coming down here before going out over the trail to Juneau. French Joe came today headed for the Stewart River. He had killed one bear coming down but nothing else.

Chris and Charley came down and stopped in our cabin. We were still working but had to thaw out the dirt with wood, and it took a lot of it. When there was a lot of ice running, we stopped working and put the boat away and went hunting. We found a good salt lick about six miles from camp with lots of fresh moose signs all over the place and also bear signs. Chris went to look around and came back late at night and said he found a den of bears on the hillside. So off we went in the morning bear hunting. We found the place and I cut a sharp stick and shoved it in and punched and out came a small bear, which we killed. Then we cut a log about fourteen inches wide and five feet long and shoved it in the hole, and chopped the soft clay on top and pretty soon out came the big bear, pole and all, and there was sure hell popping for a minute. We killed her and another cub and had plenty of meat. We then started skinning and taking out their stomachs and made a rack and piled some meat up on it and taking some meat went home tired out. The next day we packed all day, bringing the meat home and getting it in the cache.

The river froze that night and we went upriver and hollered across to the boys but they were all right. On the way home we shot a big lynx. When the skin was dried, we made mittens from it and also a cap for each of us. Chris and Charley were getting ready for their trip out. They rendered out bear fat, cooked up a big pot of beans with bear fat, baked doughnuts, fixed moccasins, mitts, caps, and socks from bear skins. The cubs were all used up.

November 22, 1886—The boys began to cut a lot of wood. The hole in the roof was too big, so we closed it up and it works better now. I am going to keep track of the date from now on.

The next day we heard shooting upriver and wondered who it was. I went upriver about four miles but didn't see anyone and killed a big black wolf. We finished cleaning the gold and when it was weighed up we had forty-one ounces.

That night I put out the quicksilver for a thermometer and we talked about what we would have for Xmas dinner, for this is the 23rd of December. As we had bear fat, I made a big plum duff and had a bottle of rum for the sauce.

We were just about to go to bed when we heard someone come up the bank and it was Chris and Charley who had come back as Charley had frozen his feet pretty badly. They told us about having some neighbors close to the Hootalinka River—eight in all. I can only remember the names of Bob English, John Penlein and Buckskin Miller. We were sure glad to have someone to visit sometimes. Chris and Charley said the reason they turned back was because the Thirty Mile River was not frozen around the shore and they could not get around the rocky points. They took over some of Stitt's flour, beans and rice and then set in to build a cabin. They made a chimney on the outside of the roof and used Charley's boat so it did not smoke so much.

The next day Chris and I set out some poison for the wolves, using bear meat as bait. We put out ten good baits and lots of wolf tracks and then came home. We waited four days and caught four wolves, but one got away. Then we put out some more bait and caught three black and one grey wolf. This was on the 10th of January, 1887.

Ben Atwater came down today and said some Indians were camped near his place and had stolen some of his number 4 large size traps. Ben wanted to go hunting, but we looked at the frozen quicksilver and that meant to stay at home. Ben's pardner is building a new cabin but Ben is staying alone—we didn't ask any questions as we didn't know what the trouble was. He went home the next day.

We put out some snares for lynx and on January 16 went to look and had caught seven lynx and one large silver fox. Today Tom Wilson and Indian Bob came up going up with the mail for Jack McQuesten. I wrote several letters and sent them with him and he charged 50¢ a letter which was all right.

Tom had an order for one sack of flour from James Stitts and he told us about a new strike at Forty Mile River but did not know how the pay turned out. It was Franklin and Red O'Brien who made the strike about thirty-five miles up the river on Franklin bar. He sure put all of us to thinking and it changed our plans. Jack McQuesten's place is at Fort Reliance about fifty miles below Stewart River and he was short of grub. We took Charley's toenails off, then cut wood and got water to cook. Our fire burns as much as a wood steamer, at least half a cord a day, and somebody must be around all the time as it throws so many sparks.

My, but it is cold today, makes you cough whenever you open the door, and there is so much mist out you can't see outdoors. We just stay indoors and pile on wood. There is not much meat, but we can't go anyplace and are getting tired looking at each other and playing cards. The cards need to be sent to the laundry. Charley's toes are getting better and he is not so cranky.

Ben Atwater came in nearly frozen stiff. We went to look at our baits and snares and got five lynx, one wolverine and two wolves. It took us all the next day to take them to camp and put them on top of the cabin. Next day we went moose hunting and separated for the hunt, but had no luck as we got only five spruce chickens. Ben went fishing in the water hole in the lake and got some whitefish and big pike. It was a nice change in grub and tasted good. We all then went hunting again and had better luck, getting one moose and two caribou, and hauled them home on Charley's sled.

Chris is not feeling good and I guess he is homesick, as it is his first time away from home at Toronto, Canada. Charley is from Maine and is an old sailor. Chris is a Dane and myself English, so we are a well-mixed group.

February 27, 1887—Buckskin came down today for some Epsom salts for Bob English and said he was sure it was scurvy. We gave him some meat and Lubeck potatoes and onions. It is still very cold and Chris is making himself a fiddle. I am making fish nets and Nick and Charley are playing poker at one cent a chip.

We made a spring camp, and Chris and I will live there as the cabin is very dusty and we are getting bored looking at each other. We have lots of blankets. Chris says he will go crazy if he stays in the cabin with the other fellows any longer. We will move soon.

Neil went to get water at the river and said someone was calling downriver. We went about a half mile and found a man talking to himself. Poor fellow had gone nuts. Had a beard all over his face and his name is Missouri Frank. He looked starved and we gave him some soup and he went to sleep for two days. Sometimes we thought he had died, but when he woke up he was plumb off his head. We did not know what to do, but in about a week he got better and we found he thought some Indians were after him on the warpath. This scared Charley and Neil. He said he had started out from Pelly River at night with the wind blowing bad and he wound up at an Indian camp and got some meat from them and kept going. He had an order signed by Stitts for one sack of flour and addressed to H. Davis—above Salmon River on Lewis River—and we thought that funny. He said he found a leg of wolf and ate it and that was what made him so sick and weak. He had a kind of toboggan he had made with moose skin, hair side down. Frank cut off his beard, and he looked awfully funny and pale and not the same man.

Charley and I went upriver to see Bob English and took some meat along. We found him very sick and were sure it was scurvy. One leg was swollen and dark with spots all over it. We made up a lot of spruce tea for him as Buckskin Miller said it was fine for scurvy. Miller is an old Cassiar miner.

Today a man named Leslie came through and asked about Forty Mile strike which we said was no good. He had no grub. Charley and Neil were talking and I heard Charley say, "What's the matter with you fellows, we can't stay here and starve," so they pulled out for Juneau for grub taking Leslie along and here I am all alone. Leslie didn't sound right to me, and I said to them I wouldn't travel with him, but he never said anything about Indians on the warpath to Missouri Frank.

March 18, 1887—Frank and Chris came in and I told them about the two men who came from Stewart River and that they had acted queer. Frank said, "Yes, I know them, one called the French Frog and the other one is Leslie, the old poisoner." He said everybody had left Stewart River except Al Mayo, the storekeeper for the Forty Mile camp. Ben Atwater came in and said Arkansas Jim was chased out of Stewart for stealing some butter and sugar from Mayo's store and that Leslie had tried to poison his pardner by putting strychnine in beans. One pardner is an ex-policeman from Seattle by the name of Jack Patterson who also keeps a saloon. Frank Densmore says he is going to work on the bar here next spring.

March 23, 1887—Chris and I fixed the boat so it will be ready for Forty Mile in spring. We will take Johnnie Quinlan along as he has no boat. Missouri cleaned up his rocker today and had about four ounces ($75). Now Chris wants to start rocking. It was all right with me and we started, but it turned cold again and we had to quit.

March 28, 1887—It turned warm again and we rocked some about noon and worked when we could until April 11 and cleaned up about eleven ounces. Frank Densmore came today. He is sick with scurvy, with his teeth all loose, gums swollen and bleeding. He had drunk spruce tea all the time but had already lost four teeth which had just dropped out. Some Indians came in with moose meat to trade for flour and tea. They told us two white men had died on Chilkoot Pass in a snowstorm. Ben Atwater came again and sold his shot gun for $90 to Chris in gold dust.

April 9, 1887—Snow is going fast and some water is running on top of the ice. Some geese went over and I killed one. A few days later an Indian came and said lots of white men were coming back from Juneau. The Indian is named Joe and talks white man's talk and said Tom Wilson had died at Healy's store and had lost all the mail. Indian Bob, his snowshoer, had gone on to Juneau and he also said some white men had fought with the Hoonah Indians.

May 5, 1887—The river is breaking up and the banks running full. It is the first time I ever saw ice break up close. We moved out of the house and put grub on the roof of the cabin. The water is still rising and the ice is jammed twenty feet at the bend below the house. We hurried to get the boat to the house and went up on the roof ourselves. We stayed here one night and two days with water everyplace—all through the woods. We ate dried raisins and dried pears but couldn't cook, and when the jam broke the water went down fast and left mud everyplace.

May 6, 1887—The river is still running with ice, and we saw a boat go by all broken up. Some poor devil got lost we think, as there was nobody on the icecake going by.

May 12, 1887—The first boat arrived and it was Jack Randell and John Reed. They said the boat we had seen had had two white men in it and that both had drowned near Hootalinka. The first thing we asked them was, "Have you any spuds?" They said, "Yes, dry ones," so we got some and cooked them so Charley could eat a lot. Pretty soon five other boats came and in them were Bob English, Miller and John Quinlan and they all stopped on the bar. All of them asked about the Indians and were fixed for them with guns ready.

We saw other boats coming downriver. One had found a dead man on Cassiar Bar and had him with them in the boat. We all got busy and dug a grave after others had made a large fire to thaw the ground. They buried him. We put lots of rocks over the grave and a head piece with the date of drowning. The man was about thirty-five years of age, dark and about five feet nine inches tall and had a fine gold ring on his finger and a gold watch. There were no other markings anyplace, and we buried all his things with him.

We bought some grub from the men in the boats and paid $1 a pound for flour, beans and sugar and were glad to get it. There was another jam downriver and we saw smoke in the hills, so our guests had to stay three days.

We now have twelve boats and crews, all wanting to go somewhere but nobody knows where. John Quinlan is the cook and I am the flunky for the crowd. We then took off, and when we reached Salmon River we saw Indian Joe and he said the Indians were not fighting white men and that the Big White Man was a liar, that the Indians were not on the warpath. We stayed all night close to Five Fingers and John Reed killed a black bear on the side of a hill and everybody ate bear that night. We reached Pelly River and saw Arkansas Jim and he looked ashamed as he was all in rags and he would not talk about the Forty Mile strike. Our next stop was Stewart River where we saw Al Mayo. He was ready to leave with the new steamer, Newracket, and said Forty Mile was good camp. We told him about Tom Wilson dying and about the poisoner and you ought to have heard what he said then. Gosh, how he could swear. We were all excited and did not sleep much that night. John Quinlan and Tom Evans were going to rock up Stewart River on Steamboat Bar. We made Forty Mile River in the morning, and talk about hard pulling—we had it. The water was swift and we only poled and pulled about eight miles and were all tired out.

Next day we put four men on the line and one on the pole and all went well. We ran into John Reed, who was upset, lost most of his grub and had to swim ashore. We picked up lots of it and stayed with him to dry it out. We were the first boat to reach the canyon and we set up a rocker and tried for two days. We cleaned up and had three ounces. This was not good so we kept on upriver and camped at Moose Creek. This was no good either so we finally got to Franklin Bar. They were just ready to begin sluicing. Skiff Michael, O'Brien, Joe Ladue and John Nelson. We did not stay long for we wanted a bar of our own. About four miles up we met Frank Buteau rocking on Bonanza Bar. Above him were Howard Hansen, Jim O'Hara and above them was Dick Hubbard, Jack Wade, Dick Poplin. They said there was a new strike about fifteen miles up south fork. Franklin and Peter Wilson had found a gulch,

That night we all talked a lot around the camp fire. The next day we kept going on and found the gulch all right. We found their stakes, and I staked a claim for myself above them. I found a big tree and cut off the side and wrote:

I the undersined, Henry Davis, a citizen of the United States do hereby claim 20 acres of ground for placer mining purposes Described as follows: Beginning at this the initial post thence running westerly direction 436 feet to post number one, thence up stream at right angles in a northerly direction 1000 feet to post number three, thence at right angle 872 feet to post number four, thence in a southerly direction down stream 1000 feet to post number five, thence at right angles 436 feet to the initial post the place of beginning.

Sined,—HENRY DAVIS.

Witness,
CHRISTIANSON

This was public notice to everybody, "keep off," that I had the prior claim, and they did. Chris did not stake. We set up the rocker and rocked about ten hours and cleaned up and had about nine ounces. This was good—the best we had ever had. We worked three weeks on this bar and had it worked out and cleaned up $1,182. The next day we went hunting and got one caribou and hung up the meat to dry and from it got about ten pounds of lard. We have lost all count of the day and date. We went hunting again and got one big fat moose which we cut up and hung to dry and kept a fire under it to keep off the flies. Some Indians came to our camp, as they had heard the shooting. My, they looked bad. They had only bows and arrows, no guns. We gave them some meat and mooseskin and they stole one blanket from us, but we did not care as we did not want trouble with them. That afternoon Jack Randell and John Reed came up and they told us my old pardner, Neil Lamont, and Indian Tom Jones had upset in the canyon and that both had drowned. My, I am sorry!

We found out this was the tenth of July. Lots of boys showed up—John Conners, B. Higgens and some more. Some are sick of the country. Some are short of grub, as they had not found what they had expected. The gold was harder to get than they had thought.

We were getting short of sugar so we started downriver for some. We met George Medlock and Percy Walker poling up at the forks. They said another man had drowned near Franklin Bar and had lost everything. It is sure tough luck after so much hard work getting this far. We stayed with Frank Buteau and French Joe who came in to get the news.

Joe was out of grub and we gave him some meat and lowered the boat through the canyon with rope. However, it was beat up bad, but we got to the mouth of Forty Mile River that night. About twenty men were there and they all wanted to know about Franklin Bar and others.

We saw Frank Densmore, John Hughes, Hank Wright, Jim Bender, Mike Hess and lots more. Hank and Jim say they are going to stay where the grub is. Somebody said, "Yes, you are afraid to go up Forty Mile River as it is too tough," and Hank Wright told him "plenty," and I believe he meant it all and would have fought a wild cat. About fifteen men were left in camp and Slim Jim of Juneau started a poker game. The Ashby brothers, Bill Bozeman, Barney Hill, Pete Coniff and Tom Edmunds. Somebody came in and said they saw smoke downriver and we were glad for it must be a steamer. I came out loser by fifty dollars by the time the boat came.

Someone raised the Stars and Stripes, the steamer blew its whistle like the band, and we all got out our guns and started shooting. My, what a racket! There was no sleep that night, for poor Al Mayo was talked blind.

Everybody helped unload the boat. There were lots of willing hands. However, it was not a big load, only about ten tons of flour, beans, bacon, butter, sugar, but no fancy stuff. Al Mayo was Captain; Henry Moore, pilot; and Bill Moore, engineer. Everybody got drunk and slept it off the next day.

In about another ten days another steamer came in with 100 tons of all kinds of grub. Al Mayo would not sell but so much to one man, money or no money—all got the same amount. Mayo then sent an Indian up to Franklin Bar to tell them grub was there now.

We played poker again and I quit about even, but was pretty drunk when I quit. Mayo told us about some creek called Beaver below Fort Yukon and Chris took off—he said he wanted to find a creek of his own. Forty Mile looked good to me so I stayed.

Three of us got a job cutting logs for Al Mayo's store. Fred Hart is clerk in Mayo's tent. Mayo started back for St. Michael for one more trip, but it will be late when he gets back. Joe Ladue, Skiff Michael, John Nelson and eight others came in for grub. Skiff said Franklin Bar was good and they were going to build a water wheel as it worked good in swift water.

We floated in forty logs, and ten men worked on the store, some whipsawing, and all in a hurry. I got a new pardner, Ira Smith, and we built a cabin on Smith Creek. John Folger and Ben Atwater came down and they had a nine ounce nugget, the biggest found so far, and it sure looked good to us. While Smith and I were working, a big moose came upriver and we killed it, and gave everybody that came along some meat. We have to make a furnace as there are no stoves here yet.

August 28, 1887—We dug a big hole and filled it with rocks. It took five days of work and then two more days on the chimney. We put in a fire and dried it out, then moved in the cabin ready for winter.

Smith went hunting staying out three nights, sleeping under trees (siwashing it). He got four caribou, one bear, and we hauled in meat. We piled the horns in a pile, he said he would use them this winter if we have to. He wouldn't say more, just laughed. There were lots of greyling coming down the river and we caught lots of them and put them on the bank where they would freeze at night. We then made a fish trap with poles in the bottom and the fish ran into a box, the water ran out through the cracks and the fish are high and dry. It is easy to catch them this way.

We then went to the Post to get our outfit. Mayo only gave us two hundred pounds of flour, one hundred pounds of sugar, fifty pounds of rice, ten pounds of salt, ten pounds of tea, one bottle of vinegar, a can of pepper, twenty-five pounds of dried apples, twenty-five pounds of prunes, a slab of bacon, twenty-five pounds of beans. McQuesten runs the store now and that was all he would give us. The bill was $500 in dust. They gave the same things to all, money or no money. It took us four days to get the grub to the cabin. We then stayed home a day to fix the fireplace and bake bread between two gold pans. It worked fine and we had lots of good bread for weeks. We also cooked lots of beans with sow belly and spread them out to freze enough to last a long time. (Note: They used to cook beans ahead of time, spread outdoors, freeze them up and leave them outside in a sack and whenever they wanted to cook up beans they went out and broke off a chunk of frozen beans, put them in a frying pan and warmed them up. This saved time and they were always available.)

September 20, 1887—Johnnie Nelson came and stayed four days with us. He lived the other side of the river, and as there was much slush running, we went hunting to bring in more meat.

October 10, 1887, On Smith Creek—It turned cold in the night and the river stopped flowing. Smith went to fix snares for chickens, made dead falls for marten and put out poison for the wolves. I started cutting birch for a sledge and snowshoes. I cut up lots of sinew (from the spinal cord of a moose) and rawhide for snowshoes, stretching them to dry. Smith got two wolves and the next morning we packed them in. Mine was a black one and full of fleas. They jumped all over me and I scratched and changed clothes and put them out on the line to freeze them out if I could. Smith had a great laugh at me.

I then went to Bonanza Bar, four miles distant, to see Fred Hutchinson, and we went upriver farther and saw Dutch John. The next day John and I went hunting. It got cold in the night, and as we had only two blankets, we took turns sleeping and the other fellow kept the fires going. My, how we did drink tea all night but got little sleep. We got nothing hunting and were glad to get home on October 20 about noon. That afternoon old man Calamity Bill came along pulling his sled by his neck with a load of grub. He stayed with us overnight and the next morning, as he was not feeling well, we hauled his sled home for him and left Dutch John with him. Five days later we went back to see him and found him dead in bed.

Andrew Maiden went downriver and he told all the boys they would know what to do with the body. In a few days Joe Ladue, Tom Ashley, Tom O'Brien and Bill Cummings came up and we buried Calamity and they went on to Franklin Gulch.

They said they had a big dance at the Post and there were lots of fine looking chickens and squaws there. Smith has done a good lot of trapping so far, has ten wolves, sixteen marten, seven lynx, and three wolverines to date.

November 20, 1887—Next day I started for the Post to get tea or coffee. Smith wanted tobacco and said to pay any price. I'm glad I don't smoke.

Some Chickenstock Indians were at the Post and plenty mad. They said some white men poisoned some of their dogs. Harper asked me who trapped upriver and I say my pardner, Ira Smith. Harper said Smith had no business trapping as this was Indian country to trap. I knew there would be trouble, so I made a thirty mile walk that day and stayed with Maiden and then made home that night and told Smith all about it. I told him what Harper had said about white men trapping and gee, but he got mad. "Hell, just let them start trouble if they want to, I'll show them how we treated Indians in Montana when they got fresh. I got as much right to trap as any Indian." No Indians came that day, and I told Smith that if Indians started any rough stuff, I would stay with him. You know what the cattlemen did to the sheepmen. Just like that!

November 22, 1887—Jim McCauley came with some newspapers and he said he had gotten $1.50 a pan on his claim. It was too late and cold for him to go back home so we played poker. He was a good player and beat Smith and me out of about $100. Then three Indians came and knocked at the door. We could see they had an axe. Smith grabbed a rifle and got ready for them. I opened the door and asked what they wanted. The Indian smiled and gave me a letter from Harper to Smith. The Indian talked heap fast, and one grabbed a sack of flour behind the stove and put it under his arm. Then things began to happen. I slowed the Indian with flour on his head with my six-shooter and he dropped, then got up and both of them ran away. It was all Harper's fault for he had told the Indians to take anything they wanted for the value of their two dogs. He said to take flour and tea and said for Smith to pay them in order not to have trouble. We were glad we did not read the letter first, for we would have been out some grub. In about four days one Indian came back and knocked and came in and laid down a fox skin for a present. We did not take it but gave him some bread and sugar. Then things were all right. Good Indians do not steal—so that's that.

January 8, 1888—Weather was cold and we finished one hole twenty-eight feet deep but it was not good, only some fine gold on bed rock—that's all. We tried 1500 feet upstream next. It was slow work firing every night. (Note: These days the method used was to take off the moss on top of the ground and to build a long fire with dry wood underneath and covered with green logs. Then get the end where it had the most draft and light the fire, covering the cracks between the logs with dirt. Next morning we took out the unburned logs and water and shoveled out the thawed dirt—and repeat this until one reached bed rock. If one made ten inches a day by fires and another six inches by picking, he was satisfied, generally speaking. The prospect hole would be about two and a half feet wide and six feet long. After reaching about eleven feet down, we could not throw the dirt on top so made a windlass and wound the rope up around a drum about seven inches in diameter, one man in the hole and the other one on windlass hoisting up the dirt and gravel. They always began panning as soon as they reached gravel and continued about every foot until bed rock was reached.)

Word came in that Jack Wade had coarse gold on the creek that he named after himself and that he had found one four and one-half ounce nugget but funny looking gold. It looked like it had copper in it, at least that is what McQuesten says it is.

Smith's foot was very bady swollen and with toes turned black. We sent for the doctor with the survey party, and he looked and said two toes would have to come off. After sewing up the foot, he left something in a bottle to put on the foot and about two weeks later he came again and said it was all right. When he started out, Smith said, "How much, doctor?" He said $25 and Smith gave him $50 and he stayed for dinner. After he left, he came back for his gloves and said, "Boys, we are going to move the survey camp and I will leave you a bottle of brandy on the boundary line behind the big dry tree." Three or four days later I went and found it where he had put it. On returning I had a hard time finding our cabin, but when Smith got the balance of the brandy his feet healed up fast, but there is no more trapping for Smith as he walks on crutches made from a crooked tree.

We ran out of butter, so Smith said to bring in a big set of caribou horns. I chopped the horns in two pieces and he said to cut that up into pieces about ten inches long. He then gave me the big pot and said to put the horns in it and that he would show me how to make butter. I filled the pot and he added water (melted snow) and we boiled this for two nights and a day, then took it off the stove, took out the bones and placed it on the floor to cool. In about two hours I looked at it and there were about two inches of white butter on top of the water. He took off the butter and put in some salt and had as good butter as any except that it was white in color. I was glad to learn how to make butter, for I won't have to go without it now.

March 7, 1888—Bill Stewart came in to see Smith and as Cummings was going to rock on the bar close by, I went to the Post—a two-day walk. Mayo hired me and three others to go upriver and cut one hundred logs and float them down as soon as water runs. Dave Dawson is a carpenter and Mayo will be the boss building the log building. Bob English is very sick and cannot walk or talk.

April 23, 1888—Some geese flew over today and Al Mayo killed one on the wing. My, but he is a good shot. McQuesten put me to whipsawing but I had my hip pocket full of gold dust and quit. I told Jack—no more whipsawing for me. He laughed and said, "Henry, they all say that, but they get there all the same." The Charlie River Indians came in with lots of fur, but we had no grub to trade them until the first boat comes upriver. All are waiting until the new store is finished so we can have a big dance there.

We started a pool of $5 each on when the ice will go out. We also played poker and spit at a crack in the floor of the store. Then one man took the right foot and the other man took the left foot and we bet a half ounce of dust the next man coming into the store would step in with his right foot first. He stepped with the left. This was lots of fun as we must gamble on something.

This is the 4th of May and I guessed on the 12th of May for the ice to move. We had a big dance and somebody made some beer. It was good stuff if you didn't drink more than two drinks.

The ice went out on May 13 and Bill Brown is the winner with $250. The ice is running hard, and I went hunting and got twenty-seven mallards. I had to make two trips to pack them home and gave nearly all away. On the 28th of May two boats came downriver and they had a big sack of mail and said fifteen boats were coming behind them. They said they all had good outfits but would not sell any. They all came and we didn't know what to do next, there were so many.

About two days later we watched a funny-looking boat coming downriver. It was a man with a boat sawed in two pieces with boards nailed on the back end. He and his pardner had quarreled and they sawed the boat, stove and everything in two and each took his half and kept going. One party split up and divided their grub. One young man from England by the name of Harry Bell, age twenty-four, was sick of the country and was going home. Said he was well fixed but that he didn't like the mosquitoes, and the gold dust didn't grow on trees like he thought. I went with him and we got to Ft. Yukon in two days. Here we met Mr. and Mrs. Canham, the new missionaries who had just arrived from Pelly River. They came down the Porcupine River. They said they heard of one man on Beaver Creek whom the Indians call Chris. This is good news, as that is the man I have been looking for, so we keep on going, but we have a hard time finding the creek on account of the islands in the river. We saw a tree blazed with the limb hanging over the creek, so we stopped and I looked and saw Chris' name on the tree. Chris came in a birch bark canoe in about a half an hour after I shot my rifle. The flies were too bad so we started downriver.

It took us three weeks to get to the Tanana River and there we saw John Folger and Ben Atwater. Folger had gotten a big birch bark canoe from the Tanana Indians and could paddle it fine. There were five other boats waiting here for a steamer to come. Hank Wright and Jim Bender came, and the next day Gordon Bettles, Lambert, Bill Moore, George Carey and Matt Hall came in and there was a minister by the name of Chapman. He sure was a good talker.

We heard about a prospector by the name of John Bremner who had been killed by Indians up the Koyukuk River, so we had a big talk and decided, "Boys, we must go after that Indian and teach them not to kill prospectors." There were not enough men here now but some were coming downriver and we waited until they came and the steamboat got upriver from St. Michael. We asked Chapman if he wanted to go and he said, "Yes, sure." Someone made a motion. "All those willing to go hold up the right hand." There were sixteen who held up hands, then the chairman said, "Now boys, no rough stuff, stay by the miner's law and do the right thing. We are here to protect ourselves and our white race in this country as there is no other law—only self-defence." The meeting adjourned until the steamer came.

George Carey tells me he cannot go as his squaw is sick but that he will lend me his rifle and cartridges as my rifle is not sure to go off. In a few days some Indians saw smoke downriver from the top of the hill (presently called Mission Hill) and came down to tell the miners. We waited three hours until the steamer tied up to the banks, and Hank Wright and a committee of six quickly got aboard. They told the Captain, "A prospector was killed up the Koyukuk River and we want you to take us there." The Captain said, no, he would not hear of going with this steamer up there. Hank then said, "Yes it will, we have already got your steamer. You go ashore, with your crew and passengers." Other men came on the boat and we put them off, in no friendly manner.

July 10, 1888—We called for volunteers to go and have nineteen white men and two Indians, John Manook and Pitka, both fine, good natives. They did not want to go much as they were afraid the Koyukuk natives would come back next winter and kill the Tanana natives. However, we talked them over.

Orders were given "No men ashore tonight for it may not be safe." Only two scouts were to go ashore. There was hardly any sleep that night for anyone. Gordon Bettles was the main squeeze, Bill Moore was acting Captain, Jim Bender was next in command, Matt Hall was chief cook, I was flunky, and Hank Wright was in command of all the men on deck.

We steamed up and got off with lots of cheering and stopped about twenty miles along to cut wood for the steamer. It did not take long as we had lots of good axmen in the crowd. We passed Kokrines and cut more wood below there. We stopped three more times and then got to the mouth of the Koyukuk River where we stopped and slept on shore. Moore said to cut lots of wood and pile it on the bow of the boat or anyplace we could find. We then stopped eighteen miles upriver to cut more wood and sleep on shore.

The mosquitoes were very bad and we looked like niggers as we greased our faces, hands and necks with lard and tar mixed together. We ate breakfast and Captain Bettles said, "Eat lots this morning, boys, this may be the last time for you to eat." Manook thought it would be two more days before we got to the Indian camp where the man was killed. This boat was the hottest place I ever saw. Firemen work in just pants, no shirt with sweat running down their backs, but the Captain gave order, "Burn the bottom out of her."

"Tie down the safety valve, and give her Hell." We went fast and the boat shook all over and soon began to leak. I told the Captain but he said let her rip, she will stand it or go to the bottom—keep her wide open.

July 14, 1888—We stopped to see if there were any signs of Indians. Yes, there was a cache full of white fish drying, and Manook said the Indians had gone up the creek for sure.

We looked in the cache and found Bremner's tools which had his name on them. We were sure then we were on the right street. Some of the boys went about a half mile up the creek and came back and said there was a fish trap all across the creek. Bill sent some men to cut it out, but two of them fell in and had to swim ashore. We got up stream and the Captain called all the men together and told us to keep out of sight as we might run into Indians any time now. All kept quiet and the creek was so narrow the sides of the boat scraped the banks just like a brake on a wheel. We had to go slow, no blowing of the whistle now, for we needed all the steam we could get. Only the boat made a noise now. We soon came to a campfire with some big sticks still burning and Manook said it was two days old but that the Indians were not very far off now.

Bill had one man on each side of the pilot house for lookouts. We were all het up, ready for anything. Some were oiling guns and getting the right size cartridges for each gun. I thought there were no three guns of the same calibre.

We saw smoke two bends upstream and all hands on the front deck got ready to jump when the boat hit the bank. Others jumped and spread out around the Indian camp. Their dogs were barking and jumping, and the Indians ran into the tents, scared stiff. Only one Indian moved for his gun and Folger hit him over the head with the barrel of his Buffalo Gun. We all got together in a bunch, and Manook asked the Chief for the Indian who killed the white man prospector. Then the Indian who Folger had hit stood out bold and said, "I killed the white man." We took him on the boat as well as their medicine man and his wife and two bad-looking squaws. Then we smashed their guns over the woodpile and threw them in the river. We had to back down the stream about a half mile to turn around and we put the two squaws off at an old Indian camp. They took to the woods like rabbits.

We got off again and got down to the Yukon by noon.

After dinner, Hank Wright called a meeting to give the Indian a fair hearing. We asked him why he killed him and he said he wanted his gun, blanket and the lot of tobacco he had. We then asked him how far above his camp he had killed the white man. He said three bends in the river above the camp. Manook said it was about three miles. When we told him he would die for killing a white man, he said he wished he could kill more whites as they were no good anyway. That's all right.

We then tried the medicine man but could not connect him up with the crime in any way, nor his wife, so we got ready for the hanging. There was a big tree bending over the river. We made a noose, tried it and it worked too slow, that is, didn't slip so well, so Hank sent me for axle grease or lard to grease the rope and it worked fine. We again put it on the Indian and everyobdy pulled on the rope and tied him up and started for home. Everybody was satisfied and in good spirits.

We got to the Kokrine Indian camp and there were lots of Indian men on the bank, and orders were given to keep out of sight, keep quiet and let Hank Wright do the talking. There was a one-eyed old man who was Chief by the name of Nicoli (a grand old man). Bill Moore ran right into the bank in the middle of them. Holy Smoke! Where did they all come from? There were no squaws in sight. Hank said, "We want to tell you—no more white men you kill—if you do, we come back and kill all of you and your families."

Nicoli the Chief said, "We won't kill any prospectors but we are not afraid of you white men, if you start anything." He asked where the Indian we had killed was and Hank said, "You will find him hanging from a tree near the mouth of the Koyukuk River. You can have him." The squaws began coming out from the woods and there were a lot of fine-looking chickens among them. Guess I will come back here and get a wife sometime, I thought. The Captain yelled out, "Let her go, Dick Poplin, all is clear." Anyway we went like a "bat out of Hell" for home.

We were sure tired and slept standing between the boiler and the boathouse. We were all fed up on not getting any sleep and not having any fighting. We stopped and the Captain said cut lots of wood for the boat—fill her up. I helped cook and got beans and bannicks and coffee for our last meal on this steamer. When we got home, there was Jack McQuesten and Captain Mayo with the steamer Newracket and the steamer St. Michael going downstream to St. Michael. We turned over our boat to the Russian Captain with very great gratitude and thanks. He said, "O.K., I am sure glad to get my boat back, everything is O.K."

That night we held a meeting and both Jack and Al made talks and said we did a fine thing for Alaska, and that both he and the N. C. Company would give us back the grub that we had used for the trip. The missionaries all talked big and said the white men were cruel to the Indians, but they didn't say how cruel the Indians were to the white men, shooting them down when their back is turned. All Oxilene, I say.

The party all scattered from here, lots of men going outside as Jack said the steamer Bertha and another boat would be leaving St. Michael before September. I felt lonesome and didn't know which way to go but decided to winter near here. There was a fine-looking squaw near here, and maybe I could get her for my pardner. McQuesten, Harper, Mayo, Chapman, Folger and lots of other boys have one or two each—why not me, I could try.

After deciding to winter around here, I got a new pardner from Boston. We were just ready to start, when another man named King came in who wanted to join us. I asked my pardner and he said, "O.K." and the man began putting his bed in the boat and climbed in. I said, "Where is your grub?" He said, "I ain't got any." I said, "Go up to the store and buy some." And he replied, "I ain't got any money." My pardner said it was all right, so we took a chance.

King didn't look good to me and I thought I smelled trouble but didn't say anything. We poled up to the Tanana River, passing John Folger where he was making a fish net. We stopped and drank some tea and ate dried fish, then kept on going but began rowing, as the water was too swift to pole. Before we left, Folger called me to one side and asked if I knew King. I said no, and he said, "He's no good, watch out for him." And I sure did. We had fair wind and put a sail and got to Fish Creek (sixteen miles) that night. There were three Indian tents here. The Indians had some fish to trade for tea.

We started upriver again and then began to have trouble. King wanted to cross the river and when I asked what for, he said that it was better going. I asked him how he knew it was better going? He grabbed his rifle and pointed it at me and I saw blood in his eyes. So I said all right and sat down and helped row. However, I had my rifle under my blanket and when we got close to shore, I grabbed it and told him to row to shore and sit down. No man can point a rifle at me and ride in the same boat. We put him ashore and put out a frying pan, some team flour and his blankets. He said, "Give me my gun." And I said, "Go to Hell, we will leave your rifle on that next point downriver along with your axe."

We left there and then rowed across the river and in a couple of days found a big Indian camp at the mouth of the Kantishna River. There were only four men there and the first thing they asked was if we had seen the Indian that the white men had killed. We said, "No." We wondered how they heard about it so quick. Indian telegraph, I guess. We had lost track of the date but I guess it was in September, as the nights were cold. We camped on a big bar where there were lots of moose tracks. We stayed there three days to rest up and greased our hands which were sore from rowing so much. They were sore inside.

We were having supper at the camp fire when all at once two moose came out on the bar. We shot and missed them, but got them on second shots. It was hard work dressing them and we worked all night. In the morning some Indians came and said they had heard shooting and thought it was some Indians. One man named Joe spoke good English. He said he stopped at St. Michael for two years. They helped skin the moose and then ate. They asked us for the balance of the moose and when we said yes, they all sure got busy.

They took the heads and skinned tnem. Then cut the meat off the cheeks, took out the brain and tongue. Then they took all the guts to the slough and squeezed the grass out from inside them and washed them in the creek.

One man took the stomach of the cow moose and got a little unborn calf from her. They said this is the most tender meat of every kind of game. It ought to be. The next day I tried to eat it and could hardly hold it on my knife, it was so tender.

One Indian said, "What is your name?" I replied, "Davis." He said, "My name is Albert—all same my father named Albert." He said lots of Indians were going to run moose out of the flats to this river bar and asked if we would stay and shoot the moose for them when they came. We stayed and about five o'clock a moose cow and calf came out of the woods. My pardner was close to his rifle so he raised up and shot. He couldn't hit a hay stack, so I grabbed the rifle and killed both animals. About fifteen minutes later a bull and two cows came out on the same trail. I killed all of them and the Indians came from every direction from the woods. They all wanted tea and began cooking meat on sticks at the camp fire. We loaded up the boat for home and had lots of meat for the winter.

When we got there, we found Frank Densmore, Fred Johnson, Hank Wright and wife Anna, Mike Hess and Tom Evans. Densmore came over and said, "King is going to kill you." I said, "Oh yeah?" He was on the bank of the river and I yelled to him to come down to the bar and we would settle this right now. I had my rifle in hand. King wouldn't come and I went up on the bank and walked up to him. I said, "King, one more squawk out of you and I will shoot." He walked into a cabin, and some of the boys saw him go and came back and said it was all right as he had said he would go away and cause no more trouble. They told him if anybody talked any more about shooting in the camp, out he would go. That settled it.

September 22, 1888—It was getting late in the year and the camp was short of grub. On September 25 the steamer showed up with some staples, and a new trader named Walker came. He gave us some grub and gave the same to everybody and said it was not on charge but was from the Alaska Commercial Co., sent with the best of luck to the miners who had hung the Indian who had killed the prospector. We didn't know how they learned our names. We may find out next year.

We went to Mr. Walker and asked if he had any sheet iron. He said no, but that he had an old stove he would sell us. When we asked, "How much?", he replied, "I'm a Scotchman boys, it will be $12." Sold, say I, and we were lucky ones. No more smoke in the cabin, no more baking bread in gold pans in the wintertime. This was October 6 and it was getting cold. Mr. Canham came over today and said he would have church every Sunday at 2 P.M. and that everybody was welcome. He said he would lend books to the miners to read.

We had a big dance tonight in the Indian sports cabin. Rev. Chapman was the fiddler. Hank Wright is going to have his baby christened at church tomorrow. I forgot whether they call him Joe or Arthur, but I know we took a vote on what to call him. Mr. Canham is much pleased to have us prospectors all there. This is the first christening that Mr. Canham has had in United States territory. Mike Hess and Pete Johnson came down from Mike Hess Creek in the ramparts and they had a big load of bear meat.

November 6, 1888—The river closed today and here we are like Robinson Crusoe, marooned and nothing to do but play poker in Frank Densmore's cabin. I lost $200 and French Pete was the winner. I think he is quite smart with the cards or something. Next day we all went out to cut wood for Tom Evans who cut his feet. Folger is the doctor.

Hank Wright is getting ready for the big dance at Xmas (we all chipped in on the makings). John Folger and I went up the Tanana to kill white-meat chickens for the crowd. We went up Fish Creek and a storm came up and my, how it blew. We started for the creek and ran into an Indian who was also lost, but we finally found an Indian dugout with two families already there. We all stayed there. Folger was the cook and we ate white fish all the time and ate together with the Indians.

One young squaw sat next to me and she was blind. She asked about me in Indian and when they told her I was a white man, she felt me all over my face and hair, talking all the time. When she lifted her hair from her face, I never saw such a sight. She had no eyes and no place for them. No eye sockets. She was born that way and was about sixteen years old and had pretty near white skin. I guess a Russian had been around her mother.

After the storm quit, we killed seventy-five chickens, and the Indians took the dog team and hauled our chickens to town. We had been gone fourteen days and found that it was the 20th of December and that Hank had all the makings ready for Xmas night.

I hurried over to ask Manook about the blind squaw. He wouldn't talk, only saying, "You die if you try and take that Chicken from her Mother." The Indians are afraid to talk about her.

Everything is ready for Xmas. Hank had the juice ready, and Mr. Walker asked everybody to dinner in his store. Four of us went and lifted the fish trap and had lots of fish. Some of them were big ones about thirty pounds called ling cod. Some black fish and white fish. We gave the white fish to Mrs. Canham and Mr. Walker.

December 28, 1888—I just woke up. We had a big time. Danced all night and it was fine. Chapman is a fine fiddler. Mike Hess played bass and Frank Densmore the fife. Al Mayo came today from Nulato along with George Carey and family, and John Burke. Hank Wright is to put on the party for New Year's. His stove is NG (no good) as we found some Russian bombs in it. We took them back in the woods and built a fire and put them in it and ran like H---. We waited three hours and there was no explosion so we put them in Hank's stove with clay between them and it looked fine. Hank built a fire and went outside to split wood and when one boom went off he was outside the house. Folger and I are going back in a few days to Fish Creek to find the blind squaw. We went but found no Indians there, so took the trail and went almost to Fish Lake and found four Indians, but they wouldn't say anything about the girl. We then went back down creek and at the camp found the girl's mother and she said the girl had died a week ago. But the Indians acted funny. We think they killed the girl, as she was not sickly when we saw her the first time. When she was feeling our faces, she was talking all the time and she must have said something to make them kill her, for I could not get anybody to talk about her. There was bad medicine someplace for that girl. John and I both took a silk handkerchief to give her.

Our thermometer has been frozen for a week (it is a bottle of quicksilver placed outside). Mercury freezes at about 40 below zero and if not frozen we go to work. If it is frozen, we stay at home. They say Mr. Canham has an outside thermometer which registered 67 below zero.

February 3, 1889—Folger and I started off this month on a long trip. We had a hard time getting dogs and got only one each. We had 400 pounds each on our sleds and had a hard trip, pulling lead most of the way ourselves. We camped at Fish Creek the first night and made Baker Creek in two more days and found lots of moose meat on cache there. As there was lots more snow, we put both dogs on the sled and myself on the Gee Pole, and Folger snowshoed a trail ahead of the dogs. We went slowly—only about ten miles a day—and finally reached the Kantishna River. On a platform were two deer and Indians and crows working on them. We covered them up and started for Tolovana River. That day we shot a lynx and ate the hind legs (just like pork), but didn't have any applesauce to go with it. We traded the skin to Chief Alexander for moose meat at Baker Creek. One boy named Sam spoke good English and I asked him about the blank-eyed squaw but he wouldn't talk. He came along with us for about three hours, left and came back and gave us two hams, having killed a young moose.

We finally reached Nenana River and stopped in an Indian cabin back of which were six dead Indians. I asked Sam how this was and he said the Nenana Indians had had a big fight last winter over trapping grounds with the coast (Keakoquim) Kuskokwim Indians, and that in the spring they would bury them on the hillside behind the cabins we were staying in.

It took about a week to get our outfit to Chena River, and we stayed with the Indians a few days resting up. One night we heard dogs barking and went out and five sleds came upriver. It was Frank Densmore, T. Burke, Dutch John, George Cary, Matt Hall, Pete Johnson and Mike Hess catching up with us. We had a big talk and they said Hank Wright had gone to the Kolkoquim River. He left his family at Kokrines. They also said King was coming upriver alone. Bettles was still at St. Michael but would come to Walker's Post next winter. Bill Eagle and his wife Mary had stopped at Baker Creek.

Next day we started up Chena slough. It was a happy bunch, but we got into trouble as there was lots of water. Some places we had to put on our gum boots, but we kept on and finally got to Salchacket River on April 2, 1889. Here the party split up and Densmore's party went to the Goodpasture (river).

There were six in my party, George Cary, Matt Hall, Mike Hess, Pete Johnson, Folger and myself all going on up the Salchacket River. We struck open water about twenty-five miles and camped there and got ready to build our boats. Mike Hess and Pete Johnson packed their outfit across a point about six miles across country. We were just going to kill the dogs when a band of caribou came close to our camp and we shot fourteen. Thus we were fat but very poor, but it saved the dogs' lives and we had lots of meat for the summer although it was hard work drying it. Cary made a rack for the meat.

Folger and I were cutting up meat when two Indians came along hunting for moose or caribou. They only had bows and arrows and a long spear with a knife made from an old file and lashed to the pole with rawhide. We filled them up with meat and tea. The Indians then made a raft with logs and lashed the logs together with willow roots and crossed the river. They came back saying a bear was on the hill and they wanted a rifle, but we would not give it to them. We went and watched them go after the bear. They crawled up hill. The wind blew away from the bear which was eating blueberries. They crawled within thirty feet of the bear and all shot arrows, several of which hit the bear and stuck in his sides. It rared up on its hind legs and came for them. The Indians let the bear come, then put the end of the spear in the ground and the bear just ran into it. The Indian held the spear all the time. It went through his breast and the bear dropped and rolled downhill throwing blood all over. It was the best show I ever saw. The Indians had more pluck than I would have had. It took the cake.

Two days after they had left us we saw a moose crossing the river and an old Indian coming after him with a bow six feet long and arrows nearly three feet long. That Indian jumped in the river in slush ice, followed the moose in the woods and came back in about three hours and said he had shot it with three arrows. Said he was going to get his family and move them up to the moose. (It was the custom of the natives to move their families to where the meat was, then make camp. They would stay there until it was eaten up and the squaw would make a roundhouse and stretch the moose skin over that and put in a smoke fire from willows. She would tan the skins with urine. I think it was taken from a virgin, if possible.) She made their clothes from moose and caribou skins. Their raincoats were made from the bloater of the big white fish. Their winter clothes were from fur animals of all kinds.

The Indian said he had followed the moose for two sleeps and indicated this by putting his hand on the side of his head with his head sideways. This meant two days.

It took us ten days to whipsaw boards, making oars and paddles and pike poles and two boats. We worked about fifteen hours a day but we finished, loaded up and started downriver. We let the dogs run on the bank. When we had gone about five miles, up came a big chunk of ice from the bottom of the river and we floated on top for about three miles until we got stuck on a sand bar. The same thing happened to George and Matt, only their boat upset and they lost all their dry meat. We picked up their clothes bag. They lost their cooking outfit and were lucky they saved their lives. We pulled their boat out of the water. It was all twisted, boards cracked and we had to wait while everybody went to the hills for pitch from spruce trees to patch it. We got about four pounds. The Indians came and said there was lots of ice in the Tanana River.

We fixed the boats and started for the Goodpasture River, but the water was too high and it took us about a month to get there. We did not see any signs of the Densmore party. We poled up about six miles, but the water was too strong and we had to camp. When we finally left the Goodpasture River, we cut off the side of a big tree on the bank of the river and wrote:

NOTICE
We the undersigned have prospected this creek
—no bars—nothing but flower gold. Mush on.

Everybody signed their names. I saw this tree in 1931, but the writing was not legible. Our judgement was proved right, as nothing has been found there since that time.

We stayed two days and returned to the Tanana River to the mouth of the Delta River and went up it. Again the water was so swift we had to quit until it went down. Here we baked some bread. The water raised instead of going down and it was as bad as White Horse Rapids. We almost got caught between two big drifts of trees coming downstream. It was a close call.

I went up a little creek and saw fine gravel and black sand. I hurried and got a pan and it had lots of fine colors of gold, so we put up a rocker on the bow of the boat and worked three days and worked it all out. We cleaned up and had forty-three ounces of sand and fine gold. I think about one third gold.

We again started up the Tanana River for the Goodpasture River (about twelve miles distant) to look for the Densmore party and about five miles along we saw them coming downriver. They did not find much gold. Only about twenty-five ounces for the whole party for all the time they were gone. They got it from a bar about thirty miles up the Goodpasture River. We didn't know where to go and somebody said, "Well, let's try the Kuskokwim River." Densmore thought it a good place for bar diggings and Summers said so too. So off we went down to the Kantishna River. George Cary wouldn't go, so that left seven in the party.

We poled for a long time. It took us twelve days to reach the big lake (Minchumina) and we met some Indians who showed us where the portage began. We had fair wind so made a sail and went along fine, when all at once a big wind came up and the other boat lost its sail overboard and we took ours down just in time. We landed about a half mile from an Indian village. Densmore's boat landed on a rocky point and broke one board in the bottom, so we had to stay three days to fix it and wait until the wind went down. We had a good time at the village while waiting.

We then found the portage and walked over it for about six miles. We were undecided what to do as our boats were too long to drag across. We decided to pack over our grub and build another boat on the other side of the portage. It was hard work but we finally got there. Matt Hall said he was going to make a birch bark canoe for himself and was going on by himself. Chapman and John Burke built the boat and we also made one. We made oar locks with wooden pins in the sides of the boat, but could take the pins out when we wanted to. We are now on the way but don't know where we are going.

It rained so hard we camped and put up the tent and began a poker game. I won about $20; Folger lost $50 and Chapman lost the balance. Dutch John cooked a fine dinner for all on the camp fire and we slept well and when the rain stopped took off again. We met an Indian coming up with lots of beaver skins and Dutch John traded his rifle for fifteen beaver skins. He made a good trade, I say.

We finally reached the old Northwest Russian Trading Post kept by a Russian with a squaw wife and ten kids. They had a fish trap, and the trader asked all of us to stay for the dance and we had a fine time. There was lots of homemade beer and the women and men all drank it.

The trader had a good-looking daughter and he came over and handed me a note written in good English saying she wanted me to come make talk with her. I said, "No, Folger this is for you." He said, "No, you go find out what she wants." I went over and she came right out and said she liked me and wanted me to stay and live with them and marry her. She knocked me cold, and I thanked her and said it was impossible. (I did not tell her I had a squaw on the Yukon.) So she said, "Come over tonight to the house," but I talked with Folger and told him I did not like the way the girl's father looked at me and that I wanted to pull out right away. He said all right, and we did. I was sure glad to get away from that Russian outfit. When the gang heard about the girl, they kidded me a lot and some wanted to take me back and have the wedding anyhow.

My, but it was hot in the boats. We couldn't find any bars in the river or gold at the mouth of any of the creeks. This is funny country, so different from what we had thought and different from the upper country. We were much disappointed.

We lost all track of time. We met an Indian named Nicoli who spoke English, and he said to take a short cut to the Yukon. Folger wanted to take it but didn't believe it was a short cut. However, Chapman, Dutch John and Folger started over it. The rest were going to the portage below the trading post and come out at the Russian Mission. We had the trader get three canoes (birch bark) from the natives. Frank took the big one, Burke and I the small ones. We tried to paddle them and got along all right until I tried to turn around. Then I upset head first and had to swim ashore. Burke was afraid to try his, so we decided to tie the two canoes together with willow sticks across the top and it worked fine that way. The trader asked us for dinner, and we had new potatoes and roast pig. It was fine, for they were the first potatoes we had had in two years.

We could not eat the pig, for it was all the colors of the rainbow and was too fat for a pig, we thought. We found out later on it was porcupine. Everything else was fine, wine and whiskey.

Next day we took an Indian guide across the portage. We killed some ducks and geese for supper and for the next three weeks went through millions of ducks and geese. At night we couldn't hear ourselves talk for the noise.

We got to a small creek and put in a fish net and got white fish and pike. We landed in a bend about three miles below Russian Mission and had to tie up, for the wind was too strong to continue. We found out that it was the 10th of August. Although it was a hard bed, we slept on the beach. Frank did the talking in Russian. Bells began to ring and they asked us to come to church. Sure we went. It was a sight for sore eyes. They were all dressed up in buckskin and beads, funny hats, and small bells ringing all the time. It was quite a show, I tell you.

That afternoon the steamer came and Al Mayo and Harper were aboard and short-handed. We fixed the busted steam pipe and Burke and I fired the boat for $5 a day for twelve hours. We got to Holy Cross and Burke quit, for he had a job at the Mission for the winter at $75 a month and board. Burke is Irish and the Mission had lots of potatoes. I think that is why he stayed there. Frank took his job firing and it was some hot place to work. When we got to Kokrines, we got dry wood and it was easier then. We got to Forty Mile and I got $45 and quit. I saw Mr. Canham and hired out to work on the new mission about eight miles upriver. Mr. Canham had lots of big logs and they had to be yawed on both sides. Mike Hess and Pete Johnson came in and said they found no gold bars anyplace they had been. Pete went to work with me. We scorged a line on the logs and it took six weeks for us to finish fifty-six logs that were thirty-eight feet long. We had no word of John Folger and thought he had had a hard time crossing to the Yukon. Maybe was lost.

September 30, 1889—A steamer came upriver today with the lost Folger. He had a hard trip and got lost for a week and lived on berries and reindeer moss until he hit the Yukon. Gordon Bettles, Hank Wright, Chapman and Walker also came. Also Tom Evans, and he got us excited, for he had about fifty ounces of dust he had gotten on a bar up the south fork of the Koyukuk River. We will go there in the spring. Mr. Canham now says he wants shingles made for the roof and it took us three weeks of hard work with the axe and wedge. John Hughes also came in from up Mike Hess Creek but hadn't found much gold. He says it is NG (no good). He got only six ounces.

October 18, 1889—John Hughes got married today to a native woman. Well, good luck to them. Pretty soon everybody will have an Indian wife. There is always something happening. Mr. Canham came up and said it was getting too cold and we must stop work. This made John blue, for he had just been married. I told him, "Sun still shining, I will lend you money for grub out of the store." We got our winter outfits and moved to our cabin on an island. John's cost came to $500 and mine $375. We then went up the Salchacket to hunt. We camped and John's wife killed a fine moose the first day. I got a bear the first day and the next killed four caribou.

We built a raft and floated down to home in running ice. We just got there in time and then cut lots of dry wood for winter. Chapman and Pete Johnson came over to my cabin to play poker. John would not play for he did not have the dough. Then the game broke up and we talked about going up the Koyukuk in the spring. We think we will try the north fork, but this is putting the horse before the wheels.

November 1, 1889—The river stopped flowing today. The wood is all cut and it is too lonesome for us so we went over to the Post on November 10 and found Walker all lit up like a Catholic church. We stayed all night but no more of that stuff for me, for my head is almost open with pain. Chapman was there working with Indians making a basket to hold fish. He was making the frame. John's father-in-law came and tried to move in with them but John gave him some tea and told him to move back, that he didn't marry the whole damn family, and he did, too.

In March we started for the Koyukuk by way of Old Man Lake and got to the forks and found Joe Ladue there with Harper and the steamer Newracket in the slough. They had been there all winter. John and I found a good bar and made a rocker and were all ready for water to rock with. We rocked on the bar (this must have been Tramway Bar), but only cleaned up one and a half ounces and had to beat it downriver when we saw some Indians. We didn't stop and arrived at Nulato and went up to the Tanana with Joe Gedna to get Mayo's family. When we got to Tanana we went to work with Dave Dawson, the carpenter, on the Mission buildings again. John Hughes came in all in rags and starved. He walked across country and had a poke with about $700 he made on his bar. He had to kill his dog and eat it.

There is nothing to do and it is the coldest ever seen here. It is seventy below zero by Canham's thermometer. We stayed until spring. I bought some dogs for $10 each, and Manook, John and I started out and I took my wife Helen along. They joshed me a lot and Tom Evans said he would not marry a squaw unless he never saw a white woman, but he fell for a Koyukuk squaw and is now a member of the squaw man union and is in good standing.

June 5, 1891—We had a good place to rock, I think, for we cleaned up four ounces, then worked another nine days and got twenty-one ounces with one $4 nugget. Then the water raised and we had to start for home. On the way we found a creek and I found gravel and black sand and set up the rocker. I shoveled it in and Helen shook the rocker, but it was no good so we went on and when we came to the place where we hung the Indian, I saw the same medicine man and the Indians wanted us to come in and talk.

I put my six-shooter in my pocket and Helen and I went up on the bank, but I did not feel easy until the medicine man said, "Indians never shoot any more white mens." They were cooking white fish on sticks and he said to me, "You good man, chuck Indian full of fat bacon one time," and then the old Devil laughed hard. We were glad to get away from them, you bet. When we got to Nulato we saw George Cary who was going back to Forty Mile with McQuesten's boat and we went along and got home on August 15. Mr. Canham got word from Bishop Bompas that he must turn over the Mission to the American Mission and go to Pelly River. This news made Mr. Canham sick and he asked me to go along.

We had a fine Xmas dinner at Walker's store, and Folger's wife had a fine eight pound baby boy. We had a vote and called him John after his father. About seventy-five natives came from Salchacket with lots of fur. I traded my shot gun for twenty marten. Chapman, John Hughes and Tom Evans are getting ready to start for the Koyukuk River again. I sold him three dogs, for Helen and I are going to the Pelly River with Mr. Canham. Hank Wright is going out next summer. Walker is very sick; I guess he had too much hootch. Hank Wright says he is going to leave Arthur with Mr. Chapman at Anvik Mission when he goes outside.

March 3, 1892—Mr. Canham came up and was well pleased with the church. We are going to put up the bell tomorrow. Some Indians came down from Rampart and are going to stay until the first boat upriver. Mr. Walker is a very sick man and he took his son David to stay with Mr.

Canham where he could go to school, for David is a smart kid. We had the first church service on April 10. Everybody went to church.

April 20, 1892—The first geese went over today and I went with the Indian Pitka up the Tanana River hunting. We got twenty-four fat geese, sixty-eight ducks and we will save the feathers for Mrs. Canham for bed ticking. The steamer Newracket came up with the Mayo family and they are all going to Forty Mile. There is no more work here as the lumber is all used up. A new minister came also by the name of Prevost who will stay here when Canham and I and his family go up on the first A. C. Company boat about the first of July. Some men came down from Forty Mile and they said all the grub was gone there and everybody was living mostly on meat.

June 23, 1892—Walker and Wright are going outside and Gordon Bettles will run the store. The A. C. Company boat named the Arctic came in. It is a fine boat. Bill Moore is Captain and Charley Hall the purser. We went one mile and stopped and cut wood all night—about eight cords—and then stopped again a little above Mike Hess Creek and then at Ft. Yukon on July 6. There we took on a trader named Bowman with lots of fur and at Charley River lots of Indians who helped wood up. When we got to Forty Mile, nobody was in sight—must be asleep. I fooled around and had dinner with Jack McQuesten and then went over to see Bishop Bompas. He hired me to help build his new church. I worked until Christmas, and then Mr. Hamilton and Mr. Prevost came. Hamilton was to work for the N. A. T. & T. Company. He had a good dog team and I went down with him and got Helen and came back up on their steamer Weare. The boat was frozen in last fall and was in bad shape. It took us forty days to get to Forty Mile. Everybody was tired out—Indians and all. John J. Healy is Captain of the Weare. We got to Forty Mile on June 11, 1893.

Here Joe Ladue showed up from Sixty-Mile River and was going up to the trading post with Harper to get the fur down. I went with them and helped Harper pack up the fur in big bales. There was a lot of tanned moose skins for the St. Michael station—also nine thousand martens and lots of fox and lynx in ten big bales. They got their fur cheap, for if an Indian wanted a rifle, they stood it on the floor and the

Indians stacked their skin to the top of the rifle. Sack flour came the same way, flat ways on top of each other. Robbers, I say they were.

September 12, 1893—Harper came up with a big stock of goods with his family of five boys and two girls, I think. Bishop Bompas paid me off with English Sovereigns (he had a big sack of them), and I put them in Harper's safe for I was afraid to leave them with Helen. Some ways I never have had any luck with money. I don't know what is the matter with my wife Helen. She gets jealous and stuck-up and we quarrel lots of times nowadays. I told her if she didn't quit getting mad I was going to quit her and go get me a white woman. She laughed and stuck out her chin and said, "Huh, I wish you would, that's good enough for you."

October 12, 1893—The steamer Weare went into winter quarters in the slough close by, and Captain Healy and the Bishop came down in small boats with two Cheechakos— greenhorns. George Carmack came down from Five Finger coal mine. Harper is staking him for half interest. He had lost his boat and everything, and the Bishop hired him to help on the school house. Joe Ladue has a saw mill working at Sixty-Mile River and Johnson is going up there tomorrow to work for him. I went upriver about one mile and cut about six cords of wood last week and will haul them in later on with Harper's dogs.

November 5, 1893—The river closed up last night. There are some Indians across the river with lots of moose meat. I bought a half moose for $10. That is cheaper than hunting them. It is cold and getting lonesome with nothing to do but play cards at night.

The Bishop is sick and Mr. Canham and I went down to Forty Mile in January. The weather got warm and we had an early breakup and lots of prospectors came. Harry Smith and Frank Brooker came and next day John Reed and Bill McCann. One other man came with a big scow load of booze. That spring, about May 30, Joe Ladue came with lumber for the Mission and took Harper and family with him. There are just the Canhams and Helen and I left here. Canham is poor company as he doesn't talk much, just sits and reads all the time.

The stores are all sold out and I traded my rifle for thirty-five marten skins but they only pay $1.50 a skin for them. In August the steamer Arctic came up and said a new strike was on below Eagle some place and brought a letter from George Cary to come on down, and hurry. It was at a place called Circle City. When we got there, the first day Helen and I bought a lot and logs from John Scott and in two weeks had a cabin up close to Tom O'Brien's store.

They have two creeks staked, Deadwood and Mastodon Creeks. Everyone has money to gamble with and as I could not get a claim, I bought six dogs from Gordon Bettles and will freight to Mastodon Creek forty-five miles distant, and to Deadwood Creek thirty-five miles distant. The steamer Weare is frozen in with a big load of grub above Ft. Yukon. Tom O'Brien hired me to haul three tons up from the steamer at 10 cents a pound.

November 18, 1894—I brought in the first load from the steamer. The river was frozen smooth and there was a fine trail, and there were only two inches of snow. I brought nearly fourteen hundred pounds. Joe Wright hauled too, with six dogs. I freighted until Xmas from the steamer and then took a good rest. I had a lot of freight for Deadwood which they called Hog-Um Creek because some people hogged it all when they staked it.

July 20, 1895—The steamer Weare came today. We have no United States flag so we nailed moose skin on poles and hoisted it where the steamer was to land. Gee, old Captain Healy was mad. Ray Stewart went up and asked the Captain if he had any horse feed on the boat and this made him madder and he said for Ray to go to Hell, he'd let him know when he brought horse feed to this camp.

A customs officer came named McMears, I think, and Mr. Baldwin who will clerk for McQuesten. Baldwin showed us the first smokeless rifle called a 30-30. My, how we all looked at that gun, and we shot it and found it shot through a twelve inch log. Everybody wanted one of them and we threw away our 45-90's or traded marten skins for a new gun. On August 8 the A. C. Company boat came and we now have lots of Kow-Kow for winter. The boat brought two horses for Ray Stewart as well as horse feed. This made Captain Healy wild.

September 3, 1895—George Snow opened up a theatre

here. After the show, we are going to have a Pioneer's meeting. We organized and called it the Yukon Order of Pioneers. We then decided on a pin with square and compass and Y.O.O.P. in the center and gave the contract for them to George Bemis. He can make the pins when he is sober.

Soon after the freeze up, Bill McPhee and Frank Densmore are going to build a saloon for next summer. The shows at the theatre are all good and some of the girls are irresistible. The squaws don't look so good now. There are a lot of people here.

We caught two men stealing grub and sent them down the Yukon after holding a miners' meeting. They went in a small boat and were told to keep going and not to come back here anymore. They started and we have never seen anything of either since then. They must have had a cold ride in the open boat. I wrote to John Folger and told him to come up here.

December 28, 1895—We had a big Christmas, fine show and Pioneer ball Christmas night with a big supper. We danced until daylight and had lots of headaches for the next week.

Circle City, March 10, 1896—I had a good winter and told McQuesten I was going outside. He said, "No, Henry, you stay here, somebody is going to make a big strike here soon for sure." So I went out to the creeks to collect for freight hauling and got every cent I had coming. I sold my place to George Cary and my dogs to Mr. Dalk and told Helen to go to her father and mother and stay until I came back. She said, "Yes, how do I know you will come back?" And I said, "I will give you $1000 to keep for me," and she said, "Yes, I now know you will come back." But I never expected to see that $1000 anymore.

Seven men left for points outside and I went to San Francisco. It took one week's wait until the big windjammer left and we paid $35 for the fare to Frisco. Jack Smith and I knew what the tubs are like so we bought a big box of sweet crackers. I took my lynx robe and nine of us had to sleep on the floor. Jack and I slept together. One of the men asked the Captain for a blanket and he said, "No, you all must furnish your own blanket." This made us mad and we decided to get even with the Captain.

We had a fair wind and started a poker game and pretty

soon the Captain came down and wanted to play with us. I said it was not good for the Captain to play with us and he said he could look out for himself and sat down. He sat between Jack and me and we all bought a $25 stack of chips and started to play. The first hand was $1 jackpots. I had three tens and opened the pot for the size of the pot but the Captain came in with $6 and Jack raised. He held his fingers all over his end of the cards, telling me he had a pat hand. I held three fingers over the end of my cards, telling him I had threes and I raised him $4 more. The Captain came in for $10 more, making $17 of his money in the pot. The Captain drew three cards and I drew one card and Jack stood pat. I opened the pot and passed, the Captain passed and Jack bet $8—the balance of our stakes. I called him and the Captain studied awhile and then called. The Captain had three aces, I had three tens and Jack a King high flush. The Captain jumped up mad and quit and said, "I will get even with you fellows." Afterwards Jack gave me my money and $12.50. We are roughnecks from Circle City and don't know nothing, I guess.

The Captain didn't speak to any of us, and two days out the cook yelled, "Come and get it" and we went to the dining room and sat down. When the Captain came in and sat down, he said, "Don't any of you fellers come in the dining room until I'm through eating." We asked what was wrong, as the cook had called us and we had paid our fares. He said, "Don't talk back to me." And then we all told him something and he left the table madder than a wet hen. Guess he did not like our looks, but we meant every word we said to him.

The next day we had no cooked dinner but we ate sweet cakes and the Captain saw us eating them and roared out, "Where in H— did you folks get them?" We said at St. Michael, Captain, help yourself. He said nothing and we asked him when we would land and he said Port Townsend in about a week. We had a tough trip and made Cape Flattery on August 27. They got a tug and we went ashore in the Captain's skiff. We went uptown but there was no place to eat except a little hot dog stand.

In two more days we got a boat for Frisco and we got aboard after we had purchased some clothes. We landed at Frisco and stopped at the Western Hotel. My, how glad we were to get there. We went out on the sidewalk and looked around at the big buildings—a stranger in a strange land.

The people on the sidewalk were just as thick as the mosquitos at Circle City.

I found the A. C. Company office and saw Mr. Wilson and Charley Hall's brother and a Mr. Turner who worked at the mint. He showed me where it was and we got our dust cashed and left most of it in the A. C. office.

We went back to the hotel and there were lots of reporters there who asked lots of questions about Alaska. We could not shake them off. Then we went to the Cliff House for a swim or rather bath. The first one since I don't know when. When we went back to the hotel, there were more reporters. You would think Alaska was a new planet out of the sky the way they talked and acted.

We went to a theater, then to a dance hall, then to see a big fighter named John L. Sullivan. Then across the street but not to bed yet. After I got in bed, I heard shots and saw two men lying in the street and the next day saw in the paper that two Chinamen were shot on Kearney Street. It made me wish I was back on the Yukon.

The next day we went to the A. C. dock and saw the steamer Bertha come in and there was Bob English, John Nelson, Harry Smith, Densmore and lots more of the boys from Circle and Forty Mile. They told us about a new strike by George Carmack on Bonanza Creek. This changed all our plans about going back. Gordon Bettles and wife were here buying goods to take back. That night the gang from the Yukon went down "South of the Slot" and had a hot time. These girls made the squaws and Circle City dance hall girls look like a Dirty Deuce in a new deck. But they came high.

November 20, 1896, at San Francisco—We sailed on the steamer Yukon and stayed in Juneau until March. Part of the time we were at Hoonah Hot Springs. I had all of my outfit with me in storage. We got away from there on the boat Sea Otter—nine of us. The Captain told us of a new route over the mountains called White Pass. We stopped at Henry Moore's and the boat left us. James Stewart, Indian Joe and I started up to see about this pass. We found it better, with only one steep pitch. We went back to timber line and slept by a camp fire. We didn't sleep much but got to Skagway that afternoon. The next morning we sent the boys out to break trail and let it freeze one night. Then everybody started with their outfits for halfway camp. It took us eight days pulling our loads by our necks to get to the summit. Then it took two days to get the outfits to Lake Atlin—two days to Windy Arm and the going was good except on Mud Lake which had frozen rough.

Mud Lake, March 27, 1897—That night the dogs were barking and I got up and saw an Indian running from my pile of grub. I grabbed my rifle and yelled for him to stop but he didn't and I shot and he dropped something. It was my clothes bag. There were no more Indians around us.

We went through Miles Canyon on the ice but White Horse Rapids was not frozen up so we packed all our stuff around it. One day out we saw two men from the new diggings which they said was rich. This made us hurry up—working late and hard.

When we got to glare ice, we put up a sail on sleds and made good time crossing Lake LeBarge and camped at the lower end. There were fifteen men here. We tried to play some poker but money was scarce, and when the river broke we started for the new strike. We got there May 17, 1897, and I sold part of my outfit to Hootch Albert from Dominion Creek. The next day I went by Carmack Fork of Bonanza Creek, climbed a hill to the dome and then to Dominion Creek where Hootch Albert had staked discovery claim. The creek was staked for four miles down in the flats, so I came back and staked a bench claim opposite and above Discovery.

May 21, 1897—Lots of men came here to stake new claims and I met Louie Hanson and Hootch Albert. Albert looked sick from one week in Dawson. He said he would give me half interest if I would put down two holes on his claim. I said it was O.K. by me and went back to Dawson for grub. I bought a lot—Block 3, Lot 7—for $1000. Paid $100 down and the balance in four payments before September. I sold it in one month for $2500 cash and paid my balance of $900 and made a good deal.

I then staked on Cheechako Hill, one hundred feet square, and recorded in Dawson. Then I met John Burke on the street. He was an engineer on an A. C. Company boat and he gave me a 250-foot lay. It looked good so I got a pardner and we went out and sank two holes, then worked six weeks and put one hole down seventeen feet and another thirty feet deep.

We got some gold but no pay. So we moved over to Dominion Creek and this packing took the cake for hard work. We went to town and I tried to hire Ed. Bartlett to pack our goods out, but nothing doing although we offered $1 a pound. Meals were $2.50, a short dance was a dollar.

We started work on Dominion Creek and it was hard digging and we could only pick about three feet a day. We picked turnabout until we got to gravel. It took a month to get this hole down and we found the first pay on Dominion. A dollar to the pan a lot of times. This was pretty good although the gold was coarse. We picked up and rocked out $1200 and then went to town for a good time. We went back after we were broke and took out pay dirt all winter but pay was spotty and we did not wash up like we thought we would.

When we went to town, the crowd had arrived from all parts of the world and we could hardly walk on the streets. Mud was knee deep. While I was there, I sold my claim on Cheechako Hill for $10,000 to the Commercial Bank. It didn't last very long—the money.

Some ways these Yukon River chickens didn't look so good, and I almost forgot Helen, too, but she is all right with her folks. I just couldn't say no to these fresh Cheechako dance hall girls that came into Dawson. Flossie, Josie, Lottie B——, Lou E——t, Cad W——n, Camille, Nellie the Pig and Cheechako Lil. Also Passionate Annie and others who were very charming, pretty and fast workers. I was sure easy picking for them.

We heard that John Hughes and Frank Densmore died outside. Too bad. We went back to work and started putting in a ditch and whipsawed the lumber for sluice boxes. On the Fourth of July we went into town. I saw a fight and it was won by Frank Slaven. I stayed in a tent behind the A. C. Store that belonged to Captain Morgan, but went back to the creek and was sick for two days and glad to get back alive.

We cut lots of wood on the side hill for winter thawing and then stampeded to Gold Creek. Saw Jack Smith—he was not doing much and we stayed all night and then went over to Sulphur Creek and killed one bear. There we stayed all night with Pete Johnson and then went back to our claim. We sank another hole close to the creek and landed on a reef and got the best pay yet but were afraid the water would come in so left it until winter to work on it and went to town for the winter's outfit. We couldn't get it but left our order with the A. C. Company. We worked all winter and sold out to the Bank of Commerce for $22,500 and we got the dump. The bank lawyer fixed up the papers and we washed up the dump and then went outside on the Bonanza King—so good bye to Dawson for a while.

We went to Vancouver, B. C., and then to Frisco and then on to New York. There I met with Tom O'Brien and we went to Montreal and from there to Ottawa, the grand city of Canada. I began to get lonesome for the Yukon, so we went to Winnépig and met Bill Eagle there. We buzzed a few nights (almost to daytime) and then I started home for good, I think. I got mixed with those elevators and things. This morning I got up and went to the elevator shaft. There were three of them. Some going up and some down, and I walked back and forth several times and none of them stopped. One of the maids came out then and I said, "What's the matter with those elevators, don't any of them stop?" She said, "Did you ring the bell?" I said, "What bell?" and she said, "Push that button." I did and finally got down stairs alive. Me for the Klondike again and as fast as I can get there. These cities sure get me mixed up.

I went back, and as I wanted to see Helen and the other Dark Bays, I stopped at Forty Mile again. No more Dawson for me, so I did not stop overnight there.

CHRISTMAS MENU
WALKER'S FORK   1899

SOUP
Cream Tomato   Consomme Royal
   Cretons

MEATS
Roast Ptarmigan Dressing
   Roast Cariboo Au Jus
      Corn Beef and Cabbage

ENTREES
Fool Hen Fricasee
   Baked Cariboo Pie
      Boston Baked Beans and Bun Bread
         Rice a la Chocolate

VEGETABLES
Cream Potatoes
Sweet Corn   Scolloped Tomatoes

English Plumb Pudding
  Brandy Sauce
    Blueberry Pie
      Apple Pie
        Black Berry Pie
          Assorted Cakes
Tea   Coffee Hot De Tas   Cocoa

January 16, 1900, Forty Mile—I got a pardner, Mike McLoy, and we took lay on Hutchinson Creek and put down three holes and drew blanks and then went to town. We then heard about beach diggings at Nome on the Bering Sea. I went to Nome that spring and found 30,000 people there, so I took a trip to Council and from there to Golovin Bay district but couldn't find anything to stake so started for St. Michaels. There I met George Carpenter, a writer of novels and war stories. We went up the Tanana River to my old cabin and got there August 16 and stayed there hunting and fishing until fall. He was well pleased with his trip and he had lots of sport.

On the way downriver we killed a big moose and sold it to the post at Tanana, as they were short of meat. I never saw Mr. Carpenter again but the memory of this summer is one of the brightest spots in my life, for he was a fine man to be out with.

After that I went up the Tanana River on the steamer Tanana Chief to Baker Creek and later on went with Ed. Anderson up the Chena to trap, but we got "froze in" near the Kantishna River. It took us four days after the ice froze solid enough to reach the Chena River and another four days to my home cabin. We had no steel traps so made dead falls. We caught fifty mink, two hundred and eleven marten and shot thirty-three beaver in the spring. Also got four wolverine. Then we went down the Tanana and on the way killed a moose and four bear and sold the meat to the post for 50¢ a pound.

May 19, 1901—Worked for Mr. Bellows at the A. C. Store for a while, then worked for Frank Sharpe cutting logs for the new government buildings and then went up again on the Jennie M. to Jennie M. Slough and into winter quarters.

October, 1902—Made a trip up the Beaver River and saw Charlie Payne working on Pine Creek, making about $8 a day. I staked on Beaver Creek and put down two holes but got no pay.

October 3, 1902—I then went to Barnette Post and sold my fur and went back to south fork on Glove Creek and prospected until New Year's day, and then went back to Barnette's and heard of the strike on Cleary Creek, so I went over there. This was January 8, 1903 and I staked a lot on river front, three lots from the Morrison hotel, and built a cabin on it.

Then I came down to Belt and Hendricks Post at the mouth of the slough but could only get corn meal and sugar for my furs. On May 20 I sold my lot to Napoleon Dupree for $800 cash and worked for him for awhile but then got a contract to cut saw logs for Noyes sawmill at $25 a thousand. Mike Sweeney and I cut sixty-seven thousand feet in four months and delivered them to the mill. The next winter I went back to Salchacket River to trap and froze my feet. That was all I got so went to the new town called Fairbanks and stayed until June and went logging for house logs. This was in June 1904.

I made one more trip across country to Beaver Creek and tried on Glove Creek but got no pay. John Folger was there and had sold his interest on Tenderfoot Creek to his pardners. I took in the Hot Springs strike in 1907 and 1908 but could not horn in anyplace so moved to below Tolovana. There I built a fine cabin and made a fine garden and have been there ever since that time just getting by. No more rambling for me, for I am seventy years old, full of rheumatism, and thank God for what I have. I have had lots of money but couldn't keep it, but what is money compared with the life I've had up here. I have never been hungry more than four days at a time.

September 11, 1931—Forgot to say that Helen died. Later on I married another native woman who only lived a few years. They were fine pardners, good workers, good fish cutters and I got used to the fish smell and loved them both very much. I busted up when they went to another happy hunting ground. There are only a few of the old boys alive. Not more than five or six who came prior to 1886, and I hope they will tell Lynn Smith, as I have done, of their experiences.

We will all soon make our last trip over the last divide and I thank God, for we all, no matter how we acted at times, believed in a Supreme Being, for we had many narrow escapes from losing our lives, and He just wasn't ready to take us to Him. Our time had not come.

Sincerely,
HENRY DAVIS

Note by Lynn Smith:

Those of you who read the Henry Davis account of his life will note he told about a party of four priests coming into Alaska over the gold rush trail and how one was lost in the rapids and could not be found. This group included Bishop Seghers and the crazy man who killed him at what is known as Bishop Mountain. There is now a cross on top of the hill which can be seen from the deck of every passing steamer. The man whom the Bishop called "my crazy brother" several times in his diary did not belong to the same branch of the Catholic church. Miller was not a Jesuit priest.

The man, Miller, who killed the Bishop, took the body on his sled down the Yukon River, stopping at Nulato, and the trader there told him to keep going so he wintered with Caribou Jim in the canal where the steamer was in winter quarters. Later on Miller was arrested and taken with Salone, one of the natives, who was a witness and given a trial at Sitka. He was judged insane and turned loose and has never been heard of since. The native witness was given a trip to the States and later returned to Nulato with a two year outfit and about $1000 in cash. When the prospectors asked this Indian boy why he killed this man, he replied that he wanted to go outside. He thought he would be given an outfit and some cash like Salone got. I believe this is correct and the incentive for the crime. The witness money that he received proved a terrible mistake and even now is, for the natives nowadays will in most cases testify to anything just for witness fees. For this reason no cases are docketed unless they are concrete, and native testimony does not carry the weight it should with most Alaskan juries. Not many Indian cases go with this court outfit, for we know them.

There is one difference in the stories told of the motive for killing the first gold prospector by the native boy. The natives claim this boy envied the man his guns and was out of tobacco. The boy's brother kidded him and said, "Kill the white man; he has lots of tobacco," never believing he would do so. But the boy took it seriously and did it.

(Lynn Smith was the U. S. Marshal for the 4th Judicial District of Alaska at the time of this writing.)

Early Days in Alaska

Jim Bender

IT WAS IN FEBRUARY 1886 when I arrived in Juneau. I came up on the old . . . , Captain Carl was captain of the boat. We left Juneau and we came up to Dyea on the little steamboat Yukon and my partners were Hank Wright and John McCloud. It was terribly stormy coming up and kept us busy chopping ice off the boat to keep from sinking. As we landed, the rudder broke and we came near running into a big rock. We milled around and finally threw a rope over the rock and landed. There were about one hundred people on the shore on the ice and they pulled us ashore. When we got off, we went over the ice up to the post about a half or three quarters of a mile. We stayed there all night and then went down the next morning to get our stuff off the boat. The ice was rough and we knew nothing about the tides and as it was low tide had difficulty landing our things.

In the morning we landed over at Douglas Island, two or three miles across from Juneau. Then we went over to Juneau. Getting off the boat we walked uptown and saw a big crowd in front of a building. I asked a fellow what was there and he said, "Witchcraft trial is coming off." I said I would just go in and hear the trial as I had never heard one before.

They had arrested an old Indian or shaman for tying his old woman up. He had tied up the old woman for being a witch. The old shaman had a daughter there and they had to throw her out two or three times as she was fighting. I thought they were going to cut off the shaman's hair so he would lose his power. Their power lay in their hair. But they settled the trial and the Judge gave the old fellow a good talking to and told him he was responsible for the old woman.

We then went up to Dyea. The first night we got there, there was a big Indian camp. We went out there and saw they were going to cremate a big squaw. I said to myself I

was going to take that in. They had a big log fire and cre-
mated the squaw. That was my first unusual experience on
the coast.

The next day we started up to the summit. We had a lot
of fun, it was nothing but a pleasure trip. However, it took
us until the last of March to get over the summit. It was
quite a contrast to what a person had seen before. Big gla-
ciers going off, roaring like big cannons, and heard in every
direction in the spring. We started on down across the lake.
There were one hundred and forty of us, and without a tent
or stove in the outfit. We just had a flylike leanto built with
big logs in front, but we came along all right.

We got downriver to the foot of Mud Lake. I and two
other fellows went to the Hootalinka about 50 miles from
the mouth of Mud Lake. We cached our stuff and then came
back in the spring after the ice had gone out. We made a
big raft and floated down big White Horse Rapids and Miles
Canyon to the mouth of Forty Mile, riding the raft through
both places. The next day we started up the Forty Mile
River to Bonanza Bar and started in to rock for gold.

Franklin Gulch was struck about fifty miles above that
and of course it was cold. Because of this we could only
make an ounce a day with the rocker, that was figured at
$17.50 an ounce so we quit and went up to Franklin Gulch.

In the fall we came downriver, and as the boats had gotten
up the Yukon, they had started to build a government post.
We loaded up with grub and came down to Seventy Mile,
staying there about a week or ten days, then came back and
went down to the New Kliatt. This was on the forks of the
Yukon River, about eight miles below the present town of
Tanana. We wintered there in 1887 and 1888. There were
about fourteen men there at the time.

Then we went across into the Koyukuk region and had an
Indian haul our stuff to the head of Old Man's River in the
wintertime when they were hunting. My partner and I went
in light in the spring. There were fourteen Indian teams
hauling our supplies out. About that time Manook and Pitka
landed on the Koyukuk at the mouth of Old John's River.

We took only rocker plates with us and built the rockers
up there. We all had sleds and when we unloaded at Old
John's River I said, "This looks like a navigable river" and
they said, "yes," so I picked up my sled and set it astraddle
the fire. I said, "I have pulled this far enough" and so the

others walked up and put theirs on and in a little while all we had left was a little iron. We had a little grub and so we built a boat. About the time we had finished it, old John Bremner came along and said he didn't have anything to eat, that he had given all his grub to the Indians. I asked him if we made him a boat and gave him grub if he would go down to the mouth of the Koyukuk. He said yes, so we built the boat and gave him six or seven days' grub and sent him downriver to get rid of him. He had a shot gun and rifle. The rifle was one barrel but the shot gun used balls and caps.

The old fellow camped about noon at the Indian village and there was a young Indian boy about nineteen years of age, a good big skookum fellow. He came out and watched the old man fry a duck, make tea and eat. He had set his gun up against the bank to catch another duck and the old man gave the boy half the duck and a cup of tea. After they were through eating, he took the frying pan and little teapot and stepped down a couple of benches to put them in the boat. While he was putting them in the boat, the Indian picked up the gun and shot him. The Indian said he jumped right over the boat into the river when shot.

We were camped on July 4 about two miles below on the opposite side of the river where a stream came in. We stayed there all night, four of us, Matt Hall, Hank Wright and a French boy called Alfonse. The Indians came down from their camp and stayed around for an hour or two, so the next day we started down the river and met an Indian who had a note for us from Mrs. Callahan's first husband. He was a Russian half-breed and could write a little. He had written us about the Indian killing old John, so we went right on downriver to Nulato about ten or twelve miles below the Koyukuk.

We went back up the Yukon River on the steamer St. Michael to Kliatt and then learned about the killing. We had passed the native about fifty miles up the Yukon but did not know about the killing and letter until we had been at New Kliatt a few days.

There were about twenty white men camped here and we went to the miners' meeting and decided we must hang the Indian. Gordon Bettles, J. M. Bender, Hank Wright, Nick Lambert, Matt Hall, Bill Moore, Henry Davis and about a half dozen other men were there and all agreed we must hang the Indian.

Lieutenant Stoney was on the boat Explorer and had stopped there as there were three or four boats met here. I was appointed the one to go and take the Explorer, which was made for shallow water. I went to the fellow and said I was appointed to take the boat and he got hot as the deuce. I said there was no use getting hot about the thing at all and he asked what I was going to do with his barges of freight and we took them and went back up the Koyukuk.

Gordon Bettles was the Captain; Jim Bender, the first mate; Caribou Johnny, captain and mate, and Henry Davis, flunky. The rest were all deck hands. When we came to the creek, there was a big tree but we got out, and though we had poling boats, the water was twenty feet deep so we cut the tree out, put the little boat up and went on up about two miles where there was a big cache. Old John's boat was all torn to pieces and we put up on the bank, for his gun was there and lots of other little things. There were also two klooches and some kids.

We took them and put them on the boat and went on up about forty or fifty miles. The river was like a dead lake. There was a big lake up there and a house. We could see they had been there, so we went on up about ten, fifteen or twenty miles and ran into a camp and took them and brought them back down to the mouth of the river. There he went up in smoke. We asked the Indian why he killed the old fellow and he said he wanted to go outside and work and get grub and money like Serete.

There were two large trees about six feet apart. We tied a pole about ten feet from the ground and threw the rope over and everybody pulled the rope. We hung him and left him hanging as an example to the other Indians so that they would not ever kill another prospector.

About a mile and a half above the mouth of the river was another Indian camp and we stopped there and told them what we had done and why we had hung this Indian. We told them to tell all the Indians that if they killed any more white men, we would do this to anyone of them. We also told this to the Indians at Kokrines and every other village along the Yukon River.

We all went back again to Forty Mile and stayed there about three years, then came to Circle when the diggings were struck. We worked on Mastodon and Deadwood Creeks.

Rivalry Among the Traders on the Yukon

Old Cap Dixon wired the N. A. T. & T. Company at Chicago, Cook County, Illinois, for the authority to handle all of our transportation. Captain Powers was to be Captain of the boat at a salary of $4,000 a year and all the other steamers necessary were wired to carry the goods.

They then had a big miners' meeting and the N. A. T. & T. Company representative John J. Healy did not stand for the meeting. He was the head man of the company and asked for a jury trial of twelve men. So they agreed to that and made a law that the jury would be picked and those who couldn't serve would be fined an ounce of gold, that is $17.50. When it came to trial, they had financial losers on both sides.

When Captain Dixon made the last trip upriver, he couldn't get any farther so wintered at Circle. He had cleared the boat at St. Michael. However, Healy didn't have a boat. They put the boat on the waves and Captain Dixon lived on the boat as watchman. When he was away, John J. Healy tore down the license on the boat and threw it on the bar and then the trouble started. Weir's brother at Forty Mile was an engineer that winter so when it came to trial Healy got bit. He was asking why he done that and here was a letter written from Weir saying he was sorry he had had trouble with Captain Dixon but try to settle it someway. Captain had a license for twenty-three years. We had lots of fun over it. I was on the jury and Healy was lucky to get out of it. He wasn't going to have no kangaroo trial—that is a miners' meeting trial.

Another Story of Frontier Law at Circle

One of the first miners' meetings we held at Circle was over a man who was brought up for stealing some grub. It was winter time and darned cold, too, but we bought him some grub and gave him a sled and started him up the Yukon River.

For a judge in Circle City, we had appointed a Mr. McConnell and he held the job really believing he was a judge and went so far as to give three French Canadians their citizenship papers for an ounce of gold dust each. He was a very precise and dignified person, who stayed strictly to the white women of the town, and always appeared well dressed when on the streets.

Living there was an old nigger wench by the name of May. She had inherited a man by the name of . . . who who thought he was her head man. He had a big dog team and they kept the dog team at her place for a long time. Finally the big blowup came and she kicked him out and brought suit against him for boarding the dogs, bodily services etc., for $2200. She wouldn't have any kangaroo court try her case and demanded a jury trial. The jury was selected and I was appointed foreman. It was held in the Pioneer Saloon. Spencer, McPfee and Densmore were on the jury and when the case was finished we were put in the storeroom of the saloon with the stock of liquor to deliberate. We did, but had to try a sample of the stock. We must have drunk at least two gallons of the very best and all staggered out to report. "We the jury find the amount sued for is excessive and fine the defendant and assess the costs of the case to the plaintiff."

We had already had it fixed for Bill Elwell to steal the dogs while the case was going on and he did and took them up the river. She went home sure mad and when she discovered the team gone, she rushed back and yelled, "The dogs are stolen," but nobody knew anything about it. Old May refused to pay the costs, so the gang got out notices and posted them on her cabin giving her ten days to come through with the costs. We issued an execution and would have sold it. We agreed among ourselves that we would sell for cash and then go into her house and spend it all with her. Some of the wiser heads stopped this idea, and May soon left the camp with her own dog team and Bill Elwell as the driver. She never came back to Circle.

Oh, yes! About two weeks before this trial, late one morning we went back to Miss May's cabin and, as stovepipes were scarce in the camp, we got a long pole, reached up on the roof and hit the stovepipe, scraped the stick along the roof and yelled, "Come down off there, Judge, don't steal May's stovepipe," then ran downtown again. The next morning the judge was still in bed when May rushed in and began beating hell out of him. The poor judge didn't know what it was all about or know anything about it. We told everyone it was the judge and he was never able to convince some of the white women it was not.

When asked if we had it pretty rough those days on account of the grub being scarce, I must say we did without, but we nearly always had butter and flour. There were more moose and caribou then than today and we would kill maybe two moose and twenty caribou for dog feed, etc. The horns would be piled up in the back yard, and when the painkiller bottle was frozen and we couldn't work, we would go out and bring some of these horns in and saw them up, put some water on them and boil them about two days. Then we would take out the horns and set the pot out to cool off, and when you put in some salt there would remain about two inches of just as good butter as you ever ate except that it was white in color.

We didn't pack any bread when we went on a stampede but would take about ten pounds of flour and put it with some salt and baking powder in a sack. It would get stirred up when we traveled, and when we got to a creek we would make a hole in the flour and pour in some water from the creek and make a ball of dough. It would be a little stiffer than for making bread, and then we would go onto the bank and cut a willow stick and trim off the bark, smooth it up and then take some bacon and grease the stick. Then we pulled out the dough just as for doughnuts, wound it around the stick and placed it on the edge of the fire in the ground, baked it and kept revolving the stick and pretty soon we had just as good bread as one could ask for.

Note by Lynn Smith:

That is all about Jim Bender I can tell you. He is eighty years old and his mind is clear and he just relives his early Alaska days and lives on his territorial pension of $25 a month. His friends just love the old boy and have forgotten his reason for coming to Alaska.

I asked him what became of Hank Wright after he gave his son Arthur to Rev. Prevost and went outside. He replied that Hank was killed by a sheriff in California—that he had had some trouble with sheepmen. Said he had gone to Montana and stayed there nine years, but thought he had stayed long enough so went to California where he married a fine white woman and went into the livery business. One day a man rode up and asked the stable boy where he could get his horse shod and the kid said the boss will do it, I'll get him. This man happened to be the sheriff from Montana and they recognized each other and the sheriff arrested him. Wright asked to go in the house and bid his wife goodbye and they went toward the house, but as they reached the door, Wright said, "No, I won't go!" Both drew their guns at the same time and the sheriff shot first and killed him. Too bad, he was a fine man!

My Experiences in the World

Frank Buteau

I WAS BORN AT Quebec, Canada, on July 29, 1856, and in 1877 moved to Lewiston, Maine, going from there to Merrill, Wisconsin, in 1879. I left Wisconsin in 1882 for Portland, Oregon, and during that same year went to Tacoma and Seattle, Washington. In 1883 I lived at Kamloops and Vancouver, B. C.

On January 11, 1886, I left Victoria with twenty-one others and arrived at Juneau, Alaska, January 18. There were ninety Chinamen employed by the Treadwell Mining Company at Juneau when we arrived there. The citizens of Juneau did not approve of the mining company employing them and appealed to us to aid them in getting rid of the orientals which we did during the month of July.

Sometime in August of 1886 we left Juneau on a schooner bound for Dyea. A party of five men headed by Bishop Seghers left about a week before we did and had trouble with the Indians at Dyea, and we also had some trouble with them there which delayed us a couple of days. After going over Dyea Pass, we arrived at Lake Linderman in the latter part of August, 1886. Our party included the original twenty-two men who had traveled together from Victoria, B. C.

Lake Linderman is a small lake not generally shown on the maps. It is south of Lake Bennett and connected with Bennett by a small river. We arrived there in the evening and camped for the night. The next morning after we had breakfasted we decided it was better for us to separate by twos and threes, but before we parted we joined hands and formed a circle. Placing one of our number in the middle of the circle, we said to him. "Talk." He spoke the following words: "Here we are in the land of ice and snow. We know not where we are going. We have seen the tears rolling down from the eyes of our fathers, mothers, brothers, sisters, and sweethearts when we bid them goodbye, our hearts full of hope to see them all once again. And now as

86

I see the tears falling here, I feel that it will be the duty of the last one of us who remains alive to tell not only of what we have done but of what we have said. So now again, forward into the land of ice and snow, and let this be for us all not 'Goodbye' but 'Au Revoir'."

As we floated down the Yukon, a party on the left hand side of the river signalled us to stop, which we did thinking that they were some of our former traveling companions. Instead we discovered as we came closer to shore that they were Indians of both sexes. When we rowed the boat parallel to the bank, the Indians grabbed the gunwale of the boat and held fast. We could not understand each other very well but managed to realize that they wanted us to stay there for the winter. Of course, we did not want to do so and tried to shove the boat out into the stream. As they were keeping such a tight grip on the boat, we were unable to shove off and began to feel a bit uneasy. My partner, Louis Cotey, said to me, "Frank, it don't look good here." So I replied, "Take off your hat—but gently." With an understanding smile, he put his hat in the boat, raised his right hand and slowly lifted his wig. The Indians were open-mouthed and open-eyed with surprise and fright. Eight or ten of them ran up the bank but others stayed holding the boat. Louie then twisted his shoulders up, uttering a gurgling noise, put his hand in his mouth and came out with his false teeth; holding them up he then turned up his head and showed his bare gums, making a nasty face and they all scooted away scared and wondering what kind of a "Skookum" medicine man that was. Louie laughed and said, "That's twice that wig and teeth saved my life."

We proceeded down the river, prospecting here and there, until we met Jack McQuesten just above the mouth of the Big Salmon River. He was accompanied by John Hughes, and they were in a poling boat headed up the river. He told us of gold on the Stewart River but knew nothing of the Forty Mile River. He also said he was on the way to San Francisco to order supplies for the miners who were located at the mouth of the Stewart River.

When we reached the mouth of the Stewart River, there was a trading post there. This trading post had formerly been located and operated at Fort Reliance, seven miles below Dawson until 1886. When we came down the river that year, Fort Reliance was supposed to be the boundary line between Northwest Territory and Alaska. There were about twenty-five white men at the mouth of the Stewart River when we arrived there. We came on down to the mouth of the Klondike River, where Dawson is today, and my partner mentioned that it was the best country to prospect that he had seen on our trip down the Yukon—and afterwards we learned it was. We then floated down to an island about a mile above the mouth of the Forty Mile River, arriving there about the 13th of October, 1886. We immediately started building our cabins—three in all being built. There were sixteen of us located on the island and about five men living near the mouth of the Forty Mile River. These five named our island "The Sixteen Liars' Island." There was no trading post at Forty Mile, and all provisions we had were what we brought with us. We had no stove, no stovepipe, and no windows, and only one-half dozen candles.

There were three of us associated together at this time—Louis Cotey, French Joe, and myself. French Joe suggested that we make a chimney out of wood, extending it through the ceiling in the center of the room and placing an open fire underneath it. He told us that the Hudson Bay Company where he used to work had done this in one of their camps. We tried it but it was too cold. So we then gathered rocks on the beach and made a stove out of the rocks and mud, and also made a chimney out of the same materials. We used a large flat rock for the top of the stove and cooked in the mouth of it. This rock broke during the winter, and we had to rustle in the snow for another one. For a window, we made a hole in the door, which opened out, and made three wooden buttons which we put around the hole. Then we went down to the Yukon and cut a clear piece of ice slightly larger than the window opening and fitted it over the hole, fastening it on with the wooden buttons. On account of the extreme cold, this window lasted all winter without thawing. It did not gather frost but remained clear all winter.

I also made three Yukon sleds—one each for the three of us. While I was making the sleds, French Joe and Louis had been hunting squirrels and lynx. The others in the island camp had been making sleds, too. After this work was completed, seven of us went hunting on the 13th day of December, 1886, to get some meat for Christmas. We had no thermometer, and therefore, no way of knowing how cold it was when on the trail. However, we had a supply of quicksilver, which freezes at about 40 degrees below zero. When we left camp on this hunting trip, the quicksilver was frozen, thereby indicating that it was 40 below or colder. When it was cold enough to freeze the "quick," we discovered that if we would hold our breath a second or two, cup our hands and exhale our breath slowly through the side of our mouths, we could hear it crackle or sizzle.

When we got to the foot of a large hill, we made our first camp. We cut spruce boughs for our beds upon which we laid our blankets. The starlit sky was our only roof; and by the position of the North Star and the Dipper, we were able to tell when to arise in order to start on our hunt just before daylight. We hunted on the surrounding hills but it soon began snowing. We saw caribou tracks but no caribou on account of the storm. When the darkness came on, we started for our hunting camp but went down the wrong creek by mistake. We became lost and had to siwash it that night.

Next morning, we went down to the mouth of the creek to the Yukon River, then down it to the mouth of the creek upon which our hunting camp was located, and on up the creek two miles to our camp. We had broken trail all this time, each one taking his turn at going ahead. When one became tired, he would drop back and another would take his place. We reached camp completely exhausted.

After resting one day, French Joe and I took a little grub but no blankets and again went out to hunt. We killed two caribou that day. Night came on and we siwashed it on a bald mountain, building a large fire to keep warm. Between eight and nine o'clock that night, which was the 18th of December, 1886, a meteor fell, lighting the whole country as light as day for about ten seconds. When it struck, we heard a report like a cannon fired at sea would make and could feel a slight jar. Later we learned that Joe Ladue, who had a trading post at Eagle, saw the meteor south of him, and as we saw it north of us, it must have fallen between Eagle and Forty Mile. This record is now made so that anyone travelling in that country can keep a lookout on the chance of finding the meteor.

We all hunted until the 23rd of December; and on the 24th, we started for our island home with our sleds loaded with meat. It proved strenuous work taking in the meat. French Joe and I were behind the others when we started. We had to cache part of our loads, taking only a small amount of meat into camp. We were the only ones to arrive in camp with any meat as the others were so worn out that they were forced to leave their sleds and meat on the trail.

They had all covered their meat with their up-turned sleds which afforded some protection from the wild animals. As French Joe and I came within a few hundred yards of the cabin and within sight of the cabin light, we caught up with a man named John Swineheart who was staggering along in the snow completely exhausted. He had taken his ropes loose from his sled and was attempting to drag his blankets to the cabin. As we were worn out ourselves, we would not help him much so rushed to the cabin as fast as we could and got others to hurry back and assist him. When they got him to the cabin, we discovered he was quite badly frostbitten in both legs. It took him several days to recover from the trip. Although the next day was Christmas, we all went back over our trail and brought the meat that had been left into the camp.

This same winter, three men—Jack Patterson, Leslie, and one other man whose name I don't remember—made a camp about twelve miles up the Stewart River. Leslie had persuaded the other two men to go with him and finance the trip, claiming that he had been there before and knew where to find gold. They didn't find any trace of gold at this camp, so Leslie began to think that his partners might make trouble for him. He decided to poison them by putting strychnine in a pot of beans which he was cooking. He avoided eating any beans by saying that he was going to visit another camp located above them and would be back later. The other men ate some of the beans but became suspicious of the peculiar taste. The small amount that they did eat made them quite ill but they recovered from the effects. They realized then that the beans had been poisoned, so when Leslie returned a couple of days later expecting to find them dead, they chased him out of their camp. Leslie went back to the camp where he had been visiting, while his two former partners went down to the mouth of the Stewart River, where there was a trading post, and told the miners there what Leslie had done. A bunch of the men went up the Stewart River and brought Leslie back. They ordered him out of the country and Leslie lost no time in going, being only too glad to get off so easily.

The following is another incident that happened that same winter. Missouri Frank and Jim Hall were camped a mile up the White River. They came down to the trading post at the mouth of the Stewart River one night and stole butter and sugar. This trading post was operated by two partners—

Jack McQuesten and Harper. McQuesten, being outside at the time, had left Harper in charge of the store. As the thieves took their stolen goods away with them on a sled, it was easy to follow them and a bunch of the miners did just that the next day. When they caught the culprits, they threatened to hang them. Missouri Frank insisted that he was to blame and that he had persuaded Jim Hall to go with him. It ended in Missouri Frank and Jim Hall being ordered out of the country. Missouri Frank left the country as ordered, but Jim Hall only went part way up the Yukon River where he spent the rest of the winter with Indians. The next spring—1887—he came down to the mouth of the Forty Mile River and promised to behave himself if we would let him stay, which we did. Both Missouri Frank and Leslie, on their way out, told the men they met on the trail that were coming to the Yukon that they were leaving on account of the Indians molesting them so much that they had to get out of the country. That frightened the men who were on their way in; nevertheless, they came on but kept a sharp lookout for any signs of hostile Indians. Needless to say, nothing happened.

Tommy Williams and a half-breed left the mouth of the Stewart River between Christmas and New Year's, 1886, to carry the news of the gold strike on the Forty Mile River which had been discovered the fall of 1886. They wanted to notify Jack McQuesten of this new strike which had taken place since he had left for the outside so that he could arrange to bring in more provisions. When they came to the summit of Dyea Pass, they had to camp there three days in a snow house which they built themselves, as it was storming so it prevented them from finding the trail down the Pass to Dyea. They had nothing to eat but dry flour. It was impossible to make a fire as there was no wood. There was no water so they had to quench their thirst by eating snow. After three days, the weather cleared and they went on to the Dyea Trading Post which was operated by John J. Healy and a man named Wilson. Tommy Williams died there from exposure a few days after his arrival there.

I have already mentioned a Bishop's party which left Juneau ahead of us. This party was composed of Bishop Seghers, two priests—Rigoureux and Tozee—Brother Fuller, and a Frenchman named Provo who had agreed to make the trip with the others and help to construct a mission building at Holy Cross in return for his board and expenses going in while working for them. When they reached Lake Linder-man, they had to whipsaw lumber with which to make a boat to go down the Yukon River. One day the Frenchman left the others working and went to camp to make a fire and prepare their meal. He disappeared and was never heard from or seen afterwards. The two priests, Rigoureux and Tozee, dropped out of the party at Stewart River, while Bishop Seghers and Brother Fuller went on with two Indian guides. They were camped in a cabin one night and all four were sleeping in the same room. In the early morning, Brother Fuller awakened the Bishop and told him to get up —that he was going to kill him. He then shot Bishop Seghers in the breast with a shotgun, killing him instantly. Brother Fuller waited until the river froze up and the snow came. Then he secured a sled and dogs from the Indians near by, and took Bishop Segher's body to St. Michael via the short cut from Kaltag to Unalakleet. The A. C. Company took charge of the body. They held Brother Fuller until spring when he was sent to Sitka to stand trial. One of the Indians who saw the killing went along as a witness. Brother Fuller was pronounced insane and released. It was afterwards thought that he had also killed the Frenchman in the Bishop's party at Lake Linderman. The Indian witness went on to San Francisco. When he returned, he told his people stories of the marvelous sights he had seen outside and of the enjoyable time he had had. This was afterward to cause another mur-der. In 1888, a young Indian boy—17 years old—killed a white prospector on the Koyukuk River; and when they questioned him as to why he had done it, he said because he wanted to get a trip outside so that he might see the wonder-ful sights that he had heard so much about. However, he did not realize his ambition, as he was hanged shortly after-ward for the murder.

Gold was first discovered on the Forty Mile River in Sep-tember, 1886, by a party of four men named Franklin, Lam-ber, Micky O'Brien, and Madden. Franklin and O'Brien located a bar claim thirty miles up the Forty Mile River. This claim was 1500 feet long, which was the amount al-lowed for one claim according to the mining laws of Alaska, and was called Franklin's Bar. Lambert and Madden located another bar called Madden's Bar. This claim was ten miles above Franklin's Bar and was also a 1500 foot claim. During the winter of 1886-87, the sixteen of us who were living on the island agreed to locate claims of 300 feet each instead of the 1500 feet allowed by the laws of Alaska in order to make room for others who might want to locate in that district.

In March, 1887, the sixteen of us started up the Forty Mile River, prospecting the bars along the river on our way up. I located a bar called Bonanza Bar which was about half way between Franklin's Bar and Madden's Bar. It was at the foot of a riffle a half-mile above Canyon Creek. My partner, Louis Cotey, located another bar also called Bonanza Bar above the same riffle and one-quarter of a mile above my claim. After the ice went out, I built a rocker and started working my ground and made from $20 to $100 a day.

At that time, there were five men interested in the Madden Bar claim, and they were trying to construct a ditch with which to carry water for sluicing the ground, as it was not rich enough to warrant working the ground with a rocker. As they did not make a success of the ditch, one of the men named Dan Spragg came on down the river and stopped at my claim, telling me that he was looking for a claim of his own to work. I offered to make him my partner and let him work my claim with me which he did. I made him a rocker, and we worked together a week taking out $200 a day. This gave us each $600 apiece for our week's work. Then a party of men came through headed for the Franklin Gulch gold strike which was 85 miles up the Forty Mile River—making it 50 miles above our claim. Dan Spragg decided to go with them although I wanted him to stay on with me. He said he appreciated my kindness to him but thought he had accepted enough help from me. So he went on to Franklin Gulch. He was unable to find any gold there.

That summer—1887—I took out $3000 in gold dust. In the fall of 1887, it developed that I had made more money than any of the others mining on the Forty Mile River so they called me the "King of the Forty Mile." But now as I write this, I find myself the "King of the Poor."

The "Sixteen Liars" spent the winter of 1887-88 at their island home above the mouth of the Forty Mile River. We spent the winter repairing our equipment for another summer's work. Some of the picks which had had hard usage the preceding summer needed resteeling, so John Nelson and myself built a cabin for use as a blacksmith shop. We had to fashion tools out of the crude materials on hand as we had no blacksmith equipment of any kind. We made a bellows out of moose skin which had been tanned by the

Indians only to find that it was porous and allowed the air to escape through the skin. We then melted moose tallow and coated the inside of the skin with it after which the bellows worked satisfactorily for our purposes. We used a boulder for an anvil and a pole axe for a sledge. We made charcoal and used it for blacksmithing as there was no coal available.

While we were building our shop and improvising our tools, Joe Ladue made a trip to the trading post at the mouth of Stewart River for some steel and borax which were needed in our blacksmithing operations. This steel and borax was all that was in the country at this time, having been brought into the country in 1883 by the three Schefflin brothers. These brothers had come from Portland, Oregon, in a small steamboat called the Newracket by way of St. Michael. They had provisions and an outfit to prospect with along the Yukon River. When near the mouth of the Tanana River, one of the brothers died. The other two sold out to the A. C. Company and went back to Oregon. Jack McQuesten and Harper got the steel and borax from the A. C. Company and took it to their trading post at the Stewart River. When Joe Ladue returned, we fixed up all the picks that needed repairing and got everything ready for another summer's work.

In September, 1887, Joe Wilson, a Frenchman, and another man left for Juneau to get word through that the miners needed gum boots in their mining work. At that time, there were no gum boots to be had in the trading posts along the upper Yukon, and the miners wanted someone to bring in a supply of them. Wilson and his partner made several attempts to get through Dyea Pass but were unable to do so until February, 1888, on account of the frequent storms which made it impossible to traverse the Pass. They had to spend the winter with Indians on the north side of the Pass. These Indians knew how dangerous it was to attempt to go through the Pass in winter and discouraged the white men from trying it.

In the winter of 1887-88, I bought one-third interest in the discovery claim of Franklin Gulch. I bought this from Franklin, the discoverer of Franklin Creek, for $1000 cash. It took me three years to get the money back out of the ground as the claim did not prove to be very rich.

The trading post called Fort Reliance was located about seven miles downstream from Dawson. Sixty Mile River is 60 miles above Fort Reliance; Forty Mile River is 40 miles below Fort Reliance and Seventy Mile River is 70 miles below Fort Reliance.

In the spring of 1887 after the ice went out of the Yukon River, twenty-five miners from Stewart River went down to Forty Mile. Skiff Mitchell and Micky O'Brien were mining on Franklin Bar, and they built a water wheel to raise the water for sluicing. The first freshet, or heavy rainfall, raised the river so high that they lost their wheel and, consequently, their summer's work. Others were making wing dams to turn the water in the river, but these wing dams were also lost during the freshet. A Slavonian, called Crooked Leg Louie, went up with his partner as far as what we called Troublesome Point, about a quarter of a mile below the mouth of Franklin Gulch. That was before gold was discovered at Franklin Gulch by Franklin. This point was very rich and was the source of much trouble between the two partners which was why it was called Troublesome Point. At that time, Franklin came along up the South Fork of the Forty Mile River. When he was talking to Louie, the Slavonian, he found out that Louie and his partner had good pay. Franklin figured that the gold at Troublesome Point was coming from the first creek above. He went on up to this creek, which after the discovery was called Franklin Gulch, prospected it and discovered gold there also. Franklin had two partners with him at the time by the name of Bill Stewart and George McCue. They located a 1500 foot claim for the three of them and one claim for the discovery.

In the fall, they came down to Forty Mile to winter, and that is the winter—1887—that I bought Franklin's interest in the claims. This same winter, there were a number of us together at our island home. The others wanted me to make some candy which I agreed to do. We had some molasses and syrup which I used to make it; and after I thought the candy had cooked enough, I put it outside to cool. I then brought it back in and got the others to pull it in order to make taffy out of it. Most of them had beards and before long had the candy tangled in their beards. I was called "Taffy Frank" for a long time after this candy pull.

We started on the 15th of March, 1888, to go up Forty Mile to our claims. Bill Stewart, George McCue and I went to Franklin Gulch, and we built a cabin the first thing. We mined all that summer without getting much gold out of the claims. One man by the name of Frank Lawson found a gold nugget worth $500.

We went back to the Sixteen Liars' Island at the mouth of the Forty Mile in the fall of '88 to winter again. In '89, sometime in March, we again started up to our claims to mine. Among the miners, there were two men named George Madlock and Pete McDonald. During the summer of '89, they went down the Yukon as far as Nulato, and each one came back to Franklin Gulch with a wife.

In the summer of 1889, the A. C. Company built a steamer called the Arctic. They loaded it with grub and started for the upriver country from their post at St. Michael but the boat struck a rock or a snag and sank, completely destroying all the provisions. The A. C. Company sent a message by the Indians along the Yukon River to notify the people at Forty Mile to come down to St. Michael to winter as they would be unable to get any grub up the river that fall. When Jack McQuesten, at Forty Mile, got the news, it was October 1; and when we got the news at Franklin Gulch, it was October 7. Just before receiving this news, Pete McDonald, George Madlock, John Campbell and myself had formed a partnership and had bought Troublesome Point. We didn't want to go down to St. Michael as we had to whipsaw lumber and build one-half mile of flume for our new claim. We decided to winter in the Forty Mile district making the best of what we had. Our food supply was very low, but we killed forty caribou which served as our main food. These caribou were all killed on a hill which was named Bloody Mountain and known by that name for years afterward. George Madlock and his wife and Pete McDonald and his wife had between them two sacks of flour, a few beans, a few pounds of dry fruit, but no butter, and all of the above were quite moldy. John Campbell and myself had nothing but one sack of flour, and a few pounds of beans— no butter or sugar—from October 10 to July 1 of the next year. It was during this time that I learned from the natives how to make "Bone Butter." About the 10th of March, we went up Chicken Creek and whipsawed our lumber for the flume, sawing between forty and fifty thousand feet of lumber; yet when the first boat came up sometime in July, we were all well and happy.

None of the miners in the Forty Mile district ever got rich. From $500 to $1500 was considered a good year's work. $3000 is the most I know of that anybody made during a year.

We made the flume, taking the water from Franklin

Gulch to our bar claim at Troublesome Point. We had twenty-four foot pressure for hydraulicking and were the first miners to use the hydraulic method in the Yukon River Valley. When the flume was completed, the dry season had set in so we didn't get enough water to do any work on the claim as Franklin Gulch did not produce enough water in the dry season. In the Spring of 1890 when the Arctic came on up to the mouth of Forty Mile, arriving there sometime in July, my partner and I went down to Forty Mile to get some provisions. That was when I got a wife, Henry Willet being the witness. We returned to Franklin Gulch; and in the fall, fifteen of us made a fish trap with which we caught about a ton and a half of fish so everybody had greyling for the winter.

In '91 I went down on the ice to the mouth of the Forty Mile to build a house. A man named Johnny Reed and I then went up Forty Mile to the kink and whipsawed lumber for a house. This is the time that Three-Finger Jack, whose name was Miller, went up to Miller Creek to prospect and discovered gold there. Davis Creek, a tributary of Walker's Fork, was discovered soon after.

In 1888, a young man by the name of Davis came up the Forty Mile River as far as Franklin Gulch and stayed with us a few days in order to get information as to how to reach the Copper River. One man went with him a short distance to show him the route to follow. The next year Davis sent word back that he had gotten through all right, but that he had suffered some hardships. He did not speak well of the treatment accorded him by the Indians.

In 1889, two men, named Johnny Folger and Ben Atwater, started from Atwater Bar, just above Franklin Gulch, for the headwaters of the Tanana River. They used a sleigh to carry their outfit—in which was included a whipsaw to enable them to build a boat of sorts in which to float down the Tanana. They prospected on their way down and found some gold in the Tenderfoot country. They did not have the necessary tools with them to mine this gold as it was so deep in the ground. It was some years afterward that this district was mined.

In July, 1890, a newspaper reporter representing the Kansas City Star, named Wells, came to Franklin Gulch. He was desirous of reaching the Copper River and following it on down to its mouth. He hired a man at Franklin, named D. Hess, to make the trip with him and also hired another man by the name of Sed Wilson to go with them the first forty or fifty miles to show them the way to the head of the Copper River. Wilson received $100 for his services and returned to Franklin Gulch after starting Wells and Hess on their way. After Wilson had turned back, Wells and Hess became confused in their directions and travelled to the head of the Tanana River instead of the Copper River. They built a raft and floated down the Tanana River. At one time, their raft became lodged on the point of an island in the middle of the river and was swamped. The river carried away all of their equipment and provisions, including their guns, but they escaped with their lives. They were held prisoners on this island for several days before they were able to repair their raft sufficiently to enable them to go on, and were forced to kill and eat the bob-tailed dog which had been their companion on the trip. They afterward wrote us a letter from Nulato telling us of their experiences and said that the bob-tailed dog was not such bad eating after all.

In March, 1887, two miners named Jones and Frenchy, who had wintered at Stewart River, left there to go to Forty Mile River. They figured on taking a short cut instead of going down the Yukon. They first went up the Sixty Mile River as far as Miller Creek and then crossed over to the head of Brown Creek. Here they built a "flat-iron" boat and travelled in this down Brown Creek to the Forty Mile River. When they reached the Forty Mile, they supposed that they were near the head of it, but in reality they were only about sixteen miles up it. They started floating on down, prospecting as they went. They soon came to Forty Mile Canyon where the water became very swift and rough. Their boat struck a large, flat rock in the middle of the river, throwing them into the water. Both of the men managed to climb out on this flat rock and Jones offered to swim ashore to see if he could find some way to get Frenchy ashore. As the water was so very cold and swift, Jones lost his life in the attempt to reach shore. In the meantime, the boat had floated on through the canyon and had been seen by a miner, Jack Trombly, as it passed his camp. He immediately started upstream to see if anyone needed his assistance. He discovered Frenchy on the rock and succeeded in getting him ashore, thoroughly chilled through but thankful to be alive.

In the summer of 1892, we mined on Troublesome Point as usual. I had intended to build a cabin at the mouth of Forty Mile River after our summer's work was over out of the lumber I had whipsawed the previous winter, but received word to come outside to attend to some business matters. So about September 1, 1892, ten or twelve of us started from Forty Mile for the trip outside. Included in the party were Harry Smith, Sed Wilson, Frank Lawson, Fred Robbin, Billy Moran, Pete McDonald, myself, and several others whose names I have forgotten. We travelled up the Yukon in poling boats to Lake Linderman on the first lap of our journey. The water was icy cold and much discomfort was experienced in handling the poles in the cold water. Each morning before starting, we would warm the poles by a fire and then use woolen mitts made out of blankets to work in, which helped us somewhat to withstand the cold. We had to portage our boat and packs at Miles Canyon. The bluffs were about thirty feet high at this point, and we had to lift our boat up to the top of this bluff, carry it a distance of about a quarter of a mile, and then lower it down the bluff on the other side of the canyon.

At Lake Linderman, we hired several Indians, among whom were two native women, to help carry our packs over the trail to Dyea. Going up the trail to the summit, a snowstorm and a strong head wind struck us, making it necessary for each one to catch hold of the person in front of him so that we might all keep together and no one become lost. When we reached the top of the summit, we could look down into the valley on the other side of the Pass and see the sun shining brightly down there. The weather cleared as we went on down the trail. Our trail crossed Dyea River seven times. It is a glacier stream, and the water is about three or four feet deep at the riffles where the shallowest water is to be found and where we made our crossings. The ice water chilled us through at each crossing, but we warmed ourselves by jumping around as we did not want to take time to build a fire each time. One member of the party attempted to make the first crossing just below a riffle. The water was so deep that he lost his footing, but he managed to reach shore safely. We then decided that the best way to cross was to take a long pole and have each one hold onto it. Then we headed across in a diagonal line with the tallest man in the lead. In this way, the force of the current was broken for those at the lower end of the pole where the women were stationed.

We finally arrived at Dyea where we embarked for Juneau on a schooner. We had not had any fresh potatoes during our six or seven year sojourn in the interior, so you can imagine our enjoyment when we were served a large platter of french fried potatoes soon after our arrival at Dyea. We arrived at Juneau thirty-seven days after leaving Forty Mile. We all went outside together on the first steamer going south from Juneau. On arrival at Victoria, B. C. we were not allowed to land on account of a smallpox epidemic there, so we all disembarked in Seattle instead. From there I journeyed to Tacoma and Bellingham to straighten up my business affairs, leaving Seattle for Juneau the latter part of November where I spent the winter of '92.

About the 1st of March, 1893, a party of four of us comprised of Francois Roy, Corbeil, Laroche, and myself boarded a schooner at Juneau for Dyea. Upon our arrival in Dyea, we proceeded to haul our outfit to Sheep Camp where we made our headquarters while we relayed our goods over the summit. Stone House was our first relay point where we cached our stuff until such a time as we could go on with it. This camp derived its name from a large flat rock extending out of the ground at an angle of 45 degrees to a height of about ten feet, affording shelter to travellers in case of storm.

While at Sheep Camp, we were surprised by the arrival of a man who had travelled from Nulato. This man's name was Hamilton, and he was an employee of the N. A. T. Company, formed by Cudahy, John J. Healy, and P. B. Weare. This company had built a steamer called The Cudahy at St. Michael in '92 which had started for the Forty Mile River late the same summer. This steamer was forced to tie up near Nulato as the ice began to run and stopped further progress, and Hamilton was making this trip to Chicago to the headquarters of the company to inform the owners that their boat had not reached the Forty Mile as they supposed it had and was frozen in the ice at Nulato. With an Indian as his guide, he had travelled from Nulato to the Tanana River, up the Tanana to its head, then north across country to the North Fork of the Forty Mile River, following this on down to the Yukon River. At the Forty Mile, he hired Johnny Reed, a white man, with his dog team, and an Indian to guide him over the trail to Dyea as his former Indian guide was unfamiliar with the trail between these two points.

After our goods were over the summit, we moved our camp to Lake Linderman which we found was covered by a foot of soft snow. As the wind was very strong, we rigged sails on our sleds, loaded on our outfits, and literally "sailed" to Lake Bennett. Here we built a boat; and by the time it was finished, the river was open for navigation. We proceeded down the river to Miles Canyon; and as we did not want to risk going through the Canyon, we portaged our boat and provisions over the bluff and around the Canyon where we again launched the boat, loaded it up, and went on to White Horse. We found the usually rough water at the White Horse Rapids quite smooth as there was evidently an ice jam below backing up the water. From White Horse, we followed the ice pack to Lake Laberge which we found covered with glare ice. Here we put our boat on two sleds, loaded our provisions in the boat, and again erected a sail. As there was no snow on the ice, we made unusually good time, crossing the length of the forty mile lake in two hours. I believe this was the most exciting ride I have ever had. Just at the head of Five Finger Rapids, we passed by a wall of ice on our right-hand side between twenty and thirty feet high. These rapids received their name from the fact that the channel split up into five separate channels at this point.

Shortly after passing through the rapids, which we navigated safely, we had an exciting adventure. We were floating with the current; I was the steersman, Francois Roy and Laroche were at the oars, and Corbeil was in the bow looking out for ice cakes ahead. These cakes were very hard to see at times, as many of them were anchored to the bottom and only extended a few inches out of the water. I happened to notice one of these ice cakes close ahead and immediately told Francois to pull hard so that the boat would get speed enough to permit me to steer it. Instead of doing as instructed, Francois turned around to look ahead, as he was seated so that he faced the rear of the boat. By the time he turned to look ahead, we had struck the ice cake. Corbeil immediately jumped on the ice and held the bow of the boat down in order to prevent the current from forcing the stern of the boat down, causing us to swamp. Naturally, I was very angry at Francois for not obeying my orders. I placed my Smith & Wesson gun by my side and remarked that hereafter if they did not obey my orders, I would use my gun on them.

There were several others going down the river at the same time. Among them was a party of three Swedes who had asked my advice about making the trip while we were at Sheep Camp. I had advised them to follow us and not to try to go ahead. This they did until after we had had our experience with the cake of ice. We had stopped to cook dinner, expecting the Swedes also to stop; but instead of doing this, they went on by, following the Day brothers who had been traveling directly behind my boat and who had made the trip before.

Another party, headed by Bertraud, had made camp with us; and when we had finished our dinner, both parties started on down the river together. As we went on, the river became much higher and the current slower which indicated that there was an ice jam somewhere below us. As our boats were close together, I called to Bertraud that it did not look good ahead to me. He replied that the others had evidently gone through so it must be all right. I said it might look as if they had gone through all right, but we did not know what might have happened to them. Soon after this, a large block of ice came in view; it was about fifteen feet high and was impossible to pass; but as we drew nearer, we discovered this wall of ice was at a bend in the river and that the channel was open. The current became much swifter as we rounded the bend; and much to our surprise, we saw a man perched on a cake of anchor ice in the middle of the channel. This anchor ice was so large that it had caused the water to fall over two feet at the lower end. When we reached this point, the bow of the boat dove down taking water and drenching Corbeil who was in the bow. The current was so swift that we were carried on by him without having any chance to rescue him. This man proved to be one of the Swedes whose boat had capsized on this cake of ice. The other two had managed to hang onto the boat and were rescued by the Day brothers. As we went on, we found the Day boys and the two Swedes camped at the next bend in the river, patrolling the river bank to see if there was not some way in which they could get the man off the ice. We also made camp there in order to help them but at six o'clock had not devised any way to get him ashore. We then cooked supper, keeping a sharp lookout to see if the ice had moved any. The ice cake he was on extended about two feet above the water but apparently was anchored firmly to the bottom. Just after supper, we noticed he had changed his position and seemed to be lying down. Then we saw that the cake of ice was moving, so we took a boat, went out into mid-stream, and waited for the ice cake to come by. We were fortunate enough to get him off safely and ashore. You can imagine how the man must have suffered on the ice for the six hours he was held a prisoner there, not only physically but also mentally wondering if he would ever get ashore safely. This accident occurred at a point in the river called the Devil's Gate about twenty miles above the mouth of the Pelly River. The Swede had evidently had enough of the Yukon River country as he refused to stay at Forty Mile with the rest of his party, going on to St. Michael and then to Juneau where he met his death that same summer working in the Treadwell Mine.

We arrived at Forty Mile the 15th of May, 1893, where I found my wife in good health. Before going out, I had made arrangements for her to stay here at Jack McQuesten's trading post. She had been busy making all kinds of mittens, moccasins, parkas, etc., and was considered one of the most skilled workers in this line in the country.

My wife and I went on up to Troublesome Point to our claim and mined there that summer. On the 15th of August, we came back to Forty Mile, and I finally built the house I had been planning on so long.

The N. A. T. Company steamer, Cudahy, came on up the river that same summer, and the company built a trading post just below the mouth of the Forty Mile River which they called Cudahy. Tom O'Brien took a contract to put up the building for them for $1,000. When the building was completed, John J. Healy told Tom O'Brien that he had lost the combination of the safe and would have to give him a note in payment. O'Brien accepted the note and endorsed it over to Jack McQuesten upon receipt of the money from McQuesten. McQuesten endorsed it over to the A. C. Company who presented it to the N. A. T. Company headquarters in Chicago for payment. This business transaction amused the other traders very much as it indicated that the N. A. T. Company had come into the Yukon country to trade without any money on hand.

Quite a large number of miners spent the following winter—'93-'94—at Forty Mile. A few men were gathered together one evening for a social talk when trouble broke out among them. Washburn, in whose cabin the men were gathered, became angry at George Madlock, one of my partners, and stabbed him in the back. Madlock retaliated in the following manner. He went to his cabin, secured his gun, and came back to Washburn's cabin. There being a light in the cabin, Madlock could see through the window; and when

Washburn happened to walk toward the window, Madlock fired at him, not with intent to kill but in order to even up the score by inflicting a flesh wound. Washburn was struck in the thigh, and both he and Madlock had to be nursed back to good health. Later on they "buried the hatchet," shook hands, and became friends again.

Washburn afterwards moved down to Circle City with his native wife where he again figured in a shooting scrape. He was in Jim Connister's saloon one night when Connister happened to come from behind the bar; he grabbed Connister's gun and threatened the others in the saloon with it. Connister turned to face him and stood with his back toward the stove and his hands crossed behind him, waiting his chance to get control of the situation. Tom King managed to slip a gun into the hands of Connister, who then walked directly toward Washburn, firing as he walked, and hit him between the eyes, killing Washburn at once. The miners tried Jim Connister for murder and found him "not guilty." He was respected and liked by all those who knew him, and it was decided that he had only killed in self defense. This happened in the winter of '96.

In the latter part of March, '94, my wife and I went up to Miller Creek where I had a claim. I freighted some material to the claim for a blacksmith shop, including steel and tools, and built a cabin there the same spring. Frank Cormier and his native wife were also at Miller Creek at this time. When my wife and I were ready to return to Forty Mile, Cormier asked us to take his wife with us as she was not feeling well and wanted to go to her home at Juneau. So in June, '94, we three left on the one day's trip to Forty Mile with just enough grub for the one day as we had to walk and did not wish to carry anything except what we would actually need. Cormier's wife proved to be so weak, though, that it took us two days to make the trip, and we were all very hungry and tired when we reached Forty Mile.

This same summer, my wife visited her father and her people at Unalakleet, taking the shortcut from Kaltag to Unalakleet. When she returned, she brought with her a nephew. This boy lived with us until he was nineteen years old when he died on June 10, 1911.

It was also in the summer of '94 that we organized the Yukon Pioneers' Lodge.

In the Fall of '94, I bought a blacksmith shop from John

I. White at Forty Mile; and in the summer of '95, I built a warehouse in which to store my stock of materials.

In the summer of 1891, Harper—McQuesten's partner—established a trading post at Fort Selkirk. There had formerly been a Hudson Bay Company's trading post at this place which had been destroyed by the coast Indians and then abandoned by the Company.

When the Day brothers came in in '93, they went up the Stewart River prospecting. At the end of that same summer, they went out to Juneau and were married there that winter to two sisters, French Canadian girls. In the Spring of '94, they came to the mouth of the Sixty Mile River with their wives, where a sawmill was being operated by Harper and Ladue. The brothers built a home here and worked at the sawmill. During the winter of '94, twins were born to Hughie Day and his wife; and later on in March, 1895, he and his wife and their twins went up the Sixty Mile River to the mouth of Miller Creek where I had my claim. A few days after their arrival at Miller Creek, Hughie's wife became ill, and he asked me to take them with my dog team to the doctor who was located at Cudahy just below the mouth of the Forty Mile River. This I did, but apparently his wife was beyond aid as she died within a week after our arrival at Cudahy. This left Hughie with the twins; and, as it was impossible for him to take care of them himself, he sent them outside to be cared for with a missionary who was going out at that time. He returned to the Sixty Mile River where his brother was still living and went to work in the sawmill again. Shortly after his return, his brother, Al, was injured at the mill. An inserted-tooth saw was used at the mill, and while the saw was in motion the setter became loose, permitting both the setter and the cutter to fly off. The setter is of a half-moon shape, pointed at one end and wider at the other end. The pointed end struck Al Day in the forehead, burying itself in his forehead at a point just above and between the eyes to a depth of one and one-quarter of an inch.

The others were at a loss as to how to remove the piece of steel, so Hughie Day took his brother down the Yukon River to Cudahy, a distance of a hundred miles, to the doctor. The doctor removed it with a pair of pinchers, holding a piece of wood from a cigar box on Al's forehead for a pry. Al eventually recovered and returned to the Sixty Mile River. Then the Day brothers tore down their cabin at Sixty

Mile, made a raft out of it, and with Al's wife drifted down to Circle City. Here they took the logs and lumber from the rafts and built a cabin. In the winter of '96, when the Klondike was discovered, they left their home at Circle and went to the Klondike on the ice. Through all their misfortunes and hard work, these two brothers never became discouraged or lost hope, always looking ahead for something better.

The first horse was brought into the Yukon River country in the spring of '93 by one of my partners, Pete McDonald. As the snow was quite deep, it was necessary to wrap sacks around his feet and legs to prevent him from sinking into the soft snow. When taking him up the steep places in Dyea Pass, steps were cut into the bank so that he could get up. At times, he balked at climbing these places, and the only way they could get him up was to withhold his feed for a while, then have a man go ahead holding a bunch of hay in his hand, enticing him up the bank. He was taken down the Yukon on a scow to the mouth of the Forty Mile River.

In the early part of the summer of '93, a party of three men arrived at the Forty Mile River from the outside and came on up the river to prospect. Their names were Charley Anderson, Gus "the Greek," and Allen. In the fall of '93, they started to drift down the Forty Mile on a raft heading for the mouth of the river to winter there. The ice had begun to form in the river when they started on their trip. When they came to a point just above the Forty Mile Canyon one evening, ice blocked the river all the way across. Before they realized that the ice had blocked their progress, their raft had drifted down and lodged against it, held firmly there by the current in the middle of the channel. They decided that one of them should fasten a rope under his arms and around his body and try to crawl ashore on the ice, leaving the other end of the rope on the raft so that it could be hauled ashore. Gus "the Greek" volunteered to go. He had managed to cover a part of the distance when the ice broke beneath him. His partners endeavored to pull him back to the raft but found it impossible to do so as his body offered so much resistance to the current that they did not have strength enough to get him back. They were forced to tie the rope to the raft and stay there all night with the lifeless body of Gus dangling on the other end of the rope. In the morning, the ice was stronger, and both men successfully crawled ashore and walked to Forty Mile, a distance of ten miles.

Frank Densmore, George Madlock, and several other men went back to the raft the next day and got the body of Gus "the Greek," bringing him to Forty Mile where he was buried. Charley Anderson, who took part in this adventure, was the same man who was credited with making three-quarters of a million dollars at Dawson when gold was discovered there later on. Five or six years after making his fortune, he had more cents than dollars.

★ ★ ★

In coming down the Yukon River in the year 1886, we met Jack McQuesten and John Hughes on their way out to San Francisco. Mr. McQuesten was on his way out to try and persuade the A. C. Company to bring in forty or fifty tons of merchandise to the mouth of the Stewart River for the needs of the twenty-five miners that were there.

On his arrival in San Francisco the A. C. Company informed him that they could not consider the proposition, giving him any number of good reasons. (The A. C. Company did not want any miners in the Yukon Valley.) Therefore Mr. McQuesten went to Portland, Oregon, with the intention of organizing a company of his own to bring goods into the Yukon Valley. When it was reported in San Francisco that McQuesten was organizing a company in Portland, it was not long until Mr. McQuesten was the recipient of a telegram from the A. C. Company requesting him to come to San Francisco, as they, the A. C. Company, had changed their minds and would be pleased to complete negotiations with regard to the shipment of the required amount of goods to the mouth of the Stewart River. They shipped the goods, and one could easily see from the brands and quality of goods received that they did not want any miners in the Yukon River Valley. The bacon was in slabs three feet long, all of which was yellow. We called it the "Yard Bacon." The flour was moldy, the rice was lumpy, the fruit was green, and in the beans were plenty of rocks and gravel. The only thing that was dry was the Black Powders (which had to be absolutely dry in order to kill fur animals). We did not receive better fare until in 1893 when the N. A. T. Company came in, after which time the A. C. Company gave us better provisions.

From the goods described in the above paragraph one can readily see the cause of that dreaded disease, the scurvy, which many of the miners contracted, and from which five or six of them died. However, being naturally strong and healthy, most of them managed to pull through.

In 1889 the A. C. Company built the steamer Arctic for their Yukon River trade, but on her first trip up the river she struck a snag and sank with her entire cargo, leaving the miners at Forty Mile without any supplies for the coming winter. As there were no supplies of any kind on the Yukon, between twenty-five and forty miners went down the river to St. Michael where there was an abundance of wet goods for the winter. In the spring, most of these men refused to pay for supplies and provisions received during that year, on the grounds that it was poor management on the part of the A. C. Company that left us destitute at Forty Mile. In the year following, the A. C. Company made claim to the Government at Washington, D. C. for the money expended on behalf of the destitutes, and received $41,000, which, needless to say, was quite a profit.

If you could see the food we had to eat from 1886 to 1893, you might laugh, but if you found yourself a thousand miles from civilization, without roads, as we were, it might bring tears to your eyes.

From the above statements one can easily see that the A. C. Company did not want the pioneers to stay in the Yukon Valley.

Today there are a few of the Old Yukon Pioneers left, but the A. C. Company, the N. A. T. & T. Company, A. E. Company, D. C. Company, and the N. C. Company are gone. The Yukon Pioneers turned out victors in the struggle. The railroad is now here and food will soon be much cheaper.

So here is Wishing a Merry Christmas to all and great success to the New Company.

Some Early Yukon River History

Gordon C. Bettles

THE FIRST PROSPECTORS to locate in the central section of the Yukon River were the Schefflin brothers who landed at Nuklukyet in the fall of 1881. They owned the first independent steamer to navigate the Yukon. It was known as the Newracket, a stern-wheeler, which was about eighty feet long and twelve feet across the beam. They remained in and around Nuklukyet until 1883, when they returned to Arizona from whence they had come to Alaska. They are the discoverers of Schefflin Creek a few miles above Tanana.

The next two prospectors who came into the interior were Pete Johnson and John Bremner, who landed at Nuklukyet in the fall of 1886. They had come up the Copper River, portaged over to the Tanana River and had come down this in company with Lieut. H. T. Allen. Upon landing at Nuklukyet (today this is known as "Old Station" and is located seventeen miles below the present town of Tanana), Pete Johnson and John Bremner decided to remain there, as they could purchase an outfit from Walker and Fredericks who were running the trading post. They remained there the winter of 1886-87.

In the spring of 1887 they necked an outfit over to the Koyukuk River, a distance of two hundred miles, and landed there before the breakup. Here they prospected the bars on the upper reaches of the river and that summer found good color.

They made rockers and took out a grubstake and returned by trail that fall to Nuklukyet. They wintered here and in the following spring outfitted again and returned by trail to the Koyukuk, necking their outfit as before. With them went John Folger, Henry Davis, Earnest Chapman and John Hughes, all of whom had come to Nuklukyet in the fall of 1887. John Minook, a half-Russian, accompanied them.

Upon reaching the Koyukuk River, John Bremner decided

to do more extensive prospecting, so Pete Johnson helped him whipsaw lumber and build a boat. John then dropped downriver, leaving Pete on the bar they had formerly worked. He hadn't gone far when he discovered a large tributary coming in from the north, so he poled up this fork some distance but had little success prospecting. This fork is now called John's River.

Leaving John's River, he dropped down to the Dolby River, and at or near the mouth he stopped for lunch. His fire attracted two natives—one an old medicine man and the other a native about twenty-six years old. They came to his camp, and although John had but a scant outfit, he fed them. After they had eaten, John started to pack the grub box down to the boat, leaving his rifle loaded in camp. When he got within a few feet of the boat, the old medicine man told the young Indian to shoot John and they would have his boat, gun and grub and no one would ever know what became of the old man as the white men were few and the Indians were many in number.

The young Indian did as he was told, through fear of the medicine man, and shot poor old John twice but didn't kill him. Then the old medicine man took the gun and shot him three more times before he was dead. They sank his body in the river and went on their way with the boat and supplies.

In due time, when John didn't show up, Pete Johnson and John Minook made another boat and dropped downriver to look for him. It was through John Minook that the murder was discovered.

The following year there were a number of men that came into Nuklukyet as the news of the discovery of gold on the Koyukuk reached Forty Mile camp. Among them were Hank Wright, Jim Bender, Frank Densmore, Tom Evans, George Cary, Frank Hawley, Captain Bill Moore, Joe Ladue, Old Herman, Jim Stafford, George Newman, Jim Baker, John and Jim McPike, Tuck Lambert and Gordon Bettles. This bunch got together and decided it was not safe to go into the Koyukuk under the circumstances, so they decided to spend the summer showing the Indians just what it meant to take the life of a white man. The Indians had killed Mrs. Bean on the Tanana in the early 80's and a Russian at Nulato a few years before that, and now poor old John Bremner whom everyone had liked so much. This posse of white men vowed they would make it their business that summer to seek every Indian murderer and hang him.

They then went down the Yukon to the mouth of the Koyukuk River. There they learned that the little river steamer The Explorer, belonging to the trader Aneasum Belkof of the Russian Mission, was expected the next day, so they took her up the Koyukuk, leaving two men to watch their barges at the mouth. The Explorer had been built for Lieutenant Stoney to explore the Stoney River in the Arctic, but when this expedition found they could not go but a few miles up the Arctic rivers on account of the canyons and falls, the boat had been brought back to St. Michael and sold to Father Zacar and Aneasum Belkof.

With John Minook as interpreter, the party of twenty-two men went up the Koyukuk River to the camp where the two murderers were living. It was some distance up the Dolby River and the exact location was not known, so they picked up a native woman who could guide them and soon found a village of about eighty natives. As this was the first steamboat to navigate the Koyukuk, the natives were very much frightened, and the prospectors had to surround them before they realized what was happening. The only two who tried to get away were the murderers. They were captured to make sure there was no one else; the Chief was told that he too would be taken if he did not give up all the men who killed John Bremner, and that they were going to hang by the neck until they were dead. He was also told that if the Indians killed another white man these same men would come back and take him and his whole family and hang them too.

Upon reaching the mouth of the Koyukuk, where the two natives were to be hanged, a dispute arose over hanging the old medicine man as the young Indian, when asked if the old man had shot John, had said no, not realizing that he was more afraid of the old medicine man than of death by hanging.

To settle the dispute, a line was drawn by the spokesman of the party who said, "All in favor of hanging both Indians step on this side of the line." Only seven of the twenty-two crossed the line, so the old man was turned loose and the party dispersed.

The young man was hanged on a cottonwood tree on the upper end of the seven mile island at the mouth of the Koyukuk River. The old medicine man returned to the vil-

lage on the Dolby River, and the relatives of the young
Indian tried to kill the old man by cutting him up, but he
recovered enough to make his way to the Yukon River, where
he died two years later. The feud between the two Indian
families lasted for three years and caused the death of six
Indians.

A Sequel to Mrs. Bean's Murder

(Author Unknown)

MRS. BEAN WAS killed in the early 80's by "Bushie Head's" tribe on the Tanana River. They had intended to kill both Mr. and Mrs. Bean and rob the store, but the Indian who was chosen to shoot Mr. Bean had wet powder in his gun. It failed to go off and he was not successful. However, Mrs. Bean was killed without a chance to defend herself, for the Indians crept up to the house in the dark of night and shot her through the window. They had no reason to suspect trouble from the Indians, for all had been peaceful in their relations with them. Had Mrs. Bean a chance to defend herself she would have put up a good fight, for she was a brave woman and a good shot.

At that time Jack McQuesten, Harper and Mayo were running a trading post at Nuklukyet, so Mr. Bean came down to them for help. McQuesten and Mayo returned upriver with Bean and helped him bury Mrs. Bean's body. Then they hauled all of the trader's goods down to Nuklukyet, and Mr. Bean left for the outside the following summer.

In the fall of 1888 I purchased Mr. Frederick's interest in the Nuklukyet Trading Post and became a partner with James Walker. We had a very good year's trade. Walker went to the States in the summer of 1889 and died sometime later in San Francisco, California. I then took over his interests and during the winter of 1889 and 1890 I was alone running the trading post. In the fall, before the freeze-up, eighty Tanana River Indians came down to hold me up. Part of them were from Bushie Head's tribe and part from Chief Evan's. They camped about seven miles above the post and sent a runner down to notify me that they were going to hold me up if I didn't make a potlatch for them.

I sent word that I would make no potlatch and that I would be there to meet them if they decided to hold me up. True to their word, they all came down and were armed with a log about thirty feet long, which was being packed on the backs of twenty strong young men. This log was to be used as a ram to break in the store door, after which they intended to rob the store.

I had with me two interpreters (Yukon natives who understood English fairly well) and I told them they would have to tell the Indians exactly what I said. I then gave each of the interpreters a new rifle, with plenty of ammunition and told them they must not shoot until I told them to; that I hoped to settle the trouble without killing anyone. I buckled my two six-guns on my belt and took my rifle in hand, and when the Indians got within fifty feet of the store we all went out in front of them. I told them to stop or I would shoot and kill twelve of them, as there were twelve bullets in my gun and I wanted to kill someone. I drew a bead on their leader, and they halted.

I told them they were like dogs, when one dog was down they all jumped on him. "I am only one. You may kill me, but I am a good shot and will kill twelve of you." When I said this they dropped the log, and as I advanced they retreated. When they had withdrawn to the river bank, a distance of about one hundred yards, I told them to go back to their camp and tomorrow to come down two at a time and I would trade with them until they all had been served.

The following morning two young Indians returned with a bunch of furs valued at about three hundred dollars. They told me the furs were sent to me by the two chiefs as a present. I thanked them and told them to come down two at a time until they had all done so. This they did. When the last one came down I told him to go back and tell all of them to come down as I wished to make them a present and bury the hatchet. They all came and I gave them goods to the amount of the value of the furs they had given me, and I never had any further trouble with natives.

Later on in the winter Bushie Head's tribe brought down the Indian who had killed Mrs. Bean and wanted me to hang him. I told them that it was a white man's job and that it always took more than one man to do it so I would have to wait until more white men came to the post. I also told them I would make strong medicine against the Indian murderer and that he would not live long. My predictions came true, for he died the following summer.

Sourdough Life

Lynn Smith

THIS IS THE brief story of a young Hoosier, native of New Castle, Indiana, who had been slaving at a watchmaker's bench in a jewelry store for eight years without saving any money. I was very much in love with a dandy girl who had a good home, but I was not willing to ask her to share my lot and go into a shanty, taking the chances. About that time the Klondike was struck, and a man working for the same jeweler in Anderson, Indiana, who had formerly been a California miner, kept hammering away at me to come along to Alaska, telling how easy it was and that he was going. He incidentally touched me for two hundred dollars to send his wife, who was living in Peoria, Illinois, to Seattle, Washington.

The day after he showed me a letter from an old partner, who had written him that he had made $16,000 the summer before in Dawson, and that on the way outside he had stopped at Minook Creek, panned on three creeks and gotten fifty cents to the pan in the grass roots, I bade goodby to old Indiana. So we left in a blaze of glory to seek our fortune, never thinking but that we would see home within one year with plenty of money to last the balance of our natural lives, as well as enough to keep our poor relations.

There were lots of men headed for the same place on the train west and the trip was full of interest. We sat up all night when we went through the Rocky Mountains and finally reached Seattle. It was full of men and women as busy as bees. When we walked through the railroad yards, we saw cars full of a specie of animal new to us and upon inquiry found they were reindeer ready for shipment to Alaska from Lapland. These held our attention for some time.

We then noticed a crowd around a man demonstrating how to save gold with a new panner that whirled around, and we left him after paying for and leaving our order for one. On the next corner on a vacant lot a man was standing, shouting "Here is what you want, save your money and time, and don't work building a boat after you get north. Let us build it here and ship it knocked down and get ahead of the rest of the bunch. You can be panning gold while they are building their boats." So we had to buy one so as not to lose any time and we paid for it on the spot. This was pretty good business for one day in Seattle, but it was not over yet.

We four innocents (two from Anderson and two from Logansport, Indiana) had to see the sights, so we headed for Billy the Mugs, and then on to the Paris House, otherwise known as the House of All-Nations. This proved to be very interesting, especially the little slant-eyed Japanese girls, who were new to us greeners. When we filed into a room which had no chairs and it was found out that all we wanted was to do a little kidding, we were politely asked to move on. We were told there were about six hundred women of all shades and colors, and about seventy-five different nations represented here.

Our next move was to a vaudeville and a dance house. We didn't dance, so we took a booth upstairs and in a few minutes two dames named the Clark sisters came in. One planted herself on Pickel's knee and said, "Come on boys, buy a bottle," and pushed the button. She was playing with his watch charm, and when one of us bright boys, who had secured a $20 bill with the No. 1000 on it on the back, showed his bank roll of ones and twos with the apparent $1000 bill on the outside, the other sister sat down on his knee and wanted to get married right away. However, we were lucky and left after spending only about four dollars, for it was soon noised around the house that the party in No. 8 were pikers and we were not bothered further. We had seen enough thrills and actions for our first day and headed for the hotel, a tired bunch after just getting our eyeteeth cut, seeing the cruel world uncut and as it was in the west in those days. Everybody was money mad.

As I recall it, we met the next morning and, after holding a post-mortem over the Paris House, turned our attention to finding a boat to take us north. We wanted a boat to take us to Skagway and one that was safe and wouldn't sink, so we began our search which took us several days.

We had been told that we must have colored glasses on account of the snow and saw a Jew on a corner selling spectacles and with a sign up which read, "We can make you read for $3." He had a card up with a pair of glasses on it, and the man said to the Polack in our party, "Can't you read the top line?" "No." "Well then try this pair. Can't you read the sign now?" "No," answered the Polack. "All right, let's try these. How are they?" "No good," answered the Polack. Then the Jew flew into a rage and said, "Can you read *anything*?" and the man answered "No." The Jew said, "You d--- fool, do you think I sell you education for $3?" The crowd laughed and we bought our snow glasses.

OUTFITS FOR THE KLONDIKE
Articles Necessary in an Outfit for One Man
One Year in the Diggings.

	Weight-lbs.	Cost
Clothing	70	$ 95

One clothes bag, 5 yards mosquito netting, 3 suits heavy underwear, 1 heavy mackinaw coat, 2 pairs heavy mackinaw pants, half dozen heavy wool socks, one-third dozen heavy wool mittens, 2 pairs leather gloves, 2 heavy overshirts, 2 pair heavy snag-proof rubber boots, 1 pair shoes, 1 pkg. needles, thread, wax, 2 pairs blankets, 4 towels, 2 pairs overalls, 1 suit oil clothing, 2 rubber blankets, 1 sleeping bag, 1 pair felt boots, 1 pair heavy rubber overshoes.

Groceries	1,200	$ 90

200 lbs. bacon, 300 lbs. flour, 25 lbs. peaches, 25 lbs. apples, 25 lbs. apricots, 25 lbs. pitted prunes, 25 lbs. coffee, 10 lbs. tea, 50 lbs. sugar, 150 lbs. beans, 90 lbs. oatmeal, 25 lbs. cornmeal, 100 lbs. rice, 5 lbs. baking powder, 5 lbs. yeast, 5 lbs. soda, 1 large box matches.

Hardware and Camp Outfit	200	$ 50

One pair ice creepers, one sheath knife and sheath, 2 miners' shovels, 1 spool wire,

4 sail needles, 2 gold pans, 2 balls twine, half
dozen 8-inch flat files, 1 handled axe and 2
handles, 1 screwdriver, 1 Disston hand saw,
1 wood jackplain, 1 ratchet brace, 4 bits
assorted sizes, 1 saw set, 30 feet of rope, 1
pack strap, 20 lbs. assorted nails, 1 pkg. bob-
nails, 3 lbs. oakum, 5 lbs. pitch, 1 set knives
and forks (six each), 6 teaspoons, 3 table-
spoons, 1 compass, 1 hunter's axe and sheath,
1 magnifying glass, 1 mixing spoon, 1 dust
belt, 1 four-quart coffee pot, cups, 1 fry pan,
1 retinned dish-pan, 1 coffee mill, 1 granite
kettle, retinned cover, 3 granite plates, 1
whipsaw, 1 gold scale, 1 sled, 1 tent and
stove, 1 box candles.

Armament   20 $ 24
   One repeating rifle, 30-30, with reloading
tools, and 100 rounds of brass shell cartridges, 1 large hunting knife and an assort-
ment of fishing tackle.

Medicines   2 $ 5
   One Chest—assorted remedies, plasters,
bandages, mosquito exterminator, etc., 1
pair dark eyeglasses.
   Cost and weight of outfit and expense of
transportation can be materially reduced by
prospectors traveling in parties of three or
four, as one camping, hardware, and armament outfit will answer for two men. In traveling by steamer or rail, 150 pounds of
baggage is checked free for each passenger.
                        Totals 1,492 $264

FROM: *The Chicago Daily Tribune—Tribune Extra Klondike
       Edition, 1898.*

★

   A little later we let our whiskers grow so that the mosquitos would not eat us up and had our last shave that night
for some six months afterwards, or until we found we had

been stung. Poor boobs from Indiana, but we were game to the core.

We boarded the little boat (a pretty one with new paint) and found people from almost every state. Doctors from Maine, dentists from Keokuk, Iowa, and sawmill men from South Africa.

We first landed at Victoria, British Columbia, on the morning of March 17, 1898. At this time I happened to realize it was my 27th birthday and left the ship to buy out the town of green ribbon. When I went aboard again, I made everyone wear the colors and we were off again—a merry bunch, all in a hurry to reach Skagway.

All of us had a mortal fear of seasickness, and before leaving Anderson while attending a seance, Jim told me I was going and how to keep from getting seasick. "Just sit down with your back up against a wall and keep your hands clasped over your head and look out over the water and the feeling will soon pass away." When we reached Queen Charlotte Sound, the boat began to pitch and roll, and I told the boys to do as I did and got my position at the end of the piano with my feet encased in a pair of patent leather shoes. Just then a guy started for the door and couldn't hold it and it went right over my patent leathers square. I took one look, got one small smell, and the feeling passed away but only after they carried me to my room and I had later been on land for six days. Oh yes, it is easy to keep from getting seasick if you only know how!

We were all uneasy and didn't take off our pants—only our socks and shoes so if we had a wreck we could swim better. After about five days we landed at Wrangell. We walked ashore and a man came up to us and said, "Have you boys got a map of the country?" We said we had none and he said, "I saw a sign up the street that read Bureau of Information. Let's go there and get one." We went (poor boobs) and stepped inside a large tent and upon entering noticed that a man stepped in front of the flap of the tent, closed it and stood inside with a rifle. We wondered at this and then noticed that there were gambling devices of all kinds. We didn't fall for them because we were short of money, having spent more with those Seattle fakers than we had intended. Upon going outside we noticed a crowd around "Big Whitie," who I recognized as having been with the Wallace's Circus in Indiana. He was working his shell game.

Doc (one of the boys on our boat) tried to guess which shell had the pea under it and a big Swede was also guessing. Doc quit, but the Swede started to double up, ran short of money and went to his belt for more. While he was at it the cappers all rushed around him and while one of them was helping him in front, another whipped out a knife and slit his belt and took his roll. About one hundred of us were watching—all afraid to make a move. At any rate we were glad to get back on the boat again—and we had learned something else. Never bet on another man's game. Boys, remember this and stick to it through your lives, you can't beat a man at his own game.

We landed at Skagway on March 24, 1898, and found thousands of people there. No beds were to be had, but we finally found a place to put our dunnage and just laid down alongside of it until morning. We were up early, and Jap and I went out to the street when we heard a shot and looked up to see a man run across the street and then drop. We hurried back and got our guns. We had 32 Stevens revolvers and put them in our pockets, with our hands ready for action, not knowing what to expect. Soon afterwards we learned from a man "that he had it coming to him—it's a wonder he didn't get it sooner." We then learned that no matter what kind of a crowd you may be in, if you keep your mouth shut and attend to your own business, you are never in danger of harm from outsiders, especially if you are Cheechakos and are broke and green as we surely showed ourselves to be.

We then held a caucus and decided to take our camp things out seven miles from town, and Padgett and I left with our first load. We found a nice spot to pitch a tent, and he handed me an axe and said, "You go get some wood and I will make camp." I picked up the implement and looked at it and said, "So this is an axe." It was the first one I had ever had in my hands. I started out and finally found a nice tree up on the hillside and began trying to chop it. I chopped all around and it finally fell, not downhill as I wanted it to fall but uphill. I trimmed it up and packed it to the camp and will never forget the crowd around looking at it. Chopped all around like a beaver, and once or twice I passed men who yelled "Hello, beaver" as I passed by.

Our next problem was the big pack over White Pass. Having read once that a man could pack as much as his own weight, I first tried three fifty pound sacks of flour on the first trip, and cussed the man who said that many times before I reached the summit. After about a week of packing, we landed our grub on top and still had a twenty-two foot boat that we had purchased in Seattle to bring up. It was hard to figure out how to do this. We finally took six boards twenty-two feet long and tied a rope near each end and slung the rope over our shoulders. Here Jap and I learned the lock step instead of at Jeffersonville. On many of the trips we were the subject of everyone's jeers and hoots, but like heroes, marched onward toward our goal laughing at the thought that we would be sitting in the sun when they were whipsawing lumber for their boats. We did, not!

At the top we found a place in a tent barn, sleeping behind horses lining the walls. We rested on the manure and straw and had our first taste of horse meat the next morning, supposing it was beef. We struck it lucky for a time after that as the weather was nice. However, the first night of sleep after that we hastily put up our tent and went to sleep during a heavy snowstorm and during the night our tent fell down on us. My, but it was heavy. We looked out and it was still dark, so we just lay there until morning. About two feet of soft heavy snow had fallen during the night and that evening we heard of the terrible snowslide that killed so many on the other or Dyea trail. About twenty from our boat were killed and we had come near going that route.

At Lake Linderman there was a regular town with everybody whipsawing lumber, making boats, etc. But we who were so wise, loaded all our belongings on the two sleds, boat and all, put up a sail and made the trip over the lake to Six Mile River above the Tagish Custom House. There were many ahead of us, but we soon had our boat put together and in the water soaking up. Then began the wait for the ice to go out.

Our neighbor had a fire outdoors. He had put a large round pot on the coals which we noticed were covered with ashes. About an hour later he went to get the pot and it smelled good, and upon investigation we found it to be a big Dutch oven full of beans. They later on showed us some bread baked the same way.

One of us had a brainstorm right there, and after quite a debate we decided we couldn't leave without a Dutch oven, so Jap said, "I'm going to be short of trickle (there was always a little trickle at the side of his mouth) and I will walk back to Skagway and get a Dutch oven and some more tobacco and see about the mail." Off he went and in four days time returned with a 60 oven on his back which he had packed the sixty miles in water. We had no time to try it before the ice broke in the lake, nor did we ever use it after toting it around for about three thousand miles further.

Our ship Hattie Sharp was ready for action, but we did not know enough to get in and see how it rode in the water with a load. What was the use, hadn't that man in Seattle told us it would carry 1600 pounds and we were only two men with about 1200 pounds. At last the word came that the ice was broken in the lake, and we broke camp "queek" and began to load our outfit. Deeper and deeper the boat went in the water as each sack was put in and when we got aboard, lo and behold only three inches of freeboard showed. Just then Jap shifted the tobacco in his mouth and we nearly capsized. We wondered what to do. Everybody was rushing past us and one "wise Mike" said, "Lash two big dry logs on each side." So back to the tall uncut timber we went and came back with two large dry logs and then went back for more. We rustled some rope and fastened them on and soon started for Tagish House where the custom house was located. We tied up there and went to get our clearance, pay our duty, etc. The Red Coat looked, listened and laughed, and said, "Are you kids crazy? You can't leave here in that craft to go on the lake. You would drown before you would get halfway across." Right then we longed for home and mother, but we sold four hundred pounds of the grub and the man said we could start, knowing full well we would come back if we could do so. The big lake ahead was filled with hundreds of boats. After we had gone about two miles, a little wave came up, hit the log aside the boat, split and half landed in the boat. Later more showed up, then lots of them came fast and one of us began bailing water while the other rowed towards shore or shallow water. We found shallow water and putting on our hip boots, one on each side, began skidding the boat around the lake on the mud and water. Finally, late that night we caught up with the fleet who were all waiting for the ice to move again.

We found our nearest neighbor was Dr. Tuller's party that had come up on the same boat with us. I thought he was Mohammed, for after giving us the once over, he said,

"Well, boys, put some of your load in our boat and we will lash your boat alongside like a catamaran." This we did and he nursed us along all the way to Dawson. It was a wonderful trip, full of thrills and kicks every minute. The first one was White Horse Rapids. Both of us had promised our girls before leaving home that we would walk around, so we had our outfit packed around on the beach and turned the boat loose to run the rapids. We caught it below but saw many boats capsize and several men drown as well as horses and mules. We got away again as soon as possible. The run was clear until we reached Five Fingers Rapids. We landed, walked down a ways and looked her over. While we were watching, there were several boats went through without a mishap, although when they took the jump off they were out of sight but bobbed up again.

We got underway and went right in the middle of the channel. I was in the back end of our boat which was tied about two-thirds behind the big boat, and we went faster all the time gaining speed. All at once I saw the two big rocks and saw Doc's boat take the high dive. I was still up in the air in our boat. Then his boat came up and I took the header and "pop" something snapped and up I came. Here is where I turned white, going about twenty-five miles an hour with a lap full of water and my boat loose from the other one. Gradually turning sidewise, expecting to upset any minute, I glanced up and saw a man in the water climbing out onto a rock as I went by. Just when I was ready to give up and get ready for the water and my watery grave, a boat hook on a long pole reached out and caught the bow of my boat and steadied it. Both boats were bobbing up, going like the mill race of Hell; Praise the Lord, Old Jasper had kept his head and saved our grub and myself. For six miles, we went in this fashion before we could land, beach the boats and put the grub on shore to dry out. About one day was lost here before we could start again. This was a relief, for we all had nervous "prostitution" all day, and we had plenty of company along the river bank, for others had the same experience.

I can't recall much of the balance of the trip other than that it was nice weather, everybody was in a good humor and there was lots of excitement. Once in a while we would see a half boat that had been sawed in half with a man riding it. Along the bank we would occasionally see a stove cut in half, for there were partners who started together with the best of intentions but fell out, and both being stubborn, would split everything up—boats, tents, stoves, and the like—and each go his own way satisfied to know he hadn't let the other fellow get the best of him. This is perfectly proper, for when you see you cannot get along with your partner or wife, quit, but don't be foolish about it or quibble over the division of your possessions. You will feel better inside if you know you gave them the best of it always. Quit friends and be friends, and don't ever hate a man or woman. Smile, even if it does hurt.

WHEN YOU GET THERE

Cost of shirts	$ 5.00
Boots, per pair	10.00
Rubber boots, per pair	25.00
Caribou hams, each	40.00
Flour, per fifty pounds	20.00
Beef, per pound (fresh)	.50
Bacon, per pound	.75
Coffee, per pound	1.00
Sugar, per pound	.50
Eggs, per dozen	2.00
Condensed milk, per can	1.00
Live dogs, per pound	2.00
Picks, each	15.00
Shovels, each	15.00
Wages, per day	15.00
Lumber, per 1,000 feet	750.00

Months that mining is possible during the year—May, June, July. These were the prices last year, but, of course, they will be no indication of the charges next summer.

FROM: *The Chicago Daily Tribune—Tribune Extra Klondike Edition, 1898.*

Not long after we came in sight of Louse Town across the Klondike River from Dawson, we passed the Klondike River and reached Dawson. Thousands of mad, wild men and women, and mud were everywhere. Everybody was on the jump. We were anxious to make some money, for we were broke, and so we sold a few sacks of flour for $1 a pound. We then wanted to go to the mines, and seeing a man packing some horses, asked him how much he would charge to pack 150 lbs. up to Bonanza Creek eight miles away. He said, "$150 at a $1 a pound." He couldn't take it before day after tomorrow. Nuf sed.

We strolled around that evening taking in the stores on the beach, the different saloons, watching the gambling games, but it was all Greek to us. We saw the big pokes of gold dust and watched the cashier selling chips by the thousands of dollars or $500 worth. Our hearts beat against our shirts.

Then the girls began to gather. They had painted cheeks and lips that would give any man painter's colic. Both Jap and I had full beards and looked too pitiful to them so not many bothered us. However, many a man was grabbed and led onto the floor for a waltz that lasted sometimes as much as three or five minutes, then was led to the bar where they had a drink and the dame was handed a pasteboard chip that went into her stocking.

This dance hall had about seventy-five girls known as dance hall girls and not all of them were by any means degenerate. All of them had nicknames such as The Virgin, Cheechako Lil, Buntie, the Oregon Mare, the Utah Filly, Bunch Grass, the Black Bear and her sister, the Cub, a light-colored Negress known as The African Queen, another called Wiggles, and so on down the line. You could pay your money and take your choice. If you didn't watch out, they would help themselves to your money. Can you imagine four Hoosiers with full beards, mouths agape, listening to the music coming from every place any time of the day or night.

Was it any wonder that when Louis Pond offered me $20 a day to take his watch bench, I wouldn't do it, and said, "Not for me, no more fixing watches, I'm going where I can get fifty cents to the pan in the grass roots." Do you wonder that we were anxious to get away from that place where everything cost dollars and everything was going out of our pockets and nothing coming in. Painted-cheeked ladies tempted us on every turn though we were all broke and wanting to get away to our grass roots about one thousand miles beyond—so off for Minook Creek or Rampart.

I forgot to say I inquired and found that there never had been any man in Dawson who had made $16,000 the winter before, so I knew we had been strung and I was glad to be rid of Padgett and did not regret the money he had borrowed from me. Still, didn't I see the letter myself that said he and Robinson who had lived in Minook had gotten fifty cents to the pan in the grass roots? It must be so or he wouldn't have written it—I thought.

That downriver trip from Dawson was a wonderful experience. The sunshiny woods were a thrill. Black bears were on every island and game was everyplace. I remember one island that had a bunch of geese on it, and Jap took his 45-90 rifle, sneaked up, shot and rushed back holding up a big goose. Not long after it was in the pot.

The little bugs (mosquitoes) were all there with their stingers, and it was necessary to get on the point of an island to sleep where there was a wind, or else wear a veil all the time. Our whiskers really came in handy after all on these islands.

We arrived at Circle City early one morning about four o'clock. On landing we saw two men come out of a saloon, holding up a third man. They took him to a small cabin where there was a watchmaker sign—and poor George Bemis was led to bed. It was the first watchmaker that I ever saw that "let his foot slip" up in Alaska. In later years we became great friends, for he was in business when I was in business at Ruby. He passed away in 1921 of cancer of the stomach, after making and spending thousands of dollars for wine, women and song.

Our next stop was Fort Yukon, where there was a lone Siwash on the bank. As soon as he saw my twenty-five cent pipe, he came out to the boat with a pair of moccasins and we traded. I found these very nice to wear in the boat and did so, and we went off again on the next lap towards our grass roots and fortune.

Near Ft. Hamlin there was an Indian camp with nobody home but squaws, and we stopped to give them the once over and spent an hour kidding them—or rather letting them kid us, as we afterwards learned. They were out of sugar and tea, and one of them wanted to trade Keteticut for Socala—sugar—but none of us wanted to trade. I recall this squaw was number 111, for her chin told us so. She was branded like a Texas pony.

On this stretch we caught up with Belden and Richmond, two other boys who had heard of our grass roots, and we went into Rampart together. Each of us staked a lot and began building a cabin up on the hill. This caused quite a few comments and remarks from the old-timers who lived there.

I remember when we landed at Rampart my partner was still in our boat and I walked uptown. In front of an Indian cabin I noticed a fat squaw stooped over picking up chips and putting them into the front part of her dress. She was about two pick handles wide and across her hips was printed, "Sperrys Flour, for Family Use." I laughed and went to the river bank and told Jap, "Come up here, there is a squaw that believes in advertising." She looked up and ran into the house, spilling her firewood as she ran.

Take myself, for instance. I'd give quite a little right now for a picture of myself at that time with the first hard-boiled hat ever on the Yukon and yellow and red whiskers that grew up to the jawbone and down to the jawbone—regular Irish "eleven ways." Jap was no better, with his long black beard and bald head. One day we noticed that nobody else wore whiskers, so we shaved ours, much to our relief. When we had a haircut, they discovered we were kids from the backwoods (near Podunk, Indiana). While the barber was working on me, I noticed about ten watches on the wall, and the barber picked one up and said, "It's a wonder some one of these fellows coming in is not a watchmaker; everybody's watch is on the bum." I said, "I'm one. You gather them up and I'll fix them and pay you for getting them." Within the next two days he handed me about ten watches. I went to work up on the hill in my cabin on a rough table. After fixing them I took them down to deliver and to pay him for collecting them, then later went to get my pay and found he was no longer in town. Upon inquiry, I found that he had been on a drunk the night before and was at that time with Skagway Kate. Thus I lost my first money earned in the country, about $80. Not being daunted, I got other watches and attended to them myself and began picking up $10 to $20 a day.

About that time the boats began to come upriver from St. Michael, and we were at breakfast one morning just as the Seattle III with iron and materials for the S. Y. T. Company store landed. Almost immediately construction was started. I told the boys I was was going down and get a job as a carpenter. I walked up to a man by the name of Mr.

HOUSE RULES — MAYO'S HOTEL

Craps—Chuckluck—
Stud Horse Poker—
Black Jack games run
by the management.

Dogs bought and sold.

Insect powder for sale
at the bar.

Always notify the bar-
keeper the size of your
poke.

Guests will be provided with breakfast and dinner, but must
rustle their own lunch.

Spike boots must be removed at night.
Dogs not allowed in bunks.
Candles and hot water charged extra.
Towels changed weekly.

Among some of the accommodations offered by the extra-
ordinary hostelry are:

Every known fluid, except water, for sale at the bar.
Private entrance for ladies, by ladies in rear.
Fire escapes through the chimney.
Electric bells "threw-out" last summer.
The hotel has a medical examiner and its rates are
one oz. gold value, $16 per day.
Indians and negroes charged double.
Special rates to ministers and to the gambling
"profesh."

Rampart, Alaska, 1898

Reed and said, "Mr. Reed, do you need any more carpenters on this job?" He asked, "Are you a carpenter?" I said, "Yes, a bridge carpenter, outside." So he said to bring my tools down at noon and go to work. When I went back and told the boys, both Belden and Richmond also got on the job. I had no tools and was puzzled where to get any. However, we started with one saw and within thirty minutes Reed had me pegged, and I was put to nailing sheet iron on the sides. I got in three and one-half days work, Richmond got in one and one-half days, and Belden about a month at $1 an hour. I made about thirty-five dollars in a few days, which seemed a lot. The boats kept coming in with freight, and as they were paying $1 an hour we put in as much time as we could. Once in a while I would fix a watch between work, so I was making from ten to twenty dollars a day. I forgot to say upon inquiry there never had been a man named Robinson who got fifty cents to the pan in the grass roots in Rampart either, so our balloon had burst and we were paupers with no hope of sudden wealth. We had been fed "Bull Con" all the time and it was a good lesson to us all in later years.

Our next problem was where we could stake a claim and we were told that there were two claims left on Jack's Gulch on Quail Creek, about thirty miles away. So the next morning in the mud, with packs on our backs, we went on our first stampede. Lord! What a trip it was, with mosquitoes in clouds in our ears, mouths and noses full, and a swarm around our heads following us. We staked and returned and had the claims recorded at $5 a claim, but we couldn't mine them until winter set in when we could freight over our grub on the snow.

About that time a Mr. Huston put up a store in a tent on the beach, and while I was talking to him, a man handed him an envelope and said, "Here is my bid on those cabins." So I got busy and asked him if we could put in our bid on the job. We did and got the contract to build two cabins. Later he rented both for that winter and a man from Honolulu froze to death in one, and the following winter the other one fell down. As carpenters from Indiana our work was guaranteed *not to stand*. But—we made about $225 each in about six days.

There were plenty of boats headed for Dawson frozen in that fall and scattered all along the Yukon River after the winter snows had fallen. Rampart was a town of about 1500 people. There were only seven white women in the camp, including one brave girl from Pennsylvania, Phoebe Hoover. Time dragged on our hands, and I induced Miss Hoover to start a private school. She got busy and went to Captain Mayo, and he said, "Sure you can take them." She asked how many children she could depend on and he replied with his big hearty laugh, "Take the whole damn kaboodle, I don't know how many there are."

About a month later I had the pleasure of attending my first Alaskan wedding. Captain Beers and Susie Raymond had a contract wedding, regularly drawn up—party of the first and second parts and so forth. The ritual said, "I Captain Beers, for the consideration of love and devotion, do hereby take Susie Raymond to be my lawful wife." They had the ceremony recorded and were very happy that winter, then storms gathered, and when the ice went out the contract was broken by both of them. She went to Nome where she afterwards married a fine man, well fixed with the goods of this world.

It then came time to work our claims, and we loaded up two Yukon sleds with our winter outfit and with a rope around our necks started pulling them. We made eight miles the first day and then tried to make a cabin up a Pup, but a heavy storm came up and left a foot of fresh snow so we couldn't find the cabin. It was pitch dark and about thirty below zero so we decided to siwash it. I tramped down a place in the snow with my snowshoes, started a fire and soon had tea ready, then opened a can of beans and had lunch. We cut a few spruce bows and placed them on the snow, but the wind was so strong we couldn't put up the tent, so we tied one end of it to a tree and spread it out over our sleeping bags and crawled in. Both fell alseep and later were wakened, as the wind had shifted and the tent was on fire. We soon got settled down again and in a little while heard a fellow go by with dogs. He hollered, "What is the matter with you fellows, why didn't you come to the cabin?" There we were within one thousand feet of a nice fire and cabin. We were just two men getting tough for what was to come—as we then thought.

The next two days were very hard ones—packing our outfit on our backs to the top of the mountain to where we could use sleds again. Here I got my first lesson of what not to do. I was famished for a drink so kept eating snow and ice. The next day we landed in the creek and found an empty cabin with ice all over one end that had glaciered up about two feet thick. We put up the stove and were ready to go to our mine by the next day.

A terrible storm was raging and it was about fifty below zero, so we did not do anything but rest and cut wood for cooking that day. That night I had a hurried call to go outside about 3 A.M. and never will I forget that first attempt—at fifty below with four feet of snow—to attend to nature's call. I made three trips before daylight and there I was, sick with dysentery and thirty miles from a doctor. After about three days without any let up, my fever was way up and I began to ramble in my mind. Poor Jap was about sick with worry, and on December 24 he went to the other cabins on the creek and told them of my illness. They all quit work, put me in a sleeping bag, lashed me to a sled and took turns pulling me to the top of the hill. Then four of them started the long run for the Doctor's. One of them went ahead and told others along the trail they were coming in with a sick man and at No. 17 above they went in for their Christmas dinner. I lay outside singing and listening to the birds, talked some about Hattie, then would have a fight with some Indians led by the Chief of the Sawtooth Range, etc. I don't remember much after that until I was in our cabin at Rampart with Jap, Richmond and Belden. Dr. Jerauld was bathing me and putting me to bed.

While they were busy I got up and was getting into my pants when the doctor asked what I was doing, and I said, "I almost forgot I had a date to take Phoebe Hoover to Christmas dinner." He said, "Get back there, you won't want any dinner tomorrow"—and I didn't for three weeks. The boys and everybody were so kind bringing nice things to eat. Never did anyone have any better care or treatment from a partner, whom I will never be able to repay, although try I did. Here the spirit of the North showed itself.

We never did go mining that winter anymore for Jap was thinking of Mollie back home in Anderson and was homesick and decided to go back. I kept working at my trade and stayed all the next summer and had saved up about $1200.

I must not forget to say that when I got to walking around town, I passed the military barracks and found my friend who had robbed me and caused me to go to Alaska. He was working on the woodpile, having been tried by a miner's meeting and sentenced to the woodpile until spring. Then in a boat with two weeks grub he left with instructions to keep moving, get out of the country. He did—just in time to get to Nome when the beach was struck and he made $4000 in six weeks rocking on the beach. He was run out of the country right into money. Luck? Well, it is all luck if you get it without any effort on your part, but no matter how hard one tries you usually can't get it. It took me ten years to find this out.

By the next fall I had what at that time looked like a million dollars and I wanted to see it all, so I took a steamer at four o'clock one morning downriver for St. Michael. The stampede to Nome was on full blast, and we could see many men all along the beach working. We took aboard our ship, the Alliance, many of them who had made a few thousand dollars. All were going out to get machinery to come back with the next spring.

We went ashore one day and alas here is where we got ours. The town and everybody in it was full of Alaska cooties, and it was a common thing to be talking to someone and see a cootie come up from inside of his shirt along his collar to see what the world looked like. However, as it was the belief that you would never be lucky until you were lousey, everybody cussed them but did not kill them all—by any means.

The trip outside from Nome stands out strong in my memory. At Dutch Harbor a big transport ship was on the other side of the dock, and when I got off our boat a fellow yelled, "O! Smitty." I found it to be a friend whom I had wintered with in Rampart. He had charge of thirty-two head of mules and was taking them to the Philippines. They had them on grass at Dutch Harbor and were going on to Japan. After a two weeks' rest there and one more stop in China, they would reach the Philippines. I was offered $75 a month and some land in Frisco, but I didn't take the trip. I have always regretted it, for if you don't see the world when you are young, you never will see it.

After a pleasant winter at home in New Castle, Indiana, I engaged passage on the steamer Ohio for Nome and returned with about forty thousand others. As it turned out, I did a turn of business here. I had gone to the Dennison Manufacturing Company while outside to purchase supplies, and they had shown me some pretty paper garlands or streamers with roses about every foot. I bought three gross at about $1 a dozen for personal use—as I thought. We reached the Bering Sea before the ice had gone out so all the boats went into Dutch Harbor. There was about one hundred of them there for ten days. We played ball—one team for each boat. We pulled out of there on a nice Sunday morning. I had been too busy to shave, so lined up for the one-man barbershop on the boat and four of us in line caught the "barbers' itch" and suffered greatly.

At last Nome came in sight. Tents were as far as the eye could see. We met friends who had wintered there and got into a rowboat to be rowed ashore when a launch with the health officers, Drs. Jerauld and Gregg came up. When it was about fifty feet from the boat, we were ordered to go back aboard the ship and up went the yellow flag. We had a case of smallpox aboard and were ordered to Egg Island in quarantine. We were a sorry and sore bunch of men and women for twenty-one days. Finally on June 21, a month later than the others had landed, we landed in Nome. I had only $16 and some tokens in my pockets.

I was compelled to go up Snake River to get a place to pitch my tent. Then I went to town to get a window in which to begin my jewelry work. They wanted $200 a month for a window and in advance, but I only had $12 left by that time.

I wanted to get to a toilet badly, but there was none in sight. A fellow said to go to the beach houses. I ran and found a wooden walk out into the water and a man selling tickets at ten cents each. They were marked The Nome Latrine Company, July, 1900. I got my money's worth all right and was a steady customer all the time I stayed there.

I recall walking uptown on the morning of July 4, very blue, and going into Tony Tubbs's tent restaurant where you could get ham and eggs for fifty cents. He was trying to decorate his place with nothing to use and I thought of my garlands, so I hotfooted it to my tent and put a sample of three kinds in my pocket. When I returned I approached Mr. Tubbs with this line of bull, "Here is what you should have to decorate this place with. Something new from Chicago." I then unwound the string and walked out to extend it. About a hundred people present said, "Gee, they are pretty." He asked how many I had and I said, "Twelve dozen," and when he asked the price, without thinking I foolishly said, "One dollar each or ten a dozen." He said, "Bring all you have." I did, and he gave me $120. Business was looking up, and I sold the balance within two hours and was again in funds and stepping high. Thus from an investment of about $30, I got about $375 and should have had more, but just didn't have the heart.

About that time I heard that Richmond was in St. Michael, so I left on a four-masted windjammer called the Ruble Richardson. We heaved on the topsail and vomited at every pull until it went up, and then I fell in a bunk down in the hole, dead as a doornail until the boat quit rocking the next morning. This was the night of the big tidal wave that did so much damage. It took friend Tubbs and his restaurant and the Latrine Company and everything else right off the map in one night.

At St. Michael I secured work trucking in the warehouse and working at my trade after hours. I made about $500 that month and when fall began to come decided to go to Rampart for the winter. Richmond fixed it so I could work my way up on the steamer Louise with Captain Dixon. I was to be storekeeper. Before we were in the mouth of the Yukon, I had my work all done and went into a stateroom and changed clothes, then went into the salon and sat in an easy chair, lit a fresh cigar and picked up a magazine and soon saw the steward and captain looking at me funny. I smelled a mouse, so went to bed and didn't get up for breakfast, but went into the galley and had a cup of coffee and bun for which I gave the cook twenty-five cents.

Then I went to the salon and just got comfortably fixed up when the steward came up and said, "Young man, ain't you a workaway?" I replied, "Yes, storekeeper and I have my work all done." It jarred him all right, but he squared himself and said, "Storekeeper, Hell, you are fourth steward on this boat. Go back and help the boys in the galley." I did and peeled spuds and washed dishes all the way upriver. I will say I never did have as nice a trip with such congenial companions, and I later lived with most of them someplace in the country.

During the winter the clerk of the N. A. T. store in Rampart was killed, and as I had good habits, led the singing in church, etc., I was permitted to clean up the joint.

There were about one thousand people in Rampart, and we had a good time with a squaw dance to watch every Saturday night and mixed crowds at the other dances. Our store manager, B. F. Baker, was a live wire, and we had a cake walk or minstrel show every winter. They induced me

MENU

OYSTERS

Blue Points .... From Sledge Island

FISH

Brook Trout .... From Extra Dry Creek
Tom Cod .... a la Gold Run

Walrus Bellies
Arkansaw Fish a la Buttons

SALADS

Crab .... a la Behring Sea
Lobster .... From Nakkila Gulch

ENTREES

Malamute Stew   Muckluck Croquetts

ROASTS

Turkey .... Chechaco Dressing
Teat Ham .... al la Reindeer Hoofs
Pork .... al la Claim Jumper
Stuffed Ptarmigan .... Eskimo Gravy

VEGETABLES

Nome Potatoes   Council City Peas
Teller Beans   Celery al la Sluicebox

DESSERT

Plum Pudding .... al la Mary's Igloo
Sourdough Pies   Cheechaco Cakes
Ice Cream a la Glacier Creek
Point Barrow Bananas   Kotzebue Sound Oranges

• • • • • • • •
Snake River Beer   Extra Dry Pribiloff
Cigars a la Undertaker's Hope
GOOD MORNING
June 27, 1901—Nome, Alaska

to join the Jolly Companions. By that time I was eligible.
They dressed me for the works and took me before the
doctor for an examination of my five senses. Then they had
to give me a shave; then with a seventy-five pound pack I
had to go up Chilkoot Pass to a ladder on the roof onto a
platform. I made the grade all right and received many

cheers. I was blindfolded all the time. The villains had built a slide along the wall and polished it slick as glass. They took off my pack and threw me on my belly and said in a deep voice, "Young man, prepare to meet your God, you are to go down the glacier through White Horse Rapids and if you survive you will ever be a worthy member of the Jolly Companions. I went down faster and faster and then jumped off into something that filled my ears, mouth and eyes, and hair. A big laugh went up and the blindfold was removed, and there were about twenty men holding a piece of canvas with fifty pounds of flour in it; everything and everybody was covered with flour.

I then had to go before the chaplain to take the oath. It was the same deep, rich voice of Captain Mayo asking me to repeat, "I, Lynn Smith, do solemnly swear that I will, etc. —always to give a brother the preference in anything, everything else being equal, etc. That I will never take another man's squaw away from him or break up his happy home. That I will never take a brother and fail him and never give a cent for tail, etc." Our group met once a week and always had a victim. Today only a few of this crowd are living, having gone on their last stampede. May their bones rest in peace.

In 1901 while I was with the N.A.T. & T. Company, living upstairs, I was awakened one morning about four by a squaw whom I recognized as Moose Mary. She waddled like a moose when she walked. She was pounding on the door of Dr. Hudgins' cabin and yelling as loud as she could. "Doctor, Doctor, get up quick. Lucy Baggage (another squaw) having Mrs. Carriage." In June, 1902, Charley Jackett came into the store for some cheesecloth and said, "Come on down, Lucy is having a baby." This was quite a surprise, as it was the first time for me to get invited to one of these parties. I hesitated, but my bump of curiosity got the better of me, so I followed him to his cabin.

There was a bedstead and they had a pole about three inches in diameter above the mattress. Lucy was on her knees with her arms over the rail, hanging over it. A native woman had one hand on Lucy's stomach and the other behind her back, and another woman was working on the bottom holding the baby's head. When her pains came on, they pressed and pulled, and the delivery was made in short order.

Lucy walked a half mile to the store that same evening to buy Canton flannel for the child's clothes.

Incidentally, three days later I called at Lucy's cabin, and it was full of men and women guessing who the baby looked like. They couldn't agree whether it had a Jew or Siwash father. Our Postmaster was a Jew and I said, "I will tell you who it belongs to," and went out to the cache and picked out a dried salmon. Holding the fish in one hand and a silver dollar in the other, I walked up to the baby boy and gave them to the mother and asked her to hold them up before him. The kid reached for the dollar and I said, "It belongs to Milt." Many a laugh did they get from this incident afterwards.

I recall another case where Lucy Sprunger was cutting fish about three-fourths of a mile from her cabin when the baby wanted to come. She ran up on the bank of the river, hung over a tree and delivered herself without help. She carried the child home later on and worked the next day.

Another amusing incident happened a few years later at Rampart when Gay Lindley Green was commissioner. They were trying Maggie Thompson for being drunk on the public streets. The Judge said in a stern voice, "Maggie, where did you get your whiskey to get drunk with?" Quick as a flash she answered, "Montgomery Ward." The Judge said, "Excused," and had to rap for order in the court.

A few months later she was up again and the Judge asked her, "Maggie, do you know the nature of an oath? Do you know what it means when you hold up your hand and swear?" She replied, "Yee, Yoho, Honest to God," stopped for breath and added, "I lie." He rapped the crowd down, and again the court proceeded with business.

In the winter of 1902 I took my first flyer in mining with Wally and Gus Conradt as partners. They left Rampart to build the cabin, and I worked another month in town to get grub for my share, then left for the creeks to help with the work. Our first job was to cut about thirty cords of wood, and I was determined to cut as much as they did and the first day was dropping timber everyplace. Wally ran over to me excitedly and said, "Wait a minute until I go to the cabin for the panning tubs—you will cut your darned legs off." We took out our dump in about seven weeks and got tied up in a lawsuit, but it was finally settled and we got our part—about $2,500 each. I went back to the store again and began to plunge, buying wildcats, grubstaking men trying to get it quick. Then the Fairbanks stampede came on, and our station was sold out of everything, our camp deserted and about twelve widows left whose husbands had stampeded. There were only three of us young men left in town to keep them from getting lonesome, and we did some team work, for we never butted in on the other fellow and always knew where the other fellow was. We would meet in my room to talk it over afterwards.

Having worked steadily since January, 1901, and having promised my sister that I would attend her wedding, I left Rampart with a dog team of six dogs that were the pick of the Yukon River, paying $125 for Banjo, the leader, and $60 to $75 each for the other five dogs.

It was quite an undertaking. Friends offered plenty of free advice, and just before I started, the American Commercial Company agent came and offered me one gallon of their best whiskey. Their bookkeeper gave me a box of cigars, and I had a large fly, a dog biscuit, 100 pounds of rice, 100 pounds of thick sow belly, a 22 pump rifle, lots of extra heavy wool socks, extra moccasins, three dozen boxes of crackerjack, some grub and snowshoes. The old trail went south from Glen Gulch down Baker Creek to the Tanana River, thence up the Tanana River to Chena and Fairbanks.

Two weeks prior to this, eleven sled loads of fur came to our trading post from Minto, and in the crowd was the blind Indian who killed the first white woman in Alaska, Mary Bean. There was also a squaw who had carried a two months old baby in a birch bark basket on her back on the trip with the weather from thirty to fifty-five below zero. They came across country, thus saving three days of travel, and I knew that about halfway across there was a crowd of my Rampart Indian friends hunting. I thought I could do anything an Indian could do; that is, take the short cut to Fairbanks as they had done—rather than go down the Yukon and up the Tanana by the easier river route.

Chief William, Mike Hess and Frank and Charley Dry Wood had told me where they would be camped and it was (only) two sleeps from Baker Creek to Monte's woodyard, then six miles up the Tanana River from where we came out. I figured this was only one stop with my powerful dog team and I could make the Indian camp the first night. They told me the Indians had come out of the woods on Claim 11 below Eureka Creek. It was forty-two below zero and there was a foot of freshly fallen snow from a week before, making a three foot average depth. The trail was broken to Claim 11 below, but there was no sign of it. I finally noticed two blazes on two trees about seven feet apart. The trail, which old Banjo easily picked up and followed, was hard and about two feet wide. If he stepped off, he would go down because of the depth of the snow.

I was on the Gee Pole on snowshoes all morning and kept plugging away until 1 P.M. when I stopped and made tea and ate some bologna sausage and hard tack. I gave the dogs a rest and off we went again. About 3 P.M. we came on to a big lake about a mile and a half across with the snow blown clear and ice slick. Banjo began to act queer, smelling the ice and finally stopping. Quite a cold breeze was blowing, so I turned the sled over on its side and went ahead of the dogs looking for a sled track. I could not see any, so went back and turned Banjo loose. All at once about three hundred feet from the dog team and off to the right I came on a spot of tobacco juice about the size of a half dollar. Nothing ever looked sweeter than that. I knew there must be more, so I took off my old Hudson Bay sash, put it down and kicked off a nigger head and put that on top of it. I began crisscrossing back and forth and finally came to another spot which I marked with my parka and from this determined my line across the lake. I started and put my eye on a tall tree on the opposite shore and came within ten feet of the good trail in the heavy timber. It was getting dark fast and was very cold. This delay had given my dogs a good rest, and I kept thinking I would get into the Indian camp, so I traveled for two hours after dark, but there was still no sign of anybody. Both myself and the dogs were dead tired and I was having trouble keeping from freezing. I got out the rifle and shot three times but got no reply so it was a case of siwash it.

Flashlights were unknown in those days, and as it was pitch dark I got into my snowshoes, stepped over to a big tree and broke off some of the lower dead branches of a spruce tree, found some birch bark and started a fire. I then sat on the load on the sled and began to get drowsy and wanted to drop off to sleep. Just then the thought came of the gallon of whiskey in the sled and I got it out and pulled the cork and filled my mouth. It was frozen and so I held it in my mouth until it melted, then swallowed it, then repeated this process.

This woke me up and I then got the axe, snowshoed off and cut down some timber. As I stooped over to pick up the wood I got tangled up with my snowshoes and pitched head-first over in the snow. Finally I got to my feet but everything was whirling. Realizing I was drunk, I crawled to the sled and got out my hunting knife, cut the sash rope, jerked the sleeping bag off, threw it down in the trail behind the sled and wiggled inside with my moccasins and all my clothing on. My back was covered with frost and there was snow on my moccasins, but in thirty seconds I was sound asleep. Don't know how long I was out but woke up and was wet as a drowned rat and my teeth were chattering. I had sense enough to know I could not get out of the sleeping bag as it was at least fifty below zero, so I just lay there and shivered for two hours. I finally dried out from the heat of my body and dropped off asleep again.

My dogs, still in the harness and unfed, were up when Banjo woke me. It was daylight and a big red sun was just coming up, so I lashed up the load, threw the gallon of whiskey away and again started. After traveling about a mile, the dogs kept pulling up, smelling, then speeding up and soon we came to two tents and a big cache of meat; there were my Indian friends except for Chief William who was out taking up his traps. They took off my moccasins. Charley Dry Wood began scraping them with his knife to get out the water and then dried them out, and I took a nap on some bearskins on the ground. I had told them to wake me in an hour and they did, and they had a big moose steak and coffee made. It was cold but a beautiful day and, against the advice of the natives, I again started, hoping to reach the Tanana River and six miles up to Monte's woodyard and a good cabin. When I was out about two miles, my sled upset and I stepped off the trail to right it and got my left foot in about a foot of overflow. Although I had plenty of socks in the sled, I did not stop to change.

About ten miles out I saw a camp fire ahead and it was Chief William. By this time my German socks and moccasin was frozen stiff but my foot was still warm. William wanted me to change. Instead I drank a cup of tea and was just starting again when he said, "No go Fla Fla (by and by)— you hit Tanana River, then wind she blow—then you freeze." I hit the river just as the big red sun was setting. Sure enough there was the wind and I had six miles to go. There was about one more hour of travel. In about fifteen minutes I noticed my heel felt like a thousand needles were sticking me, then the pain reached the front part of my foot and I knew it was freezing. I kept beating it on the trail and the side of the sled and finally pulled up on the bank to the cabin. I rushed in and there was Johnny Campbell (Minto), Calhoun and Monte. I said, "Cut off that German sock, boys, my foot is frozen solid." Campbell had already started for the river and came in with a bucket of ice and water. They finally cut and broke the socks off, and the foot was white and hard as marble. At once my foot went in the ice water, and I howled with pain but they kept adding ice, rubbing it and finally it thawed out. One of them asked Monte if he had any coal oil. There was about an inch in a lamp and they tore some rags and bandaged up the foot and kept pouring on the coal oil and I went to sleep. Later on I was awakened by a terrible pain—my heel was throbbing and a big blister had formed. I woke the boys up, and they opened the blister and I went off asleep again.

I was compelled to lay over two days, then I started for Chena and Fairbanks walking on the ball of my foot and toes. I reached Fairbanks and met Judge Dillon and Elmer Brady on the street and asked where I could put up my dogs, when a stranger said to me, "Drive on down the street, I've got a place for them." It was Senator Charley Hall, and he stopped in front of his Senate Saloon on Front Street, opened the doors and I drove in, keeping the dogs there two days and three nights. The Saloon was well stocked with everything but was closed because nobody had any money, and he still had his regular customers; they either gave him the finger or said "slop her down."

Hall wanted to sell me the Saloon for $800, and the following October it was worth $14,000. I sold fifty pounds of sugar and fifty pounds of flour for $100 and put a Gee Pole on the sled. Then I joined Bennett who had a mail contract for one trip a month from Tanana to Gokana on the Eagle-Valdez trail. We had a trail south on Cushman Street to the Tanana River but then nothing to follow—just three feet of snow. We got into our snowshoes—onto the Gee Pole and Gee Poled the next twenty-two days. We reached Chief Jarvis' cabin at the mouth of the Little Salcha River and had another foot of snow that night, so had to lighten the loads and double up, tying my sled behind his to make thirteen dogs in the team. With one behind the other, this made a team about fifty feet long.

Bennett went ahead breaking trail, and I was on the Gee Pole on snowshoes with the two lines between my legs. It was slow, hard work, making only two miles an hour. When we reached the mouth of the Big Delta River, we found an overflow everyplace and headed for timber and camped for the night. We had reached the rabbit country—rabbits by the millions—and here we had our first rabbit tea. Just before dark each day we would look for timber on the bank to make camp. The first thing was to chain the dogs up to trees, then to cut down a tree, getting two logs. We then tramped down the snow and started the campfire. Next we got the dog bucket, filled it with snow and placed it on the campfire across the two logs. We put in rice and sow belly. Then we tramped down more snow and cut spruce boughs and placed them on the snow about a foot high for our sleeping bags. We then prepared something warm for ourselves. We would try and pick out some nice clean snow and fill the teapot and place it on the fire. After a few minutes we would look to see how much water we had, usually with an inch of rabbit on top. We then repeated this, skimming off the rabbit each time, then putting in the tea. This we did for the balance of the trip to make tea.

Next morning we got out our water boots (mukluks) and bucked water for ten miles. In about two miles we again camped and thawed out. Two days later, just before dark, Bennett stopped and said, "How tired are you? You see that next bend? Well, a trapper named Nigger Bill lives there. Shall we camp or go on?" and I said, "Mush. I'll try it." The snow was about four feet deep—the dogs were tired, and I was so tired I tied a handkerchief around my wrist to the end of the Gee Pole. It was pitch dark, and I just shoved one foot ahead of the other. We kept on and passed two more bends in the river, but still no cabin. Finally Bennett, who was ahead of the dogs, said there was an overflow ahead and that we must hit for the bank and camp. I said, "Yes, you blankety, blank Scotch son of a batchelor, we've passed three bends already—show me that cabin." He took out the rifle and shot twice, we yelled and all at once a light came down to the river through the woods about one half mile away. Nothing ever looked sweeter than that light! After a short rest we traveled at right angles to the shore and then we reached the walk to the cabin. I lay down and kicked off my snowshoes and crawled on hands and knees to the cabin. When I went in, I saw a pile of bear skins and I dropped, falling asleep at once. I was awakened by Bennett and another man, who helped me to the table where they had a moose mulligan, but I was too tired to eat. I turned and asked Bennett "How much are you fined for every hour you are late with the mail?" and he replied, "Two dollars an hour." I reached inside my shirt and peeled off a hundred-dollar bill and said, "Take this, here is $50 fine. I'm not moving." He shoved it back and said, "You damn fool, you will be all right in the morning." We slept until 10 A.M., and both were as good as ever so we decided to make Myer's tent where Casey's Cache was located—ten miles up the river. But about three miles out we saw a man walking toward us without snowshoes. It was a trapper who said he left home without snowshoes because one mile up river we would be out of snow.

We reached his tent one hour after dark and turned the dogs loose until we had eaten supper and were ready to feed them. Next morning we found Bennett's valuable leader dead. This trapper was using poison and the dog had picked up a bait. This was bad luck, but I put on old Banjo and he took us along. The next day we met the Forty Mile Kid (Harry Karstens) going north and marked his trail with crackerjack boxes all across the country by putting an empty box on a willow on the side of the trail. We cut wood together and hauled it four miles to a tent that was used by travelers before hitting Summit Lake. We had a great disappointment when we discovered a turn on the lake and that we were still ten miles from the end. We hit the outlet of the lake and found water flowing south so we knew we were headed right. I went ahead of the dogs, cutting out the trail, and in four days we reached a trail across country to Gokona.

That morning we passed six dog teams headed for Fairbanks, and they told us they had struck it rich on Cleary Creek and Gilmore Creek since we had left and for us to go back. All the gold in the world would not have induced me to return. Here we met McAlpen, another mail carrier, and he took us to the Gokona Road house on the Eagle-Valdez trail. Here I sent Banjo back with Bennett and made Copper Center on the ice. Here I caught up with Bert Skinner, who was from Slate Creek and had two extra horses and double-enders, so I drove a big bay horse. We were going around Icy Point when my horse stepped off the center of the trail and was down. I ran to his head and held him. The men unhitched him, dragged the sled back and I, like a fool, wrapped the halter strap around my wrist, and when Mr. Horse got up over the bluff he went and also took a high dive into sixty feet of snow. We were both buried in snow and we lost three hours getting back on the trail.

Finally after forty-one days of heartbreaking work we reached Valdez. The steamer Farralow was at the dock, and I caught the boat which had only seven passagers. Bishop Rowe and Judge Cecil H. Clegg were on the boat. We told experiences, Alaska stories, etc. While I wouldn't dare tell all we told, I am quite sure the grand old man of the Yukon, Bishop Rowe, won't object to this one he told:

> I had just been ordered to Alaska and had my first trip on an ocean steamer. We had a rough trip and were near Unimak Pass when the storm got worse and I was frightened. I read my Bible, prayed and as I just couldn't stand it in my stateroom I made my way to the Captain's pilot house. I asked the Captain if there was any danger. He was very calm, and said, "No. Man, go back to your room. There is no danger." I stood it again for another half hour and again went to the pilot house, pale and trembling. This made the Captain mad, and he grabbed me by the arm and led me to the companion way leading to the crew's quarters and steerage passengers and said, "Listen to those men down there, if there was any danger those men would be praying instead of swearing." I listened. They were gambling and drunk and swearing terrible. I remarked, "Terrible language, Captain," and he said, "Go to your room and stay there." I went back and read my Bible some more, again prayed and stayed as long as I could and again went to the companion way, put my ear over and said to myself, "Thank God they are still swearing." Then we were in Unimak Pass and out of the rough water.

I returned to Rampart after this trip but the stampede was on to Chena and Fairbanks so I eventually went along. Before I was in Chena an hour, I had three jobs offered me but refused them all. I had by this time made up my mind that if I ever got rich it would not be by working for wages; however, as I was broke I made my spread, put up my bench again and began to work at my jeweler's trade. I kept making trips to the different creeks looking for likely claims to stake and at any rate lived through the winter and learned another dear lesson. In April, Pat Conroy, whose business I had attended to for four years in Rampart, owned No. 3 below Ester Creek. One day when he was in town he wanted me to write for him to his mother in Ireland. I did so and asked him how he was getting along, and he said it was slow work —to come out and help him put the hole down to bedrock and he would give me a half interest in the claim. I grabbed at the chance and drew up an agreement that I would be there at Monday by noon to begin work. At the completion of it he was to deed me an undivided half interest in No. 3 below. Here is where the woman comes in. There was a mighty fine looker lived across the street who was a dressmaker, and we were friends. I was taking her to choir practice and to church, and spending about three nights a week with her until eleven or twelve o'clock. On this particular Sunday night she was unusually depressed, and when I got ready to go said, "Now, Lynn, don't forget I made an engagement to play whist at Miss Fairies tomorrow night for us." When I said, "Sorry, girl, but I must go to Ester Creek in the morning and won't be back until Sunday," she began to cry and said, "If you just go with me one more day it would not make any difference to Mr. Conroy." I fell for it and said, "All right, I'll stay," and I didn't go out to the claim as I should have done but waited until Tuesday. When I went Tuesday morning, I found him in his cabin sitting on his bunk and began to apologize for not keeping my word, and he said, "Yes, I kept looking for you and when you didn't come, Ed Jes came along the creek and got on the windlass and helped me take out the thaw. He stayed all night with me and this morning I was kicking because you didn't come as you said you would and I sold him the claim this morning." My contract was no good after Monday noon, and as he had taken $35 and given a receipt for it, nothing could be done. That claim produced over $1,200,000 in three years and of course it lost as much for Pat as it did for me. Is it any wonder I have been a woman hater ever since? Here is some good advice, and you all follow it.

By this time I had saved up some money and put it into furs, deposited in a bank in Fairbanks. The famous 1906 fire came along and I lost them all. Then the next spring the flood came at Chena and I lost about $3000 more in that.

Then I went to the creeks and worked for $6 a day and board for fifteen months and took another flyer in the stampede to Manley Hot Springs with a prospecting outfit. I found a place to dig and thought we had struck it rich but worked for twenty-three months and put down sixty-four holes from three to sixty-five feet deep before I gave up and walked off weighing one-hundred and fifty-six pounds, with but $10 in my jeans.

I then borrowed a boat, put in my jeweler's tools and went down-river to Tanana where I worked from June to September and saved about $1000 and had to go home again to New Castle. After returning I started with part-interest in a general store on Sullivan Creek but without any capital. Our credit was good and we managed to have quite a stock on hand before the spring breakup came. Both Fred Howard and myself worked about eighteen hours out of every twenty-three but couldn't keep it up, and then we made another mistake. We took in another partner. The clouds began to gather and trouble started, so in order to get away from it all we sold the whole works at a sacrifice. Had we continued, there would have been a good business for years. We started with about $200 capital and in eleven months took in about $4,200 in cash. Remember this also—in business two partners can get along but three never. This cost me money to find out. After another trip home, I came back and settled down in the jewelry business at Ruby. In time it died down and everybody left, so I got into politics and accepted a deputy U.S. Marshal's job at Flat, which is the jumping-off place on earth. Thus I have learned another lesson—that it is easier to get into things than to get out of them for I have been in this job to date—May 29, 1923.

I figured up and find that I have spent over $14,000 trying to get the gold coin, and if ever a man tried, I did, but I just got close to the paystreak. If my claim had gold on it, I had soft bedrock, and the gold that should have been on my ground slid over to the one below where the other fellow got mine and his own. Thus if it is for you, you will get it without any effort on your part. It goes that way through life in everything one undertakes and has been the story of most men.

Someday I will rewrite this with more details, but I hope you heed my advice. I have enjoyed writing this—everything is fine and the goose hangs high.

ALASKA CELEBRITIES

(List of early Alaska characters given unusual names;
compiled by Lynn Smith about 1931)

MEN

Water-front Brown
Swift Water Bill
Billy the Turk
Step and a Half
Two Step Louie
Buckskin Harry
Eat-em-up Frank
Hard Luck Charlie
Muck-Luck Kid
Scurvy Kid
Skylight Kid
In and Out Kid
Malamoot Kid
The Dutch Kid
The Daylight Kid
Dago Kid
Blueberry Kid
Forty-mile Kid
Sixty-mile Kid
The Crummy Kid
Honest Ike
Deep Hole Johnson
Too Much Johnson
Husky Kid
Slivers Feiges
Slivers Perry
Powerful Joe
Blackie
Lousie Dick
Hot Air Smith
Brainey Smith
Windy Smith
Jumping Smith
Happy Jack
French Joe
Cock-eyed Shorty
John the Greek
Moose John

Butch Stock
Ham Greese Jimmy
Hungry Mike
Poker Charlie
Montana Pete
Blueberry Tommy
Dago Joe
Two for a Quart
Mush-on
Snuff Box Olsen
Snowy
Jimmy the Goat
Wise Mike
Komoko John
Long Shorty
Stone-age Bill
Tangle Foot
Tuleride Kid
Three-Fingered Bob
Dog Sam
The Black Prince
The Gambler's Ghost
The Coat
The Vest
Tripod Pete
Diamond Dick

WOMEN
The Nosey Sisters
The Limping Grouse
Passionate Annie
Bunch Grass
The Virgin
The Oregon Mare
The Utah Filly
The Black Bear
The Cub
Spanish Marie
Spanish Julia
Finn Annie
Snow Ball
Spot
Moose Mary

Short and Dirty
Dirty Gertie
Queenie
Three-way Annie
Web Foot
Diamond Tooth Gertie
Diamond Hattie
Skagway Kate
May the Cow
Allah, Allah, Allah
Kitty the Bitch
The World's Wonder
The Merry Widow
Cheechako Lil
The Chinless Wonder
French Camille
Nellie the Pig
Sweet Marie
The Sweet Pea Girl
Maggie the Rag
Moosehide Annie
Laughing Annie
Irish May
Texas Rose
Butter Ball
The School Marm
Fighting Nell
Fuzzy Knot
Box Car Aggie
The Doughnut Queen
Sixty-Nine

Indian and Eskimo Stories from Along the Yukon

Lynn Smith

ONE REDEEMING feature of a Sourdough was that no matter how tough it was coming they could always enjoy a joke; and they always enjoyed a good laugh whether it was on themselves or the other fellow. Ooksook was the name given me by the Yukon Indians in 1898. It means "too much grease."

I offer a few of the stories I have heard and things I have seen up here in Alaska, and they are offered because they are true, not because they are to be read by "Polite Society." If there are any straight-faced women reading this who cannot laugh, please pass this chapter by. I shall have to call a spade a spade and make my apologies, trusting these tales will offend no one.

When one realizes that four hundred years ago, there were more natives living in Alaska than now (1931); that they were living off the country without any doctor except their own medicine men and women; and that they had to work out their own salvation—we can take off our hats to them—for their system or way of life worked. In my many years among them I have never seen an unhappy married couple until the last few years when they learned to make their own beer mash and white mule. These were made from crude affairs of tin or anything handy, even using an old rifle barrel for a still, as was true in one case that I know about. Thus it is no wonder that when a Buck gets a few drinks into him, he beats the wife up, breaks the furniture, etc.

I remember two native men who married sisters and lived together for two years, then in 1901 decided to change their way of life. Big Bob decided that he liked Evan's wife best, and Evan decided that he liked Big Bob's wife best. They traded wives and moved down between Kokrines and Ruby and lived happily ever after—no fuss about it. Bob's wife had a baby about every ten months, and they had given many a baby away to some good family who couldn't have any children. The children were loved—educated—clothed as if they were the real children of the adopting family. Isn't that a fine idea? The natives still have the same superstitions nowadays, and no matter that they have had the benefit of missionaries and doctors for about twenty years, most of them still go to their medicine man.

It is still the custom before the big event (a birth) to put the woman in a cabin or tent by herself on the first of the month. She doesn't mingle with the other natives until it is over. And I know of one man from Holykeechuk who is about fifty years old and is still called "Under the Table" because he was born under the table in their tent.

This custom still prevails—when a girl matures, usually about two years earlier than a white girl, they curtain off one corner of the cabin and place the girl in this room. She is never allowed out of it, and they pack her food and keep her there until she completes her second period. Then she must come out of the room with her face covered (so that no Indian boy will try and flirt with her), and she is then ready for a man to get married.

Shortly after this the father and mother decide which friend of theirs they will let sleep with her and they get her ready. After this the chosen man never even looks at the girl and never again bothers her in his life. Soon after this they will say to the girl, "Susie, who do you think you want to marry? How do you like Harry Yeska? How you like mally him?" If she says, "O, fine, I like Harry Yeska," then some friend asks Harry how he likes Susie, and if agreeable Harry moves in with Susie and her father and mother and begins sleeping with her.

Soon they plan either a fishing or trapping trip, and the two go away and stay from one to six months. If they can agree and are mated and still like each other—they get married at the first opportunity. If not suited, they quit right there, and Harry quietly moves back home to his folks and never bothers Susie again. There is no such thing as an illegitimate child among the natives. If there should happen to be a child from the hunting trip, it is loved and protected by everyone. Susie will eventually try another boy and eventually find one who is suitable.

One of the most vicious customs still in existence is in holding their potlatches, where the natives from the other villages for miles around desert their traps, neglect their furs and everything else. They are accustomed to sleeping several families in one room and just dance all the time, all night long giving or performing their washboard dance, their stick dance, and the Red River jig. Finally the big day comes when they potlatch for the visitors. They must repeat it the following year.

I recall one case of Silas and Monica. Silas died and left a good home, a sewing machine, gramophone and every convenience needed. Monica was a good housekeeper, good at trapping and blest with a sunny disposition. When there is a widow in the village, the Chief takes all of the widow's things away from her. In this case the Chief took Monica's things leaving her only the cookstove, one dress, one pair of shoes, etc. Then he took her household effects and potlatched them away. This leaves the widow on the same basis as the other girls in the village. She must get her next husband on her own merits and on an even basis with the others. There are no rich widows among the Yukon Indians. Isn't this a heck of a custom?

A year or so ago Clark M. Garber of Akiak wrote me the story of the two brothers, which was told in this way:

Many, many years ago there lived two brothers in an innie on the banks of the Kuskokwim River, down where the river gets very wide and empties into the sea. They lived by themselves and had never seen any other people during their lives. Behind their innie was a small hill upon which they used to sit and look for other people.

For many years they had searched the surrounding country for a sight of others like themselves and they finally decided to start on a long trip in their kaiyaks to search for the companionship of other people.

The younger of the two brothers was a very large man and consequently was very strong, so he had built a very large kaiyak for himself. The older brother, being the weaker and smaller, had a small kaiyak. After waiting several days for good weather, they set out together, having agreed to go to the south shore of the bay which they could see far in the distance. Two long days they drove their light, sturdy kaiyaks through the water and on the third day a strong wind blew up from the south, causing them much trouble in handling their boats.

With the waves running high and the surf dashing

against the shore, the older brother in his small kaiyak became frightened and could not keep up with his stronger companion. Therefore he made for a village which he had seen through the fog. As he approached the village, the people all came out and marveled at the strange man approaching in the small kaiyak, which had a large open mouth on its bow.

The younger and stronger brother, having missed his companion, also turned his kaiyak toward the village and soon caught up with the small boat. But as they neared the shore, the stronger man became alarmed that the heavy surf might wreck his large boat, so he turned back to the sea and left the older and weaker brother to whatever adventures might befall him. As the small boat came into the heavy surf, the breakers lifted it up and carried it directly ashore where it was left stranded on the beach with its lone occupant.

As the man sat in his kaiyak, worrying and thinking about his situation, he heard a voice calling him. Directing his gaze toward the direction of the voice, he observed a beautiful girl approaching from the village. When she came to him she said, "Why do you sit here in your kaiyak so sorrowful and sad?"

He replied, "My brother has gone out to sea and I do not know how to find him. Anyway I could not follow him in my little kaiyak." After he had talked with this beautiful girl for some time, he asked her if she would marry him. She replied, "I will be glad to be your wife if you will remain here and live with me."

They then went to the girl's innie where she gave him food and became his wife in fact. However, the girl made one condition to their marriage. This was that her husband should never kill female animals during his hunting. To this he agreed but found it impossible to live up to his promise as he could not always tell which was a male or female seal until after he had killed it. When he killed female seals, he killed them for nothing for he could not take them to his wife.

After they had lived together for several years and everything had gone nicely with them, he came upon a beautiful fur seal while hunting one day and killed it for his wife. After he had killed it, he found that it was a female. However, as its fur was so nice, he did not want to throw it away, so he put it far back in the stern of the kaiyak. When he got back to the village, he hid in the willows to watch what his wife would do when she found it. Cautiously she pulled the seals from the kaiyak, and when she came upon the beautiful female seal, she became very angry and went into a veritable rage. She called to her husband, and when he came to her she asked him to follow her behind the innie. Here she turned into a fox and ran away from him. She never returned to her husband, so he lived all alone waiting and watching every day for his wife to return. However, neither his wife nor his brother came to him and he lived all his life by himself.

The natives have another custom of always cutting off the lower lip of their first-caught mink or marten, or whatever fur-bearing animal they catch. If they did not carry this piece with them, they "never no more catch any more marten." Then you will see the skull of a bear fastened over the cabin door, and if this was not done they would say, "never no more kill any bear."

These simple children of nature have hearts in them as big as anybody. If one kills the first moose of the season, it is given away, the killer keeping only the head and neck. Then when the next moose is killed, the first killer gets a hind quarter and must wait his turn for more moose. They are having it tough these days, and many of them are again living on straight dried fish and will soon become a Territorial charge.

In 1912 at Ruby, a native named Johnny Glass was being tried by a jury for beating up his old mother, who was deaf and blind. The jury found him guilty and the Judge gave him quite a talking to, pointing out how terrible it was for anybody to beat up his mother. He wound up saying, "Johnny, I have to punish you, and I'll give you three months in jail and $100 fine." Johnny did not hear him say the worth of the fine, so after being taken to jail, a few days later he called Marshal C. K. Snow and said, "Snow, the Judge say he give me three months and $100. Three months that alright, but when he going to give me the $100? I wanted to send my wife some money." This was hard to explain to him.

A couple of years later (1914) Charles Hoxie and I hired Fred Lemon with his launch and we went up the Yukekacket River for about seventy-five miles. We took along Tommy Marie, a native boy about nineteen years old. While going upstream we heard Tommy shoot—he was seated in the middle of the boat and I was in the stern with Howie up front. Tommy had killed a white meat grouse that was on the beach. About ten minutes later he shot again, killing another bird, and I cautioned him, saying, "Tommy, we want to do the shooting, and when we shoot them, we shoot them on the wing, which gives the bird a chance for his life. The next time you see a chicken, tell us and let us shoot."

In a few more mintues he said, "There chicken," and pointed toward the shore. We looked and looked and Hoxie finally said, "Where? I can't see it." Neither could I, but then it flew up and up, over the trees. Hoxie shot twice and then I too took a crack at it from far away. We both missed, and Tommy really rode us. However, there were no ducks in the river, so we shot hawks, gulls and rabbits the rest of the afternoon. We camped there all night and the next morning we got about forty ducks in an hour and came to the mouth of the river where Tommy lived. We gave him some ducks, and I had a big white owl in my hands to throw away when Tommy stopped me and said, "Don't throw it away. Mummy she eat them." So I gave him all the gulls and owls and a couple of fish ducks. Mummy was the old lady that Johnny Glass had beat up.

Jim Hagen once told me of this incident in Nenana (1931). R. S. (rough stuff) McDonald was Commissioner. Jim said:

> He called me one morning about seven o'clock and wanted me to serve a warrant at the Indian village. So I went up to the village and brought "Mr. Injun" down. He had been in jail so many times he immediately turned in but I told him, "No, not yet, Sam. You tell it to the Judge first."
>
> We entered the Commissioner's office and there was the squaw, his wife, bloody from head to foot, sitting in the corner. The Judge began to read the complaint, looking over his glasses at Sam, and said, "Sam, do you understand?" Sam said, "No savvy." McDonald said, "Your wife says you beat her up last night." Sam replied, "No, Judge. I no touch her last night, but I kick hell out of her this morning." So McDonald said, "Six months for you. Take him away, Jim."
>
> So I took Mr. Injun over to the jail and after I had locked him in the cell he said, "Jim, long time I savvy you. Long time I know you. I like long talk with you." I took a chair and moved over to the cell door and he started to talk.
>
> "Now maybe sometime you get mellied like I do. Catch em wife. She go pitcher show all time. Pitcher show—PITCHER SHOW! She come home five o'clock —four o'clock—three o'clock and one time two o'clock.

I know what you'd do." So I said, "What would I do, Sam?"

"Why," he said, "You'd kick hell out of her too. You savvy," he said, "my wife leave home six o'clock every night. Pitcher show start at eight o'clock. My wife walk down there in five minutes—my house to pitcher show. She take two hours. Where do you think my wife all that time? Maybe she see some white man." Thus he justified his crime.

Nor are the Eskimos squeamish. I saw this at Top Kick near Nome in the summer of 1900. There were some Eskimos in their igloos, and I nozied over in front of one, and there was a woman with a small baby having its "Mickinini Kow-Kow," which means "warm lunch at all hours." She was not at all disturbed by my presence and when she was through turned the child facing me. It had a trickle down from its nose, and she reached over—took the baby's nose in her mouth, took a big draw, turned her head and spit on the ground.

Thank God for missionaries and schools that have uplifted the poor, unfortunate natives until they are now partly civilized and live as we do. Though they must have their seal oil even now, one cannot help but wonder how they managed years ago without the necessities of life. Ask anyone who has ever seen or lived with these people if they have ever seen the above done before 1900. Or you might ask them if they have ever seen any of the older Eskimos or natives grab for a cootie and eat it and smack their lips. In spite of all this, they were far healthier before they knew white man's grub, since they have been polluted by disease caught from the white man, and far more prosperous before the white men came and trapped all the fur-bearing animals from the land which rightfully belongs to them. My sympathy is with the natives which our good Uncle Sammy is now called upon to help support. Just today (November 8, 1931) the government doctor drove to my house and reported thirty-one cases of measles at Nenana among the natives. He had visited their homes, and they were destitute and without food and calling for help. Nobody can doubt the report of Dr. J. A. Sutherland. It is a tough problem but must be handled in some way. This condition exists in all of Alaska—at least in the interior. What is to become of them? But I must get to something more cheerful, so will let you settle the question. "Which one, the native or the Laplander, has the better taste for Nick-Nacks?"

The winter of 1917 or 1918 I made a trip to Capt. A. D. Williams' reindeer camp about sixteen miles back from Kokrines. And there I went to the Melozi Hot Springs for baths and to reduce, if possible. In front of a cabin is a hot springs that throws out about one hundred shoots of water at one hundred and thirty degrees temperature. These run over the bank into the creek. This running water is led into a bathroom. I would soak in there twice a day, then go for a walk on my snowshoes and take up a notch on my belt every second day.

Williams had purchased his deer at Unalakleet and had hired a Laplander to stay with them and to teach him how to handle them. We will call the Laplander, Izzy.

We were out of meat so the Captain said, "Guess we had better kill a deer today." We started for the herd about four miles from camp. They soon left me behind, and I heard a shot and when I caught up with them they were dressing the deer. The head and horns were lying to one side, and Izzy said, "Smith, carry head down to the cabin and we will cook up a good mulligan."

I started back with the head slung on my back and just before I reached home they passed me. I dropped the head at the edge of a pool (about one hundred streams of hot water were shooting up around there with temperature of 120 degrees) and said, "Izzy, you skin out that head, and I'll get the vegetables ready." The Captain already had the fire started, and I began peeling potatoes, carrots, turnips and cut a half a head of cabbage. There was a large pot filled with ice and when Izzy came in he put down the biggest pot they had with the meat in it—then poured the water in the pot of meat, boiled it about fifteen minutes and put in the vegetables. I decided to make some egg dumplings, so took the vegetables out of the pot and cooked the dumplings and we sat down to eat.

We each had a plate of soup, and the Captain and I went back for more, and when I was getting it Izzy reached over and grabbed the end of a bone and splashed it out on his plate. At that point we noticed that when he had dressed the head he had split it down in front, as he held the jawbone, and there was a big, dreamy eyeball looking at us. He then tried to cut it with his table knife, but it was too dull so he went into his pocket and brought out a pocket knife with which he had been cutting his Star tobacco. This had a long pointed blade. He was holding the lower end of the jawbone in his hand and he jabbed the knife inside the eyeball, gave a circular cut all around, then turned it over and did the same thing. With his finger he then punched it out with so much force that it hit the edge of his plate and slid off onto the table toward me. I shuddered, and Izzy then picked up the eye in his hand, put his fork into it and cut off a slice in front of the cornea and began to chew it.

He then turned to me and said, "You must eat that other one, Smith. It is the greatest delicacy of the reindeer." I said, "Yeah, after a while." The Captain and I forgot to eat our soup, and when Izzy cut off another slice, I looked up and there were colored rings like an agate marble. I got up and said, "Captain, sorry, but here I go," and he followed me outdoors.

We sat down on some wood blocks and I said, "Wasn't that the darndest thing you ever saw?" He remarked, "Yes, I've heard they eat them but never believed it until now." We gave Izzy time to finish his dinner, then went into the house. By that time the other jawbone with the eyeball had disappeared. Izzy never worked as well as he did the next day. For some reason or other, I never could eat hard-boiled eggs after that without thinking it was an eyeball.

The next year this reindeer herd was combined with the one belonging to A. L. Wells and Fred Stolkey, making a herd of about three thousand deer. They engaged a native to work for them who had a round full-busted wife and a small baby. Wells and his wife had a cabin, and Williams had one, but the natives were living in a tent about fifty feet from the Wells' cabin. It was April and the deer calves were coming, and while both families were out of grub, notably cream, sugar and bacon, they did not want to lose four days making the trip up to Kokrines for provisions and so were living on short rations.

Living without cream was particularly hard on Mrs. Wells. One day at noon she saw Tommy, the native, going into his tent for dinner, and wanting to borrow something, she walked in while they were eating. She looked and saw that their tea had milk in it; at any rate it was white colored. She rushed back into her own house and said, "Shorty, those dirty Indians have stolen our cream." He replied, "No dear, you are mistaken. They had the same amount we had and they have had none for two weeks, I know."

The next day she again called on them, and sure enough, their tea was white. This made her certain they had stolen the cream and she was going without it, and she was mad as a wet hen. So she kept on the watch and the next day saw Tommy rush into the tent and without waiting for long rushed over. There was Tommy, with a teacup in his hand, milking the wife into the cup. They had used this as a substitute for cream for two weeks and ran true to form until the cow ran dry.

We must not forget that these natives have been here for four hundred years, living off the land on a straight meat diet in the summertime, fish in winter, and fish and berry diet on occasions; living without doctors and in good health. They did not know what tablecloths, napkins, diapers, or handkerchiefs were. I don't know how they managed but—.

In November 1920 I was making the trip to Ruby from Tanana with Henry Robson, the mail carrier. Two of the young dogs were not working very well, and Henry remarked, "I left those pups over a week ago and told Maggie to give them all the feed they could eat. I don't think she has done it and I am going to give her Hell tonight." Maggie Smoke was a big buxom woman, who could work like a man. She was likely the best all-round worker on the Yukon River and had a very jealous disposition and plenty of ego.

When we got to their cabin, she had a good dinner ready for us, and while we were eating, Henry, thinking he could make her jealous, said, "Maggie, I'm going to leave those two dogs with you again, and if you don't feed them all they can eat I am going to Ruby and quit you and get that school teacher." She stuck her head up, curled her lip and said, "I wish you would—that's good enough for you." They had a very charming young school teacher at Ruby at that time who had all the boys buying candy for her, but Maggie thought she was her superior.

Alaskans know that they are considered freaks by many tourists, but in turn get many kicks from them. For instance, I once was leaning on the side rail of the steamer Yukon anchored at Cordova when some lady near me stepped over and said with feminine naivete, "How much above sea level are we?" I looked over the edge at the water and said, "I think about eighteen feet." She exclaimed in marvel and ran away.

Then there was the old maid school teacher who was making the Yukon River trip and was in the pilot house with Captain Norman (Kid) Marion. She had been asking many fool questions, and he was getting quite peeved when she asked him what was the worst experience he had ever had or the nearest he had ever come to losing his life?

The Captain thought a few minutes and then said:

> I think it was the winter of 1899. Our boat was frozen in below Wood-Chopper Creek and we heard of a strike about fifteen miles back inland. I hastily put enough grub in a sack for about two days—got a lead pencil, snowshoes, rifle, but forgot to take any matches except the few I had in my parka pocket.
>
> After I had snowshoed for three hours, the wind came up, blowing snow in all directions, and as the snow came down, night came on. I siwashed it in front of a big fallen tree, keeping the campfire going all night, and the next morning again started out in the storm. I walked all day and finally came to my own snowshoe tracks. I knew they were mine as I was carrying a stick and there was the mark in the snow. I realized that I was lost and had been traveling in a circle all day.
>
> I was tired out, and it had been getting colder all afternoon so I again made a campfire and ate my last grub then and there. After putting in the night, I had to lay up all morning as it was storming so bad. In the afternoon I realized I had to do something, so started traveling and had a hard time to keep from freezing and getting awfully hungry. Night came on, and I had to keep moving to keep from freezing and I had only three matches left. I was about to drop when all at once I ran into a big moose in a bunch of willows and shot it. After opening it up, I made a fire and cut off a big hunk of meat, cut a willow stick and ran it into the meat and half cooked it by the campfire which I had used my last match to start.
>
> I forgot to say I had lost my hand axe from my pack and was having a hard time to keep the fire going without an axe to get wood. However, I kept at the fire although I was getting drowsy and all tired out. I did not dare to give up.
>
> Something had to be done, and I looked down at the steaming moose laying there and had an idea how to keep from freezing. I got some spruce boughs and

wiped out the inside of the moose, then put some of them inside to hold apart the sides and crawled in feet first, with my head and rifle at the rear end of the moose. I carefully drew the boughs out and closed the sides of the moose around my body. It was nice and warm, and I fell asleep at once.

I do not know how long I slept, but it must have been for at least twelve hours, for when I wakened it was getting dark again and the moose was frozen and I couldn't get out. There I lay in my frozen moose tomb. I lay there all night and the next day and night—when near daylight I heard a wolf howl. It was answered off in another direction and finally there were lots of howls— Ki Yis all around me. I soon felt them pulling at the moose, tearing off the meat. One big black wolf was working at the hind end within six inches of my head. I never moved, but just kept rooting for him. Another wolf began eating along side of him and they finally had a hole chewed large enough for me to get the rifle outside and then my shoulders. Action began right off, for I killed the black wolf who had rescued me and shot at the rest, crippling at least four of them, and they finally left the moose.

The weather had changed, and I got my bearings and hit the Yukon River and was back to the boat in about three hours. I think this was the nearest I ever came to losing my life, Miss Kimball. Needless to say, I was and am still here. The good Lord sure did have his arms around me on that trip.

In 1898 C. K. Snow went up the Koyukuk River, and his boat was frozen in at or near Bettles. There were about one hundred people living there, including a young native girl who always visited the different cabins begging Kow-Kow (grub). She was quite a favorite with some people. In 1933 C. K. Snow and Lynn Smith, who were residing in Ruby, composed the following song. It was sung to the tune of Sweet Marie:

THE KOBUK QUEEN

You may talk about the girls from France, from Egypt
    and Japan and Italy with all her winsome maids.
The pretty blue-eyed Spanish girl, to please the heart
    of man and the Irish girl whose beauty never fades.
But there's a girl a way up North, that's quite a proper
    thing

She lives up where the nights are very long.
And although our luck is pretty tough, you'll hear the
white boys sing
This is my one sweet song

CHORUS

My Kobuk Queen, sweet sixteen
There is seal-oil in your hair, my Kobuk Queen.
Your eyes are sore, your nose is snotty
And some say you're often naughty
But I think you're only flirty, Kobuk Queen.
Kobuk Queen, sweet sixteen, not too bold, not too green
White man's Kow-Kow are gone, My Kobuk Queen
We don't mind that seal-oil smell, or those crumbs that
bite like Hell
For your ruby lips are swell, Kobuk Queen.

There's the Ootchy-Kootchy dance that came from over
the sea
And the Can-Can that we all admit is swell
The kickers and the splitters, just as limber as can be
And the many things that we don't care to tell,
But when you speak of Muscle Dance, and everything
like that
Don't think you've seen the maid that has them all
down pat
Till you've seen our Kobuk Queen

CHORUS

My Kobuk Queen, sweet sixteen, not too bold, not too
clean
You're the simple child of nature, Kobuk Queen.
You've learned things from every nation, and boast of
white relations
For your kids are a combination, Kobuk Queen.
Kobuk Queen, sweet sixteen, not too bold, not too clean
You're the idol child of dreamland, Kobuk Queen.
You dance with the Honolulu motion, and the Coon
girls great commotion,
And the white girl's funny notion, Kobuk Queen.

There were other verses we wrote which I have forgotten.

From Valdez to Fairbanks in 1906 by Bicycle, Blizzard and Strategy

John A. Clark

IN 1906 ALASKA was a land of romance and mystery, the Mecca of the gold-seeker. The Interior, to the world at large, was a Terra Incognita, a frozen waste, inhabited by fur-clad Eskimos, whose chief occupation was supposedly the chasing of the festive polar bear from the doors of their ice igloos. To the residents of the coast towns, the finding of gold in the Interior meant that all who sought wealth in the hinterland must pass through their towns. That meant prosperity.

Gold was first discovered in the Tanana Valley about the year 1902 by Felix Pedro, one of the small number of prospectors who had each year extended their explorations from Dawson and a few of the other small mining camps on the upper Yukon River. The country was unexplored and when the prospector went forth he was generally compelled to haul all of his provisions on a small hand sled. He "lived off the country" so far as his meat supply was concerned, but all else must be carried into the wilderness.

About the time Pedro made his discovery, Captain Barnette was making his way up the Tanana River with a small stern-wheel steamer, attempting to reach some place on the Tanana River where he could establish a trading post. He left the main river near where the town of Chena was afterwards established and attempted the navigation of what became known as the Chena Slough. He progressed about twelve miles up the slough, where he encountered bars in the river beyond which he could not go, and finally dropped back about half a mile to a place where he found good timber and a high bank where he could unload and start a post.

So the town of Fairbanks, which afterwards grew around the trading post, was established purely by chance, at the point on a navigable stream that was closest to the place where gold was discovered at about the same time.

The news of the discovery of gold traveled as such news always does, and the next winter other prospectors came from the upper river. Among them was "Wada the Jap." He came, and forthwith departed for Dawson. We have always been assured that there is a particular hell prepared for the liars of the world. In Alaska it is recognized that the greatest crime that can be committed is to bring about a "false stampede." I presume Wada, being a fatalist, had no terrors of the hereafter, for when he returned to Dawson he told the most wonderful tales of the great discoveries that had been made in the vicinity of Fairbanks.

Being a convincing and conscientious liar, he named the various creeks upon which the finds had been made and named with particularity the value per foot of the ground, not only on Pedro Creek where the only gold had been found at the time of his visit, but on Cleary Creek, Fairbanks Creek, Ester Creek and on Goldstream. His news created a wild stampede, and of course he and his dog team were in demand at fancy prices for the long winter journey to Fairbanks.

When the stampede arrived at Fairbanks, practically everything that Wada had told had come true. Discoveries on the various creeks named by him had been made since his departure for Dawson, and the values were as good or better than he had stated. There is no moral to this tale. But what would the Alaskans of that day have done to Wada had he proved to be a prophetic liar?

The year 1904-5 witnessed the birth and development of a boom camp. Thousands came from all parts of the earth, as is the case wherever a new gold strike is made. Thousands came from Nome and Dawson where their boom was moribund. Regular steamboat lines on the Yukon and Tanana Rivers were established. Freight came in by way of the mouth of the Yukon at St. Michael from the west, and by way of Dawson from the east. A narrow gage railroad was projected and built from Fairbanks to Goldstream. The U.S. Army established telegraph connections with the coast, and thence by cable with the "outside."

Soon the Courts commenced to function; electric lights, steam heat, running water, and other public utilities were started; the place where timber was thickest became the town site and many houses were constructed from the timber.

Schools were started when families commenced to arrive, and jails were constructed for the accommodation of those whose actions merited that particular mark of distinction. Gold flowed in from the creeks in an ever increasing volume and a number of saloons and dance halls were started to accommodate the tired and thirsty miner. In each saloon and dance hall were set up roulette wheels, faro and blackjack and crap tables, with plenty of tables for those who preferred to lose their money at poker—stud, draw, or what have you? Civilization (?) had overcome the wilderness.

Early in March, 1906, when the steamer Oregon sailed from Seattle for Valdez it was loaded with claim owners who had spent the winter in the States and were returning for the summer work; venturesome and optimistic youths who sought their fortunes in the new field; merchants who had been out on a buying trip; gamblers, dance hall girls, prospectors—and me. The ship was loaded; so were most of the passengers, but the latter condition was speedily remedied as we took the "outside" passage. The Gulf of Alaska in March is no place for a pleasure trip.

Valdez, at the upper end of a bay, backed by towering mountains, was the only winter gateway to the interior. The narrow streets were scenes of the greatest activity when the 700 passengers landed, all eager to cross the towering ranges behind the town and be on their way. Snow from the houses had been shoveled into the streets, and in many places just beyond the sidewalks it was piled higher than the first story of the buildings. Often you could hear a dog team racing by but it was entirely out of sight of anyone on the sidewalk a few feet away. Hundreds of dog teams and double-enders drawn by horses and mules were being prepared for the 450 mile journey.

Within a few hours after the boat landed, men on foot with packs on their backs were striking out up the valley toward Camp Comfort, the first road house on the trail.

There were six in the party who believed that bicycles were the proper way to navigate the trail. There was my brother, W. Sam Clark, who had gone to Cook Inlet in 1896; had packed a load on his back over the Chilkoot Pass in 1897; who had whipsawed his own lumber, built his own boat, and shot the rapids on his way to Dawson in the great stampede that is famed in song and history. He had spent a number of years in the Dawson camp and was with the first party that ever went overland from Fort Yukon to the headwaters of the Koyukuk River in 1900. He had afterwards gone to Nome, and later had been one of the pioneers in the Fairbanks camp. Frank Black, another of the tribe, had spent a number of years in Dawson and had been one of the early arrivals in Fairbanks soon after the establishment of that camp. Fred Crouch, who was the only one who knew how to repair a bicycle, had spent some time in the Fairbanks camp. There were three Cheechakos, who comprised the balance of the party—Henry Grothe and E. E. Corecco, just out of business college in Stockton, California, and myself.

We started early the next forenoon and reached the first road house in a few hours, but decided that we would wait until morning to attempt the crossing of Thompson's Pass. Hundreds of teams had beaten down the snow until we had a fine bicycle trail to the foot of the mountain, but after passing through Keystone Canyon our troubles began.

The trail started on a long slope from the base of the mountain, across its face, ever-ascending toward the narrow pass near the summit through which all traffic had to go.

I have no idea of the geographical length of that trail, but it seemed not less than a thousand miles. The terrific gales had blown the snow over the summit and lodged it on the breast of the mountain, where it was piled up from twenty to a hundred feet in depth. Constant traffic had beaten down the snow until the trail itself was firm enough, but when you got off the trail into the loose snow it was like falling into an ocean of feathers. To make travel more interesting, a blizzard welcomed us as we started up the trail.

The steepness of the trail, and the freshly fallen and wind-blown snow made it impossible to attempt to ride the bicycles, so all we could do was to take them on our backs and start up in the face of the gale. It was interesting and exciting, especially when a dog team relaying freight or passengers came tearing down the trail for another load, or when a horse- or mule-driven rig came out of the blizzard and was upon you before you knew it. These rigs had the right of way theoretically, also practically, for the foot passenger who was rash enough to dispute it just possibly might be able to dig himself out of the soft snow by the following spring.

A man with a bicycle on his back was not only classed as a

pedestrain, but as a fool. Before we reached the top, I was entirely satisfied that both classifications were absolutely accurate. What actually happened was that when we saw a rig coming we threw our wheels into the loose snow and then ourselves on top, hoping that we would not entirely disappear into the drift. By the time we had helped each other onto the firm trail, another rig would be upon us and we would repeat the performance, and so on ad nauseum.

We became proficient as high divers but objected strenuously to the number of encores to which we were compelled to respond. That day was a nightmare and, as it was each man for himself, those of us who had been softened by office work found that a bicycle possesses the most remarkable faculty of taking on weight with increased elevation.

The lee side of a rock beside the trail presented such an inviting aspect that I, being at the tail end of the procession, could not resist its allure. I curled myself up beside the bicycle and prepared to rest. The thermometer was at about zero and the wind was shrieking down from the pass. Just as I was comfortably settled, ready to doze off, a husky pedestrian whom I had noticed on the boat stopped in front of my retreat, took one good look at me and then picked up my wheel, put it on his back, and started up the trail, merely remarking that I had better try it again. I did. That act put me on my feet when I didn't believe it was possible to go another step, much less the remaining half mile over the summit.

He made a friend for life, and afterwards we became great friends. In a small way I have been able to repay him for what he did for me that day. He was a steamboat captain going in to take charge of his steamer for the summer and I have ridden many hundreds of miles in his pilot house.

A few minutes after I again started up the trail, a dog team came down from the summit, and the driver, after being sure of my identity, delivered to me a bag of doughnuts that my brother had sent back to me, he having reached the road house at the summit some time before I did.

To a Californian, a doughnut is recognized as the staff of life. That day, to a transplanted Californian, it was not only a staff but a pair of crutches. My lips were frozen, but that didn't prevent me from eating those big, fat, greasy doughnuts. If I could have had my way about it, the Coat of Arms of Alaska could certainly have as a central figure a doughnut rampant with crossed can opener and corkscrew in the hole. Those three made Alaska great, and that day demonstrated the value of all three. By the aid of the doughnuts, I rolled triumphantly over the crest and stumbled into the road house near the top of that bleak mountain.

Never will I forget the tent road house at the summit of Thompson Pass as it appeared that day. I have no idea of the height of the mountain except that I was firmly convinced it was the mountain told of by Gulliver, thirty miles in height. The top of the mountain was absolutely bare of all vegetation, as it was high above timber line. Great outcroppings of rock, swept bare, were the only relief to the universal white of the snow, and even these were constantly obscured by clouds of snow driven before the wind howling around the peak.

When the top of the pass was reached, we experienced the full fury of the storm driving in from the hundreds of miles of bleak mountain ranges extending for an apparently immeasurable distance to the west. The road house had been built a few hundred feet from the summit and at the extreme tip of a funnel-shaped basin that had been carved out of the mountain side as if by a monstrous slide.

At the foot of the western base of the mountain was a river. The winds gathering in the canyon found an outlet up the basin, and all their fury was concentrated at the summit. Blowing up hill the winds gathered not only the snow that was falling, but great quantities from the lower reaches of the slope and hurled it all at the summit. Part of it blew over the summit and added to the pleasures of the travelers on the trail on the lee of the mountain, but most of it lodged against the peak. There a road house had been constructed in the early fall to accommodate the hordes that would travel that way during the winter.

As all lumber had to be brought from Valdez, only a little was used, merely a floor of rough lumber and a few boards around the side extending up for a distance of about seven feet. Inside this wall, using the board floor as a base, a tent had been set up. The tent was about twelve by sixteen feet. It was securely anchored with ropes to the rocks, and when a stove was installed and a few dishes and a rough table secured, the place was fully equipped and ready for business. Provisions were hauled up when needed.

When the winter winds took up their accustomed duties,

the snow was packed around the walls of the road house, and in a few days the proprietor commenced his regular winter sport of trying to keep open a tunnel to his door. When the snow had been packed down around his road house to the height of the walls, he laid a floor across the roof of his first dwelling, built a new wall and moved his tent up one story, preserving connection with the first story of his house by means of a small opening in one corner and a seven foot ladder. The day I reached the place he was living in the third story, and the prospects were excellent for moving another story before the winter was over, for in that section they frequently have fifty feet or more of snow during the winter.

I entered the road house from the side away from the prevailing winds and found about twenty men seated around a long table extending down the full length of the room. A meal was on the table, and my traveling companions were doing their best to eat everything in sight.

The proprietor took one look at me, laid another plate, pulled up a box for a chair and told me to sit down. He placed before me a great deep tin bowl holding about a quart of red hot tomato soup. I needed no further instructions as to the proper road house etiquette under such circumstances. Frozen stiff lips did not appear to affect my ability to wield an active and wicked spoon.

The next move of the proprietor was to take a pint tin cup, fill it half full of scalding coffee and cool it with an equal amount of well-seasoned Bourbon whiskey. Nectar, ambrosia, malted milk, ice cream sodas and all the other drinks of the ancients were as nothing compared with that drink. When it had gone to the place where all good drinks go, I commenced to take a more active interest in life and wrought mightily when a heaping dish of Irish stew was placed before me. Having eaten my fill, I began to shake. The proprietor led me down two ladders to his sub-basement where he slept. I lay down on the bed and had as beautiful a chill as was ever imported into the interior of that great country. I have a faint suspicion that the earth tremors noted by the seismograph in Seattle at that hour of that day were caused by something other than a subterranean disturbance in the Aleution Islands, as the worthy scientists concluded.

Having thoroughly shaken the foundations of that particular mountain and the whole coast range, I felt ready to take another chance with the storm, and we started down the mountain through snow almost waist deep, in the face of a storm that was evidently violating all union rules as to the useless waste of energy. Bicycle riding under the circumstances did not appear to offer many advantages, so hoping to placate the wheels for the hard usage given them the day before, we decided to carry them on our backs. I have often heard boys who were trained during the war claim that the War Department arranged that they should carry articles that would make their packs most uncomfortable, and I am thoroughly convinced that the Department overlooked a golden opportunity when it failed to include bicycles in the doughboy's pack.

Fortunately it was downhill, and about dark we reached Ptarmigan Drop, a road house at the foot of the mountain on the shore of the frozen river. We had out-traveled most of the people who were at the Summit Road House when we left there, as they had teams and loads to attend to and their progress down the trail through soft snow consisted of many upsets and more profanity, especially at the "drop" at the foot of the hill.

It was interesting to us ahead of them, in a good warm road house with bunks reserved, to look out of the window and watch the performance on the last hundred feet of the trail. "Drop" it surely was, and often the load would reach the bottom somewhat in advance of the horse or mule attached to it. First would appear a swirl of snow as a heavily loaded double-ender attempted to overtake its motive power on the last half mile pitch of the trail before the "drop" was reached. When the top of the drop showed up, the speed was generally so great that there was no stopping for any purpose, and the next thing we would see was a rig pitching over the edge and a swirl of canvas-covered load, sled runners, wildly waving legs of horse and man, and a great cloud of snow as the whole mess settled in the great drifts at the bottom. Fortunate was the man whose rig landed on the trail at the bottom, for all he had to do then was to turn his heavily laden sled over, dig out his kicking horse or mule, gather up his loose articles that had shaken off during the descent, dodge a few other similar rigs that were apparently falling out of the sky, and be on his way. The outfit that missed the trail at the bottom and went into the drifts occasionally had a little difficulty in getting straightened out, especially as in one case when I saw three rigs piled up together in the same drift over the edge of the river bank. The trail took a sharp turn at the bottom, and the rig that missed that turn in its descent went over the bank into drifts probably twenty or thirty feet deep. The drivers who had been over the road before knew the conditions at the bottom and hence checked their speed on the long slope before the drop. Having a sense of humor, they failed to warn those who traveled the trail for the first time, evidently considering the matter from a sporting standpoint; they probably made bets with themselves as to whether or not the driver in his first descent would make the turn or do the high dive.

Before we had been in the road house at the Drop for an hour, every available bunk was taken, and some of the late-comers decided to stop long enough to feed their horses and then push on to the next road house a few miles up the river. The storm had passed, the stars were out, and they could drive at night.

Road houses on that trail that year were much alike. They had been built in a hurry to meet an emergency and were spaced from fifteen to twenty miles apart—too short generally for a one-day journey, and yet so far apart that for the ordinary horse-driven rig it was difficult to make two road houses in a day.

Meals at the Valdez end, for the first hundred miles, were $1.50 and beds $1.50 to $2. "Beds" is a misnomer, for generally they were only bunks against the wall, usually in tiers of two or four, depending upon the height of the roof. The bunks were constructed of round spruce poles and the mattress and springs of the same material. Some of the road house keepers, having evidently been accustomed to luxuries before they came to Alaska, sprinkled a few spruce boughs over the poles, and some of them actually had a few blankets to spread over the boughs. After sleeping on one of them, I concluded that the blankets were for purposes of concealment. But after a day on the trail, even the presence of a few boulders, cannon balls, broken glass, and other trifles would not have been noticed.

In the center of the room was generally an "oil tank stove," that is, a hundred-gallon steel oil tank. In place of the bung was a door for the purpose of feeding into the beast, and at the other end on top was a hole cut for a stovepipe. Some of them had a few holes below the door for the purpose of draft, and when a fire was started in the stove it soon gave a good account of itself and nothing better could have been devised.

Above the stove, near the roof, and all around the pipe, was a rack made of small poles or sometimes wire, over which were drapped wet socks, soaked shoes, shoe laces, moccasins, and wet et ceteras. A "musher" or dog team driver would come in, find a box or log or whatever was used for chairs, sit down and remove his wet foot gear, hang it on the rack and after skirmishing around in his "war bag," find dry foot gear, his pipe, matches, etc. When his pipe was started, he might then condescend to speak to whoever might be in the road house. I have seen hundreds of men come into road houses and follow out the above ritual before speaking a word, and while so engaged no one would speak to them. In fact, each man's business was his own particular business, and unless he chose to take others into his confidence he was let strictly alone.

A table was generally in evidence in the main room, in many cases the only room in the road house. Sometimes a kitchen was built on as a lean-to, but more often all of the cooking, eating, sleeping, drying of clothes and shoes was done in the one room. For ventilation there was generally a small aperture near the roof, about four inches square, and this was supposed to furnish all of the fresh air that ten or fifty men needed. It is not a matter of wonder that a traveler was always ready to start out the next morning, regardless of what reports he had received as to the trail ahead. In fact, most travelers were early risers!

I recall one road house on the Gakona River, reached by us late at night after a very hard day, where there were only four bunks in a room not more than eight by ten in size. There were boughs on two of them, and by boughs I mean a few branches that did not even cover up the rough poles beneath. No blankets were in evidence to conceal in any manner the beautiful simplicity of the sleeping accommodations.

A freighter who was hauling apples, oranges, and eggs to Fairbanks had reached the place first and for the protection of his perishables had unloaded his freight, piling it up in the only open space between the bunks and the other wall. When we got there, our bicycling party by this time having been reduced to four, we entered the room by climbing over the freight, bumping our heads on the roof, and sliding down the other side into a small lean-to kitchen where we dined sumptuously, at $2 per, on a stew made of ptarmigan bones, water, and a little flour. Others had been there before us. In fact, a whiskey drummer had pre-empted the best bunk, and I am thoroughly convinced that he had also appropriated all of the spruce boughs from the other beds. My belief is founded upon the fact that when he wasn't looking I lifted a corner of his wolf robe and found an eight-inch mattress of boughs beneath. We didn't question his ethics, for we knew that had we been the first to arrive, we would have done the same; besides, we had no bedding and desired to acquire a robe from him, as we knew he was traveling in style in a basket sleigh and must have other robes or blankets. After we had praised his whiskey and treated him to a cigar that one of us had, which in some manner had weathered successfully the various vicissitudes of the trail, he finally loaned us one blanket and one robe. Two of us in each bunk, poles and weather underneath, and a blanket or robe on top, served us for the night.

It afterwards became my duty as attorney for one of the companies here to cause that drummer to be indicted by the Grand Jury for selling whiskey at wholesale price without paying a Federal license. I was not sorry, however, when the indictment was quashed by reason of an error of the District Attorney. Besides, his house paid the expenses of defending him.

When I was a small boy in California, I frequently had occasion to try to walk the ties on the railroad and I always marveled at the skill of the trackwalkers in being able to travel the ties. For three days after leaving Ptarmigan Drop I had cause to recall my early aversion to railroad ties.

The Signal Corps had established a great many stations along the Valdez Trail and was engaged in hauling their supplies for the summer. This was done on double-enders, and the motor power of each was one transplanted Missouri mule. They had about twenty mules at work and had been relaying the freight for a couple of weeks. The mules, being methodical, stopped each time in the same place as before. As a result, for more than seventy miles, about every eighteen inches was a trench across the trail made by the mules' feet. The trail being about two and one half feet wide and cut up with cross trenches made bicycling anything but a joy. It was like trying to ride a wheel along the ends of railroad ties. What we said about the Signal Corps, mules in general and those mules in particular, was sufficiently slanderous to have caused us to be imprisoned for several lifetimes. In fact, we had to walk and shove our wheels beside us for the full distance until we passed the last station to which supplies were being hauled.

We had our revenge, however, for on the last day when we were experiencing such rough going, as we rounded a turn on one of the river banks, we came face to face with twelve mules, each attached to an empty double-ender, returning for another load. There were only three soldiers with them, as it was not necessary to have a driver for each, since the mules soon learned what to do and were allowed to do their own navigating. There was a driver for the front sleigh for the purpose of setting the pace and another for the rear sled to prevent straggling.

The three soldiers were with the last sled and were entirely unsuspicious of disaster. When four of us on wheels rounded the bend and confronted those long-eared calliopes, they took one look and started away from there. One started up the mountain side but didn't go far, for in a few moments he was back on the trail with the sled on top. The rest of them could not go back, and they followed the line of least resistance; that was over the bank onto the river about a dozen feet below. The river was fortunately shallow, but swift, and the ice was thin. When a dozen mules hit the surface of the ice practically all in one place, the ice gave way, and inside of ten seconds there were eleven mules, three doughboys, and sleds galore splashing around in the river. Mule drivers are generally accorded the palm for original and flowery profanity. Add to this a mule-driving soldier and you have a work of art.

The first mule that broke through the ice and reached the farther bank started through the woods. When we left there, we could hear sounds of falling timber and other disturbances sounding like a band of stampeding elephants. One mule managed to tangle his sled with a tree too large for him to pull down, and there he was, standing on his front legs and trying to kick his sled to pieces. What those soldiers said when we sat down on the bank and laughed was sufficient to have caused every one of them to have been "churched" in a church where every deacon or elder was a mule driver. We forgot all of our troubles and the terrors of the road for the past two days, and, fearing that some of those doughboys might have a gun, mounted our wheels and in spite of the rough trail made a record for Alaskan travel for the next mile. I hope they found all of their pets. It is certain we never made inquiries. We were not to blame for the mules' lack of bicycle culture and their superstition.

The very name of Ernestine Road House is enough to call up memories of discomfort and congestion, not to mention dirt and disorder. We reached the place just at dark about the third day out and found to our sorrow that there were many others ahead of us, the tag ends of the last boat load of passengers preceding the Oregon.

By traveling on wheels and traveling light, we had outdistanced virtually all the other passengers, and consequently we were in hopes of being able to secure accommodations at the various road houses. As I now recall, this road house was presumed to have accommodations for about twenty-six people. When we reached the place, there were more than fifty already there, and before midnight the number had swelled to seventy-three. The bunks were all taken, and I did not have a look into the portion of the building where the beds were located.

We could not go on, as we were tired out and the thermometer stood at about twenty below zero, and the next road house was distant more than twenty miles. We decided to stay. There was little difficulty about meals, for the proprietor had plenty of provisions. Besides, we were hungry after twelve or thirteen hours in the open, pedaling over different and indifferent trails. Ham and cold storage eggs, sourdough bread, Lubock potatoes, and canned butter, at $3 per meal, was living in luxury, and we kept clear of the kitchen part of the establishment as its reputation had reached us before we reached the road house. What we didn't know would not hurt us.

As for beds, that was something else again. For the sum of $2 I rented a blanket for the night, and a part of the contract was the privilege of trying to find a place to lie down. Against one wall of the main room was a small bench or settee, consisting of one twelve-inch board attached to the wall by wooden brackets. As a finishing touch and to lend distinction to the structure and to simulate a couch, another foot board about two feet long was fastened to the wall and thus feebly imitated the sloping head part of the couch.

The whole structure was about four feet long, and as the pole floor did not appear very inviting and all of the floor space was already appropriated, I decided that the couch should be my bed. I was young and inexperienced in rough-and-tumble sleeping in road houses, and those who chose the floor were not.

However, by removing my shoes, wrapping the blanket about me and lying down on my side on the couch, I felt that I might "pull through." My backbone was twisted and my pedal extremities stuck out over the lower end about two feet, and I was in imminent danger of falling off when I went to sleep. Outside of that, for a few minutes it was quite comfortable. The chief drawback was that the table was right in front of me and the lamp, which they kept burning all night to enable late arrivals to locate the sleepers on the floor, was within three feet of my eyes.

This disadvantage was overcome by making friends with a large well-fed cat that lived there. When cordial relations had been established, I placed the cat on the table between me and the light and induced the cat to go to sleep. With this feline lamp shade in place I managed to get to sleep, after pulling the table up so that I was wedged against the wall and could not fall forward.

I didn't lie awake to listen to the gentle and ungentle cursing of those who tried to sleep upon the hard floor, as it was apparent that their troubles were none of mine. The lamp was turned low and comparative quiet reigned until about midnight, when a stage loaded with passengers bound for the Interior pulled in.

There were six men and two women aboard, and they were anxious to enter and get warm and have a meal. They opened the door and stepped in. It was no longer quiet, as the sleeper in front of the door objected verbally to having his midsection used as a floor. The first man in weighed about three hundred pounds, and his weight was enough to waken the soundest sleeper. He hastily apologized and stepped one step forward, and then the disturbance was increased by exactly one hundred per cent as he stepped on another man's face.

Having left a little space behind him, the rest of the passengers came in, and as every foot of the floor space was occupied by tired men, the result is better imagined than described. The dim light was of little assistance and the presence of ladies was no deterrent to the disturbed sleepers, who faithfully, conscientiously, and fervently consigned the whole lot to the lowermost torture chamber of the hottest Hades that they could think of.

The heavy man managed to work his way to my side of the room, and in the dim light, perceiving a couch there and desiring to rest his feet from the labor of smashing bodies, sat down. It chanced that the so-called couch was the two feet and more of my legs that extended beyond the lower end of the couch. Three hundred pounds applied to that caused the other end of my body to rise up and the passenger to descend.

Fortunately for him, but not so for the sleeper, another man was lying on the floor at the foot of my bed, and the first intimation he had of impending trouble was when the heavyweight sat down on his face. Being out of bed and the better to express myself, it being difficult to do justice to such a subject in the dark, I turned up the light, and we were then able to see what was going on.

The sleepers who had been walked on were dragging themselves out of harm's way, with the exception of one big fellow near the door, and he gave the best exhibition of gallantry that it has ever been my good fortune to witness. One of the ladies was standing on his chest, and he wasn't saying a word but was pretty red in the face. When she saw where she was, she gave a little shriek and moved on, without waiting for an apology from her animated door mat.

The proprietor was routed out, and the stage load demanded something to eat. A space having been cleared for them, they huddled there while the cook built up a fire in the kitchen and cooked their meal. When it was ready, he called them to come into the dining room, which was a lean-to arrangement with a stove in one end and a table running the rest of the way down the room.

A bench was provided, and when they sat down and put their feet under the table, another howl of protest was registered, as every bit of the space under the table was occupied by sleepers who couldn't find room in the main room. They ate their meal with their feet resting on faintly protesting mushers, and then the question arose as to sleeping accommodations.

The stage driver came to the rescue of the ladies; he took one of the seats out of the bob sled stage and made a bed in the bottom of the stage, using all the wolf robes he had. The women crawled into bed, and he covered them over and then replaced the seat, and even though the thermometer was 25 or 30 below zero, they were thoroughly comfortable.

Where the men passengers slept, if at all, I don't know and didn't care. Some of the sleepers who had been disturbed got up, put on their shoes and started out in the starlight to mush to the next road house, about twenty miles further on.

We arose early and before daylight were on our wheels going away from there. Two of the six of us who essayed the trip by bicycle abandoned the wheels here and decided to do the rest of the traveling on foot. The trail was good and we made good time, as we were traveling over a great plateau. About noon when we were ravenous we reached a road house which had a reputation bad even for that trail that winter.

I was the victim chosen to reconnoiter and ascertain the temper of the lady proprietor and the state of her larder. I ascertained the first. It was bad. The larder ditto. In fact, to accept the lady's tale as true, it was the same cupboard that Old Mother Hubbard formerly owned.

Not caring to go back to my traveling companions empty handed, fearing that they might in their state of hunger suggest cannibalism, I attempted to secure some provisions, even if we could not get a meal. I succeeded—one weevily hardtack for which I paid $1, the price of one "light lunch" at her road house. It being round and not capable of being evenly divided into four parts, and not caring to cause dissension, I ate the hardtack myself. In fact, the other three insisted that I eat it and stood by until I did so!

The first hundred miles of our journey had all been a consistent upgrade, and when we reached the plateau country we thought our troubles were over, for we were then on the downgrade toward the basin of the Copper River. Magnificent mountains were ahead and from one of them to the east, Mt. Wrangell, a great cloud of smoke was constantly issuing, as it was then and is now a live volcano.

The trail here, by reason of the great amount of travel, was in excellent condition, as there had been no snow for a couple of weeks and it was a perfect boulevard. When we started down the long slope, many times, for miles, all we needed was a good coaster brake. Frequently our brakes would become so hot that we would have to stop and throw the machine into the snow to let it cool off.

Just before reaching the Copper River valley, I chanced to be in the lead and was going at a decidedly fast clip down the trail when from around a bend came a dog team headed my way. I was going so fast that I could not stop, and to avoid a collision I turned out into the deep snow and went headlong into a drift, nothing but my feet showing above the surface. The passenger in the dog team got out, and he and the driver, each taking hold of one of my feet, managed to pull me out. I then rescued my bicycle, and after thanking them for upending me I mounted my wheel and went on down into the valley.

Fifteen years later, while discussing early experiences with a mining engineer friend of mine whom I had known intimately for over ten years, I discovered that he was the man who had pulled me out of the drift. He was then en route to Nome, and after spending a number of years there, had come to Fairbanks.

My recollection of most of the road houses we encountered on the other end of the trail that spring is not very distinct. They were much alike, with the exception of a few that were a little worse than the others, while the one bright spot beyond the Copper River valley was the night we spent at the Tonsina Road House.

We had bunks with blankets on them; we had good meals and everything, except the travelers, was clean. We were definitely ahead of everybody who had come up on the Oregon. We had passed most of the stragglers from the earlier boat and were making from 35 to 50 miles a day. Prices were $2 per meal and the same for a bunk. At one road house my brother and I secured a real room for ourselves and paid $3 each for the privilege of sleeping in a real bed and being enabled to take off something more than our shoes. As for appetites—well, our patronage of the road houses was no asset to the proprietors thereof. We were a floating liability.

Though we were doing the hardest kind of work, I gained twelve pounds in the twelve days we were on the trail.

When we reached the Copper River, our trail was on the ice of the river for sixty miles or more, and it was like riding on a pavement. The road house keeper kept the trail scraped for about fifteen or twenty miles south of his place of business after each fall of fresh snow. As he had no snow scraper available, he used a dead horse for that purpose. Even though the horse was thoroughly frozen, it was pretty well worn out before spring.

Three of my companions were Alaska wise, having been in the country many years, so I was not handicapped like many Cheechakos by dressing too heavily. We wore medium-weight woolen underwear, a heavy woolen shirt, denim trousers, a light and a heavy pair of woolen socks inside shoe pacs, i.e. rubber shoes with about fourteen-inch leather tops.

For a coat I had a khaki jacket. A fur cap with ear flaps that could be turned up and tied when not needed completed the outfit. For extra clothing we each carried two pair of dry socks.

A tooth brush and tooth powder, a shaving outfit, and a few clean handkerchiefs completed our baggage, and it was all made up into a package that could readily be tied under the saddle of the wheel or stuck in one of the pockets of the coat. We wore woolen mittens inside large leather mitts.

With this clothing, when exerting ourselves there was little danger of perspiring too much. In that kind of travel the less perspiration the better; otherwise one is in danger of becoming overheated and then cooling off suddenly. The denim, being closely woven, keeps out the wind, and this is true of khaki. The only place where we might feel the cold was on our hands or faces. The hands were protected by wool on the inside and leather on the outside to keep out the wind. The ears and cheeks were protected by the fur cap. The rest of the face had to take its chances. Noses appear to have been made for freezing, and a peeling nose was a sign of the trail traveler. Without it people might think you had come in by stage.

In the early mornings when the sun was still attempting to get up its own circulation, and before the universe was "het up," it was sometimes pretty cold; but during the middle of the day we were frequently compelled to shed our coats and ride with bare hands. When it commenced to get dark and we were hungry and there was no road house in sight, then we felt the cold. That trip taught me that a good meal is better than a thick overcoat, and hunger makes a liar out of a thermometer.

Speaking of liars, during the year 1906, Alaska, I believe, held the per capita world record for liars. I do not know what the white population was at that time, but whatever it was, that was the exact number of white liars running at large within the confines of the Territory, and I believe that the entire population was on the trail.

Of all the liars, the distance liar is the worst. We would meet someone on the trail and ask the distance to the next road house. He would gravely ponder the matter for the moment and then tell us it was about four miles. We thought he was taking time to think in order to be more accurate, but we soon found he was sizing us up to ascertain how large a lie we would swallow without being suspicious. Feeling cheered, we would speed up and speculate as to whether we would have moose or caribou or mountain sheep for dinner when we got in. When we had ridden eight or nine miles, we would commence to worry as to whether we had passed the road house without seeing it.

Frequently we would meet another traveler and ask him the same question and find that it was about four miles further. We would then ride another hour or two and be cheered by a sign beside the road, "One mile to the road house," and then we would feel that our troubles were over and would desist from cursing the road liars we had just met.

Our education as to the length of "one mile" was a slow and painful affair. We never found such a sign closer than three miles from any road house, and when we did reach the road house and expressed our opinion of a man that would put up such misleading signs, the proprietor was always apologetic and surmised that some- - - -fool had moved the sign, as he had paced off an even mile to where he first put it up.

After all, the misinformation was beneficial in a way, for many times if the traveler really knew what was before him, he would give up. The psychological effect was good, since the weary traveler was so intent upon finding the road house around the next bend that he forgot how tired he was.

We soon became adept in conveying misinformation, for when we met some poor devil going out over the trail, especially if he was afoot and looked tired, we shortened the distance to the next road house by several miles. In after years there was a rearrangement of the road houses so that they averaged about fifteen miles apart and a reasonably good walker could make that distance in between five or six hours.

After we left Copper Center on the Copper River, we went up that river near its junction with the Gulkana River and then ascended to the great plateau that separates the watersheds of the Copper River and the Tanana River.

My recollection of that part of the trip is of endless trails that seemed to stretch into infinity—road houses few and far between. Great mountain ranges, scores of miles away on each side; trails cut through the timber where nothing could be seen but the trail straight ahead; or, when not in timber, endless wastes of dazzling snow that made snow glasses a necessity.

There was a hundred mile nightmare of hard pedaling through about an inch of new snow and then a sudden descent to the very headwaters of the Gulkana River at Summit Lake. The lake is six or seven miles long, situated above timber line in a basin in the mountains.

From one end of the lake flows the Gulkana River, which ultimately empties into Copper River and it in turn into the Gulf of Alaska in the northern Pacific. From the other end flows the Big Delta River, which empties into the Tanana, which in turn pours its muddy flood into the Yukon, which empties into Bering Sea, and the driftwood carried by the parent and tributary streams is sometimes cast up on the Asiatic shores.

The trip across the lake, coming as it did at the end of a day of ceaseless toil, was almost the last straw, and if there had been timber near we would have been mightily tempted to "siwash it" in the timber that night. We had reached the home of the winds, and they had done their worst to the trail and the drifts were so numerous that riding was out of the question.

That stretch seemed endless, and it was sheer will power that kept us going, as we understood that Yost's Road House was only a short distance beyond the end of the lake and on the right bank of the river.

We finally turned the end of the lake and entered the narrow canyon of the Big Delta just at dark, and we figured that we would be able to ride the few remaining miles on the glare ice of the river. We didn't. We ran into overflow on the river, and the surface of the ice from shore to shore was covered with water to a depth of about a foot, and the current was swift. There was nothing to do but put our wheels on our backs and start downriver with the water, as the walls of the canyon were precipitous.

It was now thoroughly dark, and the gloom was rendered worse by the high walls on either side. The winter trail followed the river and so did we. We were unable to judge as to whether there was open water ahead and we didn't much care. The water ran over the tops of our shoe pacs, and frequently one of us would slip on the smooth ice and go down into the water. We seemed to flow with the black water—black water underfoot, with black night ahead.

Some time later we saw a light on the bank and left the water for the road house. Small, poorly ventilated, none too clean, beds of the softness of granite, meals fair, but it was a paradise! Even the knowledge that we had to take to the water on the river in the morning could not take from us the enjoyment of the warmth and dryness of that road house.

Before daylight, we were on our way again, hoping to get onto the ice and down the river ahead of the overflows that were generally at their worst in the late afternoon and evening. They slacken as the chill of night comes on and generally freeze over during the night as the thermometer was about thirty below zero.

The day was clear, but the terror of the Delta region had come during the night. That was, the wind. The Cave of the Winds must be located in that region. The natives say that the Mother of Winds lives in the high hills there and if that is true her progeny are numerous and lusty, and the terror of all winter travelers who perforce must go that way.

For once fortune favored us, for the wind blew down the river and would be at our backs. We congratulated ourselves upon that piece of good fortune and blithely pedaled forth to the middle of the river where we would have a straight shoot and the wind would save much hard pedaling.

The difficulty with us was that we always congratulated ourselves too soon. That was perhaps fortunate, else we never would have enjoyed congratulations. The wind was there all right, and when it got a good chance at us our brakes were the only things that saved us from annihilation. It was blowing about sixty miles per hour, and all we could do was to put on the brakes and hold the bicycle straight and trust to luck, and even then we must have traveled at times at the rate of fully thirty miles per hour.

You will note that I said "at times," for that speed never continued long, because the ice was uneven and, as we had no "skid chains," when we struck a sideling place, down we went, and unless we held onto the wheel in falling the wind would whirl it downriver on the glare ice, even though it was on its side.

Try some time to run on glare ice with ice-covered soles on your shoes, and then imagine four men trying to catch as many wheels as they pursued an erratic course down the river. Once caught, the task was to remount. We found that the only way was to put one leg across the saddle and put on the coaster brake and then mount in a hurry and hope for the best. I have ridden bucking horses and been bucked off many a time, but I never saw a bucking horse that could get from under me as quickly as that wheel. There was no escape, for inside of a mile after we left the road house we found that there was open water on both sides of us. There was no possibility of reaching the shore, and all we could do was to go ahead and hope that we found no open water in our path.

To vary the monotony of falling on glare ice, we frequently ran into overflow on top of the ice. This was water that had not frozen during the night or ice that would not hold us up, and when we struck the water we went down again. We would have to pick up our wheels and carry them on our backs and splash through, until propelled by the wind we found clear ice. Then we would have to kick the ice off the chains and other parts of the wheel to enable us to go on, as the water froze the moment we picked up the wheels.

We made shore at Casey's Cache for lunch and then resumed our gyrating down the river. If we fell once, we fell a hundred times in twenty miles. Once we rounded a bend out of the wind and, having clear calm sailing, prematurely considered that we were out of the worst of it. Again we were mistaken. I was in the lead, and we were strung out about a hundred feet apart for safety. The wind, not being able to reach us from the rear, dropped down over the western wall of the canyon, and I went down as though I had been shot. As I struck the ice, I looked back, and one after the other of the riders at about two second intervals went down as I had done. It was funny in spite of our discomfort. For two weeks after I reached Fairbanks, both of my arms were black from my wrists to my elbows, to say nothing of other parts of my anatomy.

We witnessed a good example of what we would have been compelled to undergo had the wind been from the other direction. During the afternoon, we met several teams toiling up the river, and one man on a bicycle who had decided to go out that way. He had been hugging the bank for several miles until just before we met him, when he was compelled to come out in the open and face the wind. We had taken refuge behind some rocks on the shore to rest and had a good view of the final act of the little comedy. He tried to ride the wheel and was promptly blown over backwards. He then tried to push the wheel ahead of him with negative results.

He struggled manfully for about ten minutes and made about fifty feet backwards. He then laid the wheel down on the ice, untied a small sack under the saddle and put the package in his pocket. He took up the wheel, carried it to a pile of rocks on the shore, lifted it as high as he could above his head and then slammed it down on the rocks and started up stream on foot. In the few minutes that we listened to him we learned more about the genealogy of bicycles in general and that one in particular than all of us combined had known before. In fact, after learning the origin of bicycles from the brief remarks he made, we felt that it was almost immoral to be seen in the company of one of them.

Late that afternoon as we were sailing down the river and looking for a road house supposed to be on the right bank, we saw a man on foot a mile or more ahead of us, running before the wind. Suddenly he disappeared. Taking warning, we steered more to the right until we reached the place where we had seen him last. At that place the river was open, and it was evident that he was going so fast that he was unable to stop when the open water showed up before him and was swept in. Who he was or where he came from we never learned, for there was no compulsory registration at the road houses and no way to check up on the travelers.

Soon it was dark and no road house in sight. Fortunately the wind had died down, so we were able to go slower and watch the shore for a light. We did not see the light until we were an eighth of a mile past the place. We were in the middle of the river, which at this place was about a half mile wide. We started for the light and had only gone a few rods when we came to the edge of the ice. Before us was open water for about a hundred feet in width. The edge of the ice was resting on a gravel bar in the center of the river, so when we climbed down to the edge of the water we were standing on the gravel.

We had no idea how far up or downstream we would have to travel to find an ice bridge or solid ice and were too tired and cold to do any searching in the dark. We put our wheels on our shoulders and stepped into the icy current and started across, dodging the floes of slush ice that traveled on the surface. We couldn't tell how deep it was and we didn't care much.

Cold! I never felt such cold water in my life and never want to again. Fortunately that branch was only about three feet deep, and we soon clambered up on the four foot ice on the other side and went toward the light.

About fifty feet from the shore we reached the edge of the ice again and saw a real river between us and the bank. We called until someone came out of the road house with a lantern, and from him we learned that the nearest ice bridge was almost a mile downstream, and he didn't know for certain that it was still standing. Neither did he know the depth of the water between us and the bank, but he opined that it was damned deep and swift.

Again we took up our wheels and after going upstream a short distance warned him to be on the look out to grab us if we came by his way. We went in one at a time and found the water almost to our chins, the current swift and floating ice covering most of the surface. Fortunately the weight of the wheels held us down, so we were not swept off our feet and one at a time he dragged us up onto the bank. Donnelly's Road House was a brilliant spot in the memory of that trip. Plenty of room, hot fires, dry clothes, and good beds. Again the proper use of a corkscrew saved our lives, and when we had done full justice to an excellent dinner, we turned in and slept the clock around.

My experience traveling by bicycle ended here. I was not accustomed to the use of shoes with as low heels as the shoe pacs and as a result the unwonted strain on the tendon of Achilles caused it to swell so that I could not walk.

It was decided that we would lay up for a day to enable me to do some poulticing, and a young fellow who chanced to be at the road house for the night borrowed my bicycle to see if he remembered how to ride. He did. He returned the wheel in a few days, neglecting to tell me that he had tried riding it over broken glass. We had lost our repair kit, and there I was 140 miles from Fairbanks, the nearest source of supply.

The others decided to go on, and I was to follow by stage when it came through. The last we had seen of it was the memorable night at the Ernestine Road House, but we knew that it would be through in a few days. I rested and proved the efficacy of tea-leaves poultice and hot water. A little pin that I chanced to have sticking in the bosom of my woolen shirt was the means of introducing me to two chicken dinners, and when the stage arrived I was sorry to leave.

The stage, carrying a capacity load, apparently offered little opportunity for one partially crippled traveler. It was not possible to carry the passengers' baggage on the stage so they had secured a double-ender upon which the baggage was piled and which was attached to the rear of the bob sled. Emulating the gypsy's victims, I "crossed with silver" (only it was a gold piece) the palm of the driver, and he informed me that when the stage pulled out if anyone climbed on top of the baggage he certainly would not come back and put him off as the attempt to ride that rounded pile of canvas-covered baggage would be punishment enough for the trespass.

When the stage pulled out, I was astride the baggage, trying to find some place to put my feet so they would not drag on the ice of the river. Lacking a lap robe, I picked up a worn-out mackinaw coat. Thursting my feet into the arms and throwing the skirt up across my knees, I had a lap robe of shorts and a support for my feet.

Again congratulations on my good fortune were in order, and again they were premature, for when we got out on the open river where the wind could have a fair chance, I soon concluded that it was easier to ride a bicycle on glare ice than to stay on that athletic sled.

The first mishap was when the lashing that fastened the shafts of the double-ender to the rear of the stage broke, and one of the shafts, slipping up the back of the bob sled, passed under the back of the fur collar on a passenger's overcoat and gently but firmly lifted him from his seat and suspended him in the air. The outraged passenger had formerly been a sea captain and he was neither dumb nor ineloquent. The damage being repaired, we again started, I being still enthroned on top of the baggage, the driver having completely overlooked me when refastening the lashings.

The wind, unable to accomplish its purpose when blowing directly from the rear, veered a few points to the south and in a few seconds I was further downriver than the team and bob, and the horses were headed upstream, as we had been blown end about. The driver had to drive into the lee of the shore in order to get turned around, and then for several hours it was his task to keep the wind directly astern, otherwise there was confusion and loss of time, with an abundance of profanity.

While I was enjoying the driver's discomfiture, even though my own teeth were chattering, the wind gave me a sideswipe and I was thoroughly dismounted and tangled in my combination lap robe, while the stage was being whirled down the river. There was no use for me to yell, for the roar of the wind would drown all sounds. Moreover, officially I was not there at all, so how could a non-existent human make any noise and why should a driver pay any attention to a noise that really could not be?

It was incumbent upon me (non-existent though I might be) to perch myself on that load "without the benefit of clergy" or the favor of the driver. With badly swollen ankles that next quarter of a mile represented an experience that I would not care to duplicate. For once the wind favored me and when I reached the sled, I was out one perfectly good lap robe, considerable breath, and "in" a large amount of pain and considerable experience. For the balance of the day, I rode face down on the load, holding on with both hands.

We reached Butche's Road House at dusk. Being crippled, I was unable to get into the road house ahead of the passengers and when I did get in there, all of the bunks were appropriated. There were eight bunks, each capable of holding two people, provided they were not too well fed. The method of securing a bunk was to get to it and throw some of your personal possessions into the middle of it. That proved your appropriation, provided you watched it close enough until time to turn in. The two days' delay at Donnelly's had permitted some of the passengers whom we had distanced to get ahead. Some of the overflow had appropriated a tent near the house. It had a board floor, and there was some hay in the barn. The proprietor couldn't watch the hay and cook supper for about thirty people, hence the occupants of the tent soon had beds, provided they had enough robes to keep themselves warm.

I had no bed, no robe or blankets and an almost overwhelming desire to go to sleep. The passengers had been in such a hurry to get in and appropriate bunks that they had neglected to remove their wolf robes from the sled. It was dark. The edge of the woods was only a few feet distant, and two of the robes crawled into the brush with the evident intention of reverting to their wild state; or perhaps they had heard other wolves howling in the woods and desired to rejoin the pack.

A few minutes later the owner of the robes went to bring them in and make up his bed which consisted of the usual poles and a few spruce branches. What was said when he found that the robes he cherished, and for each of which he had paid about $150, were gone is better imagined than repeated. The words can undoubtedly all be found in the dictionary (unexpurgated edition), but it was the peculiar arrangement of the words that made them interesting. The owner of the words and robes weighed about three hundred pounds and was the same man who had seated himself on my projecting legs at the Ernestine Road House. Everyone sympathized with him.

Now, two young fellows had a lower bunk, and one of them had a blanket large enough to cover up the nakedness of the spruce boughs, but nothing to put over them. I asked them if they would let me crawl in with them if I could get some sort of covering to go over us. They looked at my not-over-puny frame and then looked at the bed, evidently mentally calculating what would be left of the room after I was in, and finally consented to the arrangement.

I then casually entered into conversation with the irate passenger and incidentally asked him if he could give the finder of the robes one of them for the night. Evidently considering one robe better than none, he consented, but he could have been sent up for life for what he thought of me at that time. This merely illustrates how one can be misunderstood and one's motives misconstrued.

Having had some previous experience in California with wild animals, both Democratic and Republican, I tried to think as the wild animals would think under given circumstances and concluded that the robes had heard the "call of the wild" and were sneaking off in the brush. This proved true, and I soon returned in triumph to the road house with both robes which I had caught without injury to their skins. Of course I didn't doubt the outraged passenger's word, but I dropped one robe outside the door until he confirmed the agreement, and then presented myself and the other robe at the bunk that I was to occupy that night. I chose the middle; the thin chap next to the wall spent the night trying to keep himself supplied with breath and the stouter one on the outside kept himself awake trying to keep from falling out of bed. I slept well.

The next day was a repetition of the previous day's experiences, except that the driver, about a mile from McCarty's Road House, discovered that he had one more passenger than had been reported by the various telegraph stations along the road, and he made me get off and walk before we were in sight of the telegraph station.

In passing, I would mention that the heavy passenger who supplied me with beddings at Butche's afterwards became one of my best clients, and it was not until more than ten years later that I explained how I happened to find the robes. The explanation was made in the presence of about twenty men in the Tanana Club, and as it was unanimously decided that the joke was on him, he had to buy for the crowd. The next Christmas he sent me a box of excellent cigars.

When the stage left McCarty's the next morning, my throne was empty, but about a mile down the trail, well out of sight of the road house, the stage overtook me and that was that. That afternoon we were on the Tanana River. Spring was approaching, so the driver avoided the main river as the ice there was treacherous because of the swift current underneath. He followed the sloughs as much as possible. The ice there was none too thick, and a dozen times that half-day the ice gave way, and horses, stage, and trailer were afloat, sometimes in water three or four feet deep. The top of the baggage load was about two and a half feet above the ground, when on the ground, but otherwise when in the water. I thought I had signed up for a land cruise, but to my sorrow found that the voyage by water was thrown in without extra charge.

That night we reached Joe Henry's Road House on the Tanana River, at a point where the town of Richardson was later built after gold had been found on Tenderfoot Creek, just across the ridge from the road house. The next time I visited the place was two and a half years later when I went in a steamboat. That town has been compelled to move three times by reason of the encroachment of the river, and this year (1926) the few remaining residents moved back a quarter mile to the base of the hills on a rock foundation. The place where the road house stood in 1906 is now approximately the center of the river; there is a small island there where geese each year rear their young.

That night at Henry's was my introduction to Alaskan wolves, for a band of them had evidently pulled down a moose a half mile from the road house and they were holding a wake.

The next forenoon we traveled by land and reached Munson's Road House about noon. After lunch, the driver took me out by the stable and informed me that he had just learned that I had been riding on his trailer and that was strictly forbidden; that I must cease, stop, desist, refrain, and forebear breaking any more regulations; besides, the next telegraph station was down the road a short distance, and they always reported to the office in Fairbanks the number of passengers on every stage that passed. Without being compelled to tear his clothes, I prevailed upon him to accept a souvenir in the form of a metallic disc extracted from my purse, and we parted good friends.

Two years later I went out over the line as a passenger, and as I was attorney for the stage company at the time and as he drove the stage for a portion of the trip, I have wondered what he thought about it. As he still retained his position, I presume he concluded that I had never told the company of his defective eyesight. Incidentally, on that second trip under the then-existing circumstances there never was any difficulty about good beds and meals at any of the road houses.

From Munson's the last forty miles was made on a freight team returning empty after delivering a load of baled hay at one of the Stage Company's Stations. Wearily I climbed aboard, spread out a lot of empty grain sacks and horse blankets, and lay down on them. Covering myself with some other material of like nature, I turned my face up to the falling snow and went to sleep. It would have taken more than a snowstorm to keep me awake. The weather had be-

VALDEZ TRAIL

	Miles
Valdez	0
Camp Comfort Road House	10
Keystone	13
Wortman's Road House Telegraph Station	20
Eureka Road House	30
Ptarmigan Drop Road House	31
Siana Telegraph Station	34
Beaver Dam Road House	40
Tiekel Road House	48
Tiekel Telegraph Station	53
Ernestine Road House	58
Tonsina Road House	77
Tonsina Post Office and Hotel	77
Willow Creek Road House	89
Copper Center Telegraph Station	103
Copper Center Post Office and Hotel	103
Tazlina Road House	110
Gulkana Road House	128
Gakona Road House	132
Hart's Road House	152
Gillespie's Road House	159
McMullen's Road House	183
Timberline Road House	192
Yost's Road House	208
McKinley Road House	215
Rapids Road House	225
Nigger Bill's Road House	250
Bennett's Road House	252
Joe Henry's Road House	272
Salcha Telegraph Station	296
Chena Slough Road House	300
Dolan's Road House	333
Murray's Road House	342
Fairbanks	350

The Home Restaurant, Charles G. Horsfall, Proprietor. Opposite Hotel St. Elias, Valdez, Alaska, 1906.

come mild; we were out of the wind belt; the runners slipped smoothly over the freshly fallen snow on the beaten road. It was no effort to sleep. I roused myself at the next road house long enough to eat, then slept the remaining eighteen miles into town. At about four-thirty on the twelfth day after leaving Valdez, I reached Fairbanks, ending a trip of almost four hundred miles.

About three years ago Frank McCafferty, Master Mechanic for the Alaska Road Commission—during the summertime —in a remade, revamped, rebuilt and stripped "flivver" made the same trip in nine hours and twenty minutes.

My trail companions of that far-off time have since become scattered all over the landscape of the West. My brother, after spending five more years in Alaska, making fifteen in all, returned to Stockton, California, where he has made a name for himself as a developer and grower of a new fig which now bears his name. Frank Black added a few more years to his already respectable record of life under the Arctic Circle. He then returned to California and afterwards went to Mexico where his experiences with Villa's playful but erratic brigands made him long for the peaceful solitude of the Alaskan blizzard-swept wilderness. He afterwards bitterly complained of the Mexicans' lack of hospitality, and especially their crude manner of inviting him not to return, by using his head as a target as he swam the Rio Grande. He said he was perfectly willing to leave their damned country, but contended that they should have permitted him the use of a bridge in so doing. Fred Crouch spent several years working for an electric power company near Fairbanks and then married; he and his wife returned to the Pacific Coast. Corecco and Grothe worked around this part of the country for four or five years, and then departed for their old haunts in sunnier climates. Of the six who blazed the way for bicycle travel over the trail, I am the only one left to tell the tale and emulate the old soldier in one of Goldsmith's poems, who "shouldered his crutch and showed how fields were won."

Fairbanks in 1906

John A. Clark

IN 1906 FAIRBANKS was a wooden town and a new one. Most of the buildings were only one story. There was no necessity for false fronts, as is the custom in so many western country towns. Besides, false fronts cost money as lumber was high and anyway people were more concerned with what was in the buildings than how the buildings looked from the outside.

The residences were, for the most part, built of logs, which in many instances had been cut on the very lots upon which the houses were erected. The rights of the possessors were "squatter's rights" and possession was everything. Paint was expensive and many of the buildings in the business portion of the town were as yet unpainted. Wherever there was a vacant lot or piece of ground upon which no building had been erected, there the stumps were in evidence as the residents had not had time to dig them up. This was rather easily done, as in this country, where the top covering of moss has not been disturbed, the ground does not thaw down for a distance of more than two or three feet each summer. All of the tree roots are within a couple of feet of the surface as none of the trees could grow tap roots through the frozen ground. The frozen stratum so close to the surface serves the same purpose as "hard pan" in other countries and retains the moisture, so there is no necessity for the roots to go very deep.

The main business street was on the water front, as the town was built along the Chena Slough, which was, in part, a branch of the Tanana River and in part a continuation of the Big Chenoa (Chena as Anglicized) River. The town stretched for a distance of more than a mile along the bank of the river and the upper part of Front Street was marked by the tallest building in town, a brewery. The lower end of the street had a similar marking and between the two they

194

managed to forestall any drouth that might choose to visit the land.

North of the town proper and across the river was Garden Island, so named because one man decided that he could make money market gardening. He did. A bridge constructed on piling connected the two settlements and this bridge "went out" each year at the time of the "breakup" when the ice left the river. The time of the going out of the bridge officially marked the commencement of spring and all bets as to the time of the breakup were settled on that basis.

On Garden Island was the railroad depot, as a narrow-gage railroad had been built the previous year to connect the town with the creeks upon which pay had been discovered. A hospital, some machine shops, lumber mills, and residences were built there and as they were outside of the incorporated limits of Fairbanks had all of the advantages of the town with none of the taxation burdens. Between the time of the breakup and the going out of the bridge, until the water went down and the ice ceased to run, a ferry was in operation between the two places. This served all needs save that of fire protection, for the fire engine could not carry its hose across the river when there was no bridge. Luck favored that settlement, as there was never a serious fire over there at any time when the bridge was out.

Three banks were in operation, all of them buying gold dust from the miners and loaning money at three per cent per month. This was afterwards reduced to two per cent, and then when a suit was instituted under our law to recover double the amount of usurious interest so collected, the rate was reduced to the legal rate of one per cent per month and has remained at that figure ever since.

The president of one of the banks was, as was afterwards disclosed, an ex-convict who had served time for embezzlement in one of the states. The president of another bank was formerly the best-known professional gambler in Dawson in the boom days of that camp. He ceased to gamble when he went into the banking business, as three per cent per month beat poker or faro which were his specialties. He was known, and rightly so, as a "square gambler"; and in spite of the fact that everyone knew his former occupation, he established and maintained a splendid bank, the only one that has withstood the vicissitudes that have beset the banking institutions of this country. He was universally trusted and through aid that he extended, frequently in violation of the rules that governed national banks, his bank being such, he helped in the development of the bank. His mind becoming affected, especially on religious subjects, he retired, and after being restored to capacity entered business in one of the middle western states, where he now holds a rather commanding position.

The third bank was organized by the now-president of the Dexter Horton National Bank of Seattle, who acted as its president here. Some years later the stockholders sold out and two of the banks were merged with disastrous results.

The courthouse was a two-story affair and made a very beautiful fire a couple of months after our arrival here. The two incidents, as will hereafter appear, had no connection.

There was one three-story building, erected by one of the fraternal orders. The Northern Commercial Company had a power plant and supplied the town with water, heat, light, and power, as well as fire protection. A few days after my arrival, at about midnight, the fire siren shrieked its warning and people from all parts of town dressed and went forth to help fight fire. At that time there was no contract with the water company providing for maintaining pressure in the water mains, so when a fire started and pressure had to be secured in a hurry, desperate measures were resorted to. The fire promised to be a bad one, as it started at one end of a five hundred foot block of wooden buildings. Wood was the fuel used under the boilers in the power house, but that was not sufficient to enable them to get up steam and secure the necessary water pressure to save the town. The company ordered its men into its warehouse near the power house and in a few minutes truck loads of sugar-cured bacon were being dumped beside the boilers. While some broke open the crates, others pitched into the firebox bacon that was selling at 65¢ per pound. After about two tons had been so consumed, they had sufficient steam and were able to keep it up thereafter by using wood. Two months later, at the time of the great fire that destroyed most of the town, they again had to resort to bacon and so saved the power house and most of the food supply of the town.

There were three Protestant churches in the town and a Catholic church across the river on Garden Island, where the latter church also maintained a hospital. St. Matthew's Church (Episcopal) had a hospital in the town. Practically every industry, including manufacturing, was represented, and the latter made a pretty good showing with two breweries and two or three well-equipped saw mills. These mills running to capacity could not keep up with the demand, for there was a great deal of lumber used in the mines on the creeks and in the building of small towns on the different producing creeks. Berry was the name of the town on Ester Creek, named after Clarence Berry, one of the big operators on the creek and now one of the oil operators of California. Cleary City furnished the supplies for the operators on Cleary Creek, named after the brother-in-law of Captain Barnette, one of the early stakers on Cleary Creek. Meehan was the name of the town on Fairbanks Creek, named after Matt Meehan, one of the first operators on a large scale on the splendid paystreak that he uncovered. Gilmore was situated at the mouth of Pedro Creek, upon which creek the first gold was discovered, and was named after Tom Gilmore, who first established a roadhouse at that place. Lower down on Goldstream was the town of Fox. It took lumber to build these towns and supply the mine operators, and not being able to get all they needed from Fairbanks, a mill was placed on the Chatanika River at the mouth of Cleary Creek. When Dome Creek proved rich and a town of that name was started there, still another saw mill was erected.

Beer and lumber were the principal products of the manufacturing industry. The law of supply and demand was working under high pressure. There were provision houses, wholesale and retail; shoe shops, ladies' furnishings, hardware stores, gun stores, stores where baby buggies could be purchased (and they were needed); cigar stores, butcher shops, and clothing stores. Three jewelry stores were flourishing, where in addition to selling ordinary jewelry they manufactured and sold nugget jewelry and jewelry made of a combination of gold and native old ivory from the various mastodon tusks uncovered in this region.

Barber shops and bath houses; hotels and rooming houses; saloons and dance halls; they were all there. At first glance one would conclude that there were more saloons and dance halls than of all the others combined. They occupied the most conspicuous places and gave the impression of being more numerous than they actually were. While every saloon was not a dance hall, yet every dance hall was a saloon. Gambling was wide open and games were running night and day in practically all of the saloons. To one who sought excitement and had the money to lose, the choice was various. The rattle of the ball and the call of the operator called many to the roulette wheel, while others had a system by which they believed they could overcome the dealer's percentage at faro. The crap table attracted those who desired noise with their recreation, while the less venturesome preferred blackjack. To those who desired a stiff game with big stakes, or who fancied themselves as poker players, the tables in the private rooms or in the back of the saloon had an irresistible fascination. Money was plentiful and the "sky was the limit" at most of the games, so men went broke with neatness and dispatch. The dealers worked twelve hour shifts for which they received $15 per day, and generally when one of them went off duty he went and had something to eat and then went and lost the balance of his wages at some other game in some other saloon. The fool killer was so busy elsewhere that he had not attended to business in Fairbanks.

At night the saloons and dance halls were busy places, and as the camp was young and most of the people here were in their twenties or early thirties, they had to have some way of letting off steam and gambling was the most available and attractive. The men who were here at that time were the pick of the world physically. I have seen crowds in dance halls at night where out of perhaps four hundred men fully sixty per cent were six feet and more in height and strong in proportion.

There were no gun fiights, as I do not suppose one man in five hundred carried a gun. Fist fights were few, for while men would get drunk occasionally, they were not a quarrelsome lot, being young men who had come here from a spirit of adventure. They were strong, fearless, and, for the most part, clean living young animals. Many of them did not drink at all. Hundreds never gambled a cent, although no one apparently considered gambling a vice and the games were square. They gathered in the saloons and dance halls at night as there was no other place to go. Many of them were newcomers who had not been able to secure work. Others were men who had worked in the cold and wet drifts all winter and were taking a layoff for a few weeks in the spring before the water commenced to run and the cleanups would start. There were others who worked in the stores and shops by day and when these closed there was no other place to go until bedtime. If you wanted to find anyone, all you had to do was to make the rounds of the saloons and dance halls and some time during the evening you would find your man.

The heaviest players were the mine owners and operators, for they seemed to be obsessed with the idea that the supply of gold in the ground would never run out. There were exceptions to this rule, however. The gamblers and saloon men were mostly former residents of the camps on the Canadian side of the line. Whatever might be thought of their business, it was legitimate under the law, and the saloon men were respected for their own intrinsic' worth, regardless of the character of the business conducted. They gave liberally to every worthy cause; assisted the churches and hospitals, and many of them were church men and their families were active in church work. Some were elected members of the City Council and some of them have served on the School Board. They sold liquor at 25 cents per drink to those who had the wherewithal to buy. They gave credit to anyone worthy of trust. They gave money to those in need, and many a prospector who had dissipated all of his wages was given a grubstake and sent back into the hills by some saloon men. They were trusted by the miners and practically every saloon in town had a safe in which different miners or prospectors had placed their pokes or rolls for safekeeping. I have on several occasions seen the proprietors of saloons refuse to give up to a miner the poke he had left there for safekeeping, telling him that he had had enough to drink and to go home and come back in the morning and they would give it to him. With but few exceptions they were trustworthy business men; honorable and respected by the community. While they conducted gambling games in their places of business, yet those games were absolutely on the square and never during the two years that gambling was conducted after my arrival here did I ever hear anyone so much as intimate that any crooked work was being done. If a man wanted to gamble, that was his privilege. If he chose to drink, he could do so; if he drank too much, his friends were urged to take him home. No one was encouraged to drink or gamble, but every person was a free agent and could do as he pleased.

There were no locks on people's doors and the hotel bedroom doors were in many cases entirely without locks, much less keys. There was no poverty, for the population consisted almost without exception of able-bodied men and women, and work was plentiful and well paid. There were no sneak thieves, no burglars, and no criminal element in the common acceptation of the term.

There were those who toiled not, neither did they spin, and who outshone the Queen of Sheba and the lilies of the field in the gorgeous hues of their raiment and whose furs and diamonds would dazzle even the most blasé New Yorker, but their wealth and splendor were not forcibly wrested from the rightful owner. The lesser lights of their great fraternity who danced for their percentage might have been grouped with the working class. Their satellites, messengers, and general utility men came nearer to being of the criminal class than any others, but none of them sought the property of others—save such as might come their way "legitimately" in their pursuit of life, liberty, and happiness. Prudence, not virtue, was in all probability their guiding star. If a man was fool enough to get drunk and purchase the same bottle of champagne three or four times, paying $5 per pint each time, that was his mistake. If he was such a poor judge of wine that he couldn't distinguish champagne cider from the real article and was willing to pay ten dollars a quart therefor, that showed that he either had more money than he should have and that someone should relieve his distress, or that his lack of judgment in wines was such that he should be penalized for his utter ignorance. Some of them were hard to teach.

One peculiarity about the camp was that, while it was a gold-producing community and a man's wealth was measured by the amount of gold dust that he extracted from the ground, there was practically no gold in evidence. Paper money was the medium of exchange in all amounts over five dollars. The smallest coin in use was a quarter. Nothing could be purchased for less than twenty-five cents and that condition prevails, with but few exceptions, even unto this day. A few weeks after my arrival I saw a nickel and two dimes pasted on a piece of cardboard which was hung up in the newspaper office and underneath was inscribed: "What are these coins?"

There was but little money in evidence even at the gambling tables, particularly at the faro and roulette tables, as chips were used in the betting. The banks paid checks or purchased gold dust with currency until after the panic of

1907, when a change was made to gold coin. When the banks here were on a scrip basis, the scrip was so little like real money that the holders thereof spent it much more freely than they would real money. As a result, when the banks resumed specie payments, many people found their bank accounts badly depleted and for fear that the banks would not continue to pay out real money, they withdrew their money in currency and cached it around their cabins or buried it. The banks depended upon the purchase of gold dust for a good part of their profits and when they made a purchase and the operator demanded cash, it soon reduced the bank's cash to an alarming state. It cost the bank about $3 per thousand expressage to ship in currency, and when they were paying out for gold dust five or six million dollars each year, this was quite an item. To solve the difficulty, the banks shipped in great quantities of gold coin and when an operator demanded cash for his cleanup and the paying teller counted out to him ten, twenty, thirty, or forty thousand dollars in gold coin, he became discouraged, as he couldn't carry that much around in his clothes. As a result, he would shove the money back and open a bank account and use a checkbook. Thus everybody was satisfied.

When the "financial stringency" of 1907 reached Fairbanks and the banks found it necessary to cease paying out money, they were confronted by a rather peculiar situation. There was no clearing house and but three banks. There was but one solution and that was to call a general meeting of depositors and explain the situation and seek a solution. One bank was closed and the other two in danger of having to do so. The depositors appointed a committee of five, as I now recall, who were instructed to examine the loans and discounts and securities of the bank and report back. When the reports of the various committees were made to the respective depositor groups, it appeared that the banks were solvent and the trouble arose from their inability to secure real money from their correspondents in Seattle. The depositors of two of the banks decided to pool their interests, and a committee of three was appointed to whom the securities were transferred in trust, and this committee was authorized to issue scrip up to about eighty per cent of the appraised value of the paper so delivered to them. The depositors of the third bank acted independently but took similar action. The committee in each case consisted of the principal men of the town who were judged of the value of the paper submitted to them as collateral for the scrip. The respective committees went to the local newspaper office and had a few million dollars' worth of scrip printed, and when this was signed by the committee, the banks opened again and resumed operations with "business as usual." There was one great disadvantage so far as the possessor of the money was concerned and that was that the paper was very thin and when a man left a bill lying on the top of a wet bar for a few minutes while he was busy expounding some obtuse principle of international law or the best way to thaw frozen ground to someone who was equally anxious to expound his theory in regard to infant damnation, by the time the owner of the bill was ready to pick it up, it was ready to fall to pieces and generally did. As a result if the barkeeper would accept the fragments in exchange for further quantities of liquid refreshments, he was generally given the opportunity to do so. If however, the owner of the bill was particularly good humored, he would give some sort of a discourse concerning the lack of value of the money and tear up the fragments or drop them on the floor. It was good business for the bank.

Speaking of different kinds of money brings to mind a lesson that one big operator learned in 1905. He had secured an option to purchase a mining claim on Cleary Creek, the time of payment of the final and larger part of the purchase price being extended until about the middle of the summer of 1905. The attorney who drew the option was probably fresh from the "outside" and did not appreciate the various quirks and angles of the money situation in this country, so he had stipulated that the purchase price should be paid in "Gold Coin of the United States." Nothing was thought of this until the next spring when the particular claim involved had been proven a regular Bonanza and the option price was but a fraction of its real value. The proposed purchaser, being rather "canny," consulted his attorney to see if the contract was "horse high, hog tight, and bull strong," and his attorney assured him it was, *provided* he would be ready on the fifteenth of September to pay the full amount of the purchase price in gold coin of the current weight and fineness. The holder of the option went to see the owners of the claim to ascertain whether they would accept currency in payment. They had also been advised by an attorney and they were feeling rather cocky as they realized that there was not in the whole camp one-tenth part of the amount of gold required. They had probably never heard of Shylock and his experience in trying to force someone to live up to the "letter" of the contract but they did see a chance to retain the claim that had proven so rich. They gravely stated that they were willing to abide by the terms of the contract but they must have gold coin in payment and no arguments could budge them. The purchaser was by this time in rather a panicky state, but he sent men out over the creeks to gather in all of the gold coin that anyone might have and he secured all of the gold coin in the banks and still he was several thousand dollars short. It would take weeks to get money from Seattle and he couldn't wait. He couldn't get it from Dawson, for they were using nothing but Canadian currency. He finally telegraphed Nome and found that the amount MIGHT be procured by scouring the camp. He wired authority to "scour" and jumped on a boat that was about to leave for St. Michael on Bering Sea, more than fifteen hundred miles downriver. When he reached St. Michael, he caught a boat to Nome and found that the required amount had been raised. He paid for it, caught another boat, and started on the long, wearisome journey up the mighty Yukon against the current. The day for final payment was dangerously close and if any sand bar should force its attention upon the boat, he would be too late. Fortunately nothing happened and at Tanana he caught another boat up the Tanana River and reached Fairbanks the night before the payment fell due. He was able to make the payment in gold coin and so secured title to a claim that produced over a million dollars and put him on his feet for life.

A rather interesting method of securing nails was resorted to in the early days of the camp. A man wanted to build a house, but others had been of the same mind and when he started to build, he found that there were no nails to be had, so he advertised for nails, agreeing to pay a cent apiece for every nail of a certain size that was brought to him. He then went ahead with the raising of his log walls, feeling certain that he would have nails when he needed them. People not otherwise employed at the moment went nail hunting, breaking up packing boxes, etc. The nails commenced to pour in but not fast enough, so he increased the price to two cents per nail and when it came time to use them, he had all he needed.

Merchants were compelled to make their purchases of goods and supplies during the short summer, as the open season for navigation in those days did not exceed three and one-half months, as everything had to be brought in by the river route. The ice didn't leave the mouth of the Yukon River until about the middle of June, so no freight by the lower river route could reach here before the first of July. The upper river route by way of Lake Laberge opened a few days earlier. The last freight had to leave Seattle by the fifteenth of August to insure its delivery. The merchants, therefore, had to guess as to the amount of all commodities that they might need. They had to figure out what people might need or desire and they therefore put in their spare time during the winter on their guessing list. Sometimes they overestimated and had thousands of dollars tied up for a year or more. Again they guessed short and before spring they would be very short on some article. Some of the small merchants tried to take advantage of this condition and to charge exorbitant prices, and in a few instances they succeeded. Thereafter, when it appeared that they had underbought, the big firms either rationed their customers on that particular commodity or ascertained the needs of their regular customers for the year, and then set aside that amount to each customer putting his name on the pile. They made delivery to the customer as required, charging him at the regular price when he took the merchandise. The others went without, but it prevented gouging.

No human being could possibly guess correctly as to what might be required. When I came over the trail in March, I had my typewriter boxed at Valdez and sent it in by freight at fifty cents per pound. When it arrived, the frame was broken on both sides, all of the type had collapsed, and the various parts were tangled and twisted out of shape. It was a complete wreck and looked hopeless. At that time there was stationed here a mechanical engineer, who was also a mechanical genius, and when I showed the machine to him, he walked around it a few times and expressed the opinion that he "would be eternally damned" if he had ever seen such a mess. He said he had never tried to repair a typewriter but for the sake of the experience would "give it a whirl." A couple of weeks later he brought the machine to

my office and it was in excellent shape and wrote as well
as ever. He had been compelled to MAKE the tools with
which to repair it, as no merchant had ever thought to bring
in tools for repairing typewriters that had fallen over a cliff.
The life of the machine was short, however, for within a
month after he repaired it, during the great fire that destroyed the greater part of the town, I attempted to carry it
out of the building where I had my office, after the building
was well afire. The flames met me at the head of the stairs
and in attempting to protect my face I forgot the machine
and it rolled down the stairs, beating me to the bottom by
about three stairs. The name on the front of the machine
was all that was left that even remotely resembled a typewriter and I sadly surveyed the wreck and left it to the
tender mercies of the flames.

Watching My First Breakup

John A. Clark

DURING THE LAST days of April in 1906, each day I noticed larger crowds congregating on the bridge across the Chena River in front of the town and heard a great many people speaking of the "breakup." Each day there appeared to be more water on top of the ice and the ice itself appeared to be rising but I had no idea that there was or would be anything spectacular about the affair when it did come. At about eight o'clock in the evening of April 30th, I heard the siren at the power plant commence to shriek a warning, and as everyone in my part of the town started on a run for the river front, I decided to go and see what the fuss was all about. I lived six blocks from the water and when I got out of the house could hear a strange rumbling and crunching sound as of a million bones being crushed. The nearer I got to the river, the louder the sound and when I reached the river bank, it was readily understood why everyone was on hand to see the spectacle.

Three hours before, when I had last seen the river, the water was about ten feet from the top of the bank, and now it was bank full with the surface a solid mass of great ice cakes, some of them an acre or more in extent. As they ground together, great pieces would be thrown in the air and there would be a great tinkling as the small fragments fell back on the swirling floes. The rumbling and the dull booms were caused by the immense floes striking against the banks and bulkheading that protected the bank in front of the town.

I hurried up Front Street to a place where I could see up the river to the nearest bend, about a quarter of a mile above town. The water was running like a mill race and there were millions of tons of ice being carried along. As far as could be seen upriver was a never-ending procession of ice floes,

grinding and swirling; turning up on edge and sticking up for
a dozen feet or more above the surface of the water. The
main current set into the bank right in front of the town,
being cast there by a projecting point on Garden Island. The
fall before, the Cold Storage Co. had brought one of its
steamers, the Lotta Talbot, up to the town and had most ill-
advisedly tied it up to the bank in the exact spot where the
current was strongest. The vessel was loaded with cold storage meats and they had used it for a winter warehouse.
Between the boat and the bank was a small barge, probably
fifteen feet across and twice as long. It was used as a landing
barge from the vessel. The boat and barge had been left
there and had frozen in. There was no chance to move them
before the breakup, so they were there to assist in making
the breakup spectacular. Just as I reached the vicinity of
the boat, a great ice field, probably two acres in extent and
eight feet in thickness, swept majestically around the bend
and headed right for the boat. As the current of the river
was probably flowing at the rate of twelve or fifteen miles
per hour, I will leave it to the mathematicians to figure out
the striking power of that field of ice. One corner hit the
boat just about amidships, and the barge between the vessel
and the shore was crushed in an instant and seemed to
explode as the timbers were thrown twenty feet in the air.
The ice went right through the side of the vessel, as if it
had been made of paper, wrenched the wheel (it was a stern-
wheeler) from its fastenings and calmly pursued its journey
toward Bering Sea. It didn't even hesitate in its course; nor
did the boat hesitate after the ice passed on in making a
record journey to the bottom of the river. In less than half
a minute after the ice had struck the boat, it was a wreck,
and all that could be seen was the upper works sticking out
of the water. In a few minutes other floes had autographed
the exposed part and a good many thousands of dollars'
worth of frozen meat and a first-class river steamer were
total losses. A few weeks later when the big fire came along
it took care to burn all of the vessel that remained above the
water line.

When the ice run started, the first thing that went was
the bridge across the river. It was built on piles and they
snapped off like so many straws and the bridge itself mounted
a floe and rode away. Just below the bridge was one of the
steamboat docks, the outer edge of which was supported

on piles. A cake of ice nuzzled into the bank, snapped off
the protective piling and carried away most of the supports
under the center of the dock and left the outer edge sagging
down where the ice cakes could, by reaching a little, tear
off the corrugated iron that formed the walls. A short distance farther down stream the ice repeated the performance, but was more thorough, as the structure undermined
was a warehouse in which some goods were stored. The
same cake of ice that cleared out the piling received in passing the whole building and contents and the last anyone saw
of it was as it rounded the bend below the town; just a
huddle of broken and twisted timbers.

The whole story of the upper river was written on the
floes as they passed. There were piles of tin cans from some
cabin probably miles above the town. Dead dogs that had
met their end during the winter; embers of camp fires where
someone had camped on the river and built a small fire to
boil some water for tea; pieces of trails that had either followed the river or crossed it. Snowshoe tracks in the snow
on top of the ice were all that remained of some hunter's or
trapper's journey. There were great trees that had either
fallen during the winter or had been undermined by the ice
and carried away in its mad rush. There were live rabbits
that had been caught out on the ice when the run started,
while tracks of moose, wolves, lynx, marten and mink could
be plainly seen in the snow blanket on the ice. Patches of
rabbit fur or scattered grouse feathers recorded a wilderness
tragedy.

It was the great cleaning up time of the year. The rivers
are the great scavengers of the North. They clean and scour
the banks and carry away to the sea all of the winter's
accumulation of trash or carrion. In those days, with the
ice, went the shut-in feeling that the people had when the
water ceased to run. It meant that soon the steamboats
would be whistling round the bend and the necessities and
luxuries for another year would pour in. It meant the end
to their winter of discontent.

I have seen a score of breakups since that time but never
one that caused the thrill that that one gave me. One could
not help but feel the futility of human effort to oppose or
withstand the terrific forces of Nature. It was a magnificent
sight to see the endless stream of ice cakes swinging around
the bend above town, now in orderly rows, again in irregular

ranks like the retreat of an army. It was the retreat of an army; the cavalry of winter retreating before the forces of Spring.

At times the millions of tons of ice, blue and glittering, would sweep by without sound, and one had the feeling that the river was standing still and the earth and the spectators were moving. Again great masses of green anchor ice would break loose from the bottom of the river and surge half their length out of the water and then fall back with a splash. It is the anchor ice that makes traveling in small boats within a few days after a breakup so dangerous. Many a traveler has been floating along on the swift current, with no thought of danger, when, without a second's warning, some great mass of ice that had been anchored to the gravel on the bottom of the river all winter would come loose and come to the surface with a rush right beneath the boat. When that happens, the boat goes into the air and rare indeed it is that the passengers ever escape, for the water is terribly cold and the current too swift to swim and the water so impregnated with silt that in a moment the swimmer's clothes are full of sand and he sinks. Many a traveler who thought he was in a hurry and who would not take the advice of the old-timers has procured a small boat and "followed the ice," as the expression is, down the river; and many of such travelers have never again been seen or heard of. Their boats have occasionally been found, invariably bottom up. Such disasters have occasionally been witnessed, and in a few cases some of the victims have escaped.

Several friends of mine were going down the Tanana River several years ago in a launch. They waited about five or six days after the river had cleared of ice before they started. A couple of hundred miles down the river they were approaching a rather sharp bend in the river and could hear a roaring in front of them around the bend. The man who was steering noticed that the speed of the boat had materially quickened and that they were rushing toward the bend at a terrific speed. He was an old-timer in the country and a fast thinker. He turned the bow of the boat toward the shore, reversed his engine, and yelled to the others to get ready to jump ashore with a rope or to grab hold of some overhanging trees or brush. By that time the current was so swift that even the powerful motor boat could make no headway against it, but he managed to reach the shore by angling across the current. The passengers grabbed hold of some small trees and held on until the boat could be tied up and then they asked the steersman what in the devil was the matter. He told them to come with him and he would show them. He led them around the bend of the river and then they understood. The ice had jammed clear across the river and the entire current had been forced into a comparatively narrow lane of ice until it reached the jam and then the whole river dived under the ice. Had they gone another hundred yards, no power on earth could have prevented them from being sucked down under the ice and another mystery would have been added to the already long list chalked up against the northern rivers. On the Yukon River in 1900 a scow loaded with several horses and half a dozen men with their whole outfits ran into such a jam and every one of them was lost. It was witnessed by some other scow travelers, who managed by frantically manipulating their sweeps to get their barge ashore before it was taken over by the increased current. The barges had no power, but were used for going from upriver points to some downriver points and the river was the motor power, the sweeps being for steering purposes only.

Fairbanks' Great Fire

John A. Clark

AS IN THE EMERALD ISLE where everything dates from the "great wind," so in Fairbanks everything dates from the great fire in 1906, when a large part of the town was destroyed. It was and had been for several days extremely hot and dry. Sluicing of the winter dumps on the creeks had been in full blast for two weeks or more, and the "dust" was coming in to the banks in a steady stream. There were three banks in operation and the gold dust tellers were, on that particular afternoon in the latter part of May, extremely busy receiving the pokes of dust, weighing them and giving receipts therefor. The creek train arrived at about four-o'clock, and at four twenty, in all three of the banks, the operators were lined up before the teller's window awaiting their turn, each having deposited at his feet one or more pokes.

There was a three-story building on Cushman Street between First and Second Avenues, and on the second floor were offices. A lace curtain in a dentist's office, swayed by the breeze through the open window, came in contact with an open light and in ten seconds the room was ablaze. On the corner of Second and Cushman was the Washington-Alaska Bank and right across the street was the First National Bank. I, unfortunately, had chosen the Washington-Alaska Bank Building as the place for my office and had been settled there just about a month. That building was connected on the second floor with the three-story building where the fire started, there being an iron door between the two hallways, which joined at right angles. Someone came into the office and told me that there was a fire in the next building, and I went to the opening where the iron door was located and could see the smoke pouring out of the transom down the hall. Carefully closing the door, I went back into my office and told my partner and our stenographer that there was abundant evidence that we had better vacate "muy

pronto." The stenographer was sent down the stairway opening on Second Avenue, distant at least eighty feet from the
place where the fire was located. I gathered up the typewriter
that I had recently had mended, together with a bundle of
valuable papers that we had just laid out for inspection, and
stepped to the head of the stairs and started down. There I
met the flames coming up. It seems that someone opened the
iron door in escaping from the burning building and forgot
to close it. When our stenographer opened the door at the
foot of the stairs, it evidently drew the flames along the hall-
way, and the dust that had accumulated did the rest. I lost
my eyebrows, part of my hair, my typewriter, which I
dropped in order to use my hands to protect my face, the
papers which I abandoned for the same reason, and in addition was scared out of several years' growth. The fire was
roaring behind me and the only thing to do was to go down
through the fire. When I reached the bottom, the wreck of
my machine was already there. Fortunately someone opened
the door onto the street just as I arrived.

My partner had just come down from Dawson with a lot
of promissory notes given to one of our clients in Dawson
by people that had moved to Fairbanks, and when the alarm
was given, we had just opened them up and computed the
total amount at a little over $300,000. Part of these papers I
dropped and they were promptly destroyed. My partner was
to follow me with the balance. Less than ten seconds after I
left the office he attempted to follow and was met at the door
by an attorney from the building where the fire started, and
a solid sheet of flame. He pulled the other attorney in and
closed the door, opened a window and draped the other attorney over the window sill, where he could get some air, and
then poked his own head out of the window and commenced
to yell for a ladder. No ladder was available. He was an
impatient man and possessed of a varied and lurid, sul-
phurous vocabulary when really aroused. He told the whole
world what he thought of it and then centered his attention
on the absent fire department, and, when he got started on
that subject, he really did a wonderful piece of word paint-
ing, and even the paint on that side of the building where
there was not as yet any fire shriveled up and showered down
upon the sidewalk. The fire soon got into the office and then
he climbed through the window and held on with his hands
to the window sill and continued his dissertation. A ladder

was in sight by this time and he then centered upon the man who was carrying the ladder. When the ladder carrier got close enough to distinguish what was being said, he stopped and listened with awe and admiration to Tom's eloquence, for he at one time had been a "mule skinner" and appreciated a good piece of work when he heard it. By the time the ladder was shoved up where Tom could reach it, he was about all in and slid down the ladder to the street, where, when he had recovered his breath, he pronounced the benediction upon everyone in general and the ladder bearer in particular for his lack of speed. The half-fainting attorney draped over the window sill was carried down the ladder, none the worse for his adventure, except that they had to seat him firmly on the ground and rub him around a bit to extinguish the fire that had started on that portion of his trousers which would be his north exposure when he was headed south.

When Tom found that he could not get out of the office, he threw the remaining papers out of the window and one of the bystanders took them to the log jail, situated a block away, for safety. Inside of half an hour thereafter the jail burned, together with all notes and other papers. Of the total of over a quarter of a million in notes so destroyed, we afterwards collected less than two thousand dollars.

Inside of two minutes after the fire started, the whole of the building in which it had its inception was a mass of flames and the windows of the buildings across Cushman Street were crackling and falling and the buildings themselves were afire. At the First National Bank they had not as yet constructed a vault and had some iron safes for the storage of coin and dust. The employees threw as much of the dust as possible into the safes, slammed the doors, and bolted out the back way, leaving a good-sized pile of buckskin pokes of gold dust on the counter. The fire spread in every direction and the fire department centered its efforts upon preventing its spread to the power house and in this they were successful. Everything else went. The flames crossed First Avenue and soon the Lotta Talbot and the Pacific Cold Storage Company boat that had been sunk by the ice a few weeks before were on fire and burned to the water's edge. Two of the three banks were burned. The other one was saved by the fact that the building closest to it was the Court House, constructed of lumber but with sawdust-filled walls, so it did not burn rapidly. Heavy woolen blankets were hung from the cornice of the bank building and these were kept thoroughly soaked with water.

The fire burned all night and utterly destroyed the very heart of the town. One man who owned a building on Front Street, about three hundred feet east of the place where the fire started, took one look at the fire and the progress it was making and then hurried past his, as yet, unburned building and kept on going for about an eighth of a mile to a saw mill. Before his building was on fire, he had placed his order for sufficient lumber to rebuild, and at midnight that night, while the fire was raging on three sides of him, I saw teams unloading that lumber in front of his lot. At eleven-thirty that night I saw a crew of men with shovels digging trenches through the glowing embers and laying down heavy timbers for the foundation of one of the saloons and dance halls on Front Street. The floor was laid before the ashes were cold and the place was open for business inside of forty-eight hours after the fire started.

While the Washington-Alaska Bank building was still burning, the officials announced that they would open for business at the regular hours the next morning at the same old stand. They failed to live up to their agreement by thirty minutes, but at ten-thirty the next morning they had a floor laid, walls up part way with a canvas roof, rude unplaned lumber counters, and no other furniture, but they were taking in gold dust and paying out good money for it. The First National Bank across the street had erected a tent over their site and had a crew of miners at work with gold pans, panning the ashes to recover the gold that they had been unable to save the previous afternoon.

Fortunately the river was open and both of the saw mills had received a drive of logs, which were still in the water. All the sawed lumber was ordered within a few hours, and thereafter teams were in line at the mills receiving the new lumber straight from the saw, cut from green logs hauled a few moments before from the river. There were dozens of good carpenters here and the town was reconstructed with amazing speed. To be sure, the lumber, after it was in place, shrank as it dried, so that in some of the buildings there were more cracks than boards, but it was boom times with the camp and who cared?

Practically no one carried insurance, so it meant the finding of new money to build a new town. The banks furnished most of the money, as the greater part of the men whose property was destroyed had a credit with the banks. Operators on the creeks came to the relief of their business friends in town. No one was discouraged or downhearted. Even old Bill McPhee, whose new $20,000 building was destroyed by a fire in March, rebuilt in April and May, and destroyed in the latter part of May, resolutely went to work and built his third building. Assistance was offered by other Alaskan towns, but it was declined with thanks, as the people were able to take care of themselves.

As a fair example of the spirit with which the people met their losses, I well recall that of an old jeweler who lost everything but his violin. The other merchants and business men were comparatively young men and could start again, but he was well past middle age and it would be supposed that the future would look pretty black to him. My brother and I had an extra bed in the cabin where we were living, so we asked him to spend the night with us. He brought his violin and spent the early hours of the morning playing to us. He was as hopeful and buoyant of spirits as the youngest of them; rebuilt his store on borrowed money; afterwards went to Tanana, where he accumulated quite a substantial fortune before his death.

While the fire was still burning, the merchants were preparing their telegraphic orders to be sent to the Seattle wholesalers. Fortunately the fire was stopped next door to the telegraph office. Many hundreds of dollars were paid that night for telegrams.

Oddities of a Pioneer Town—
Including Dogs, Cats and Chickens

John A. Clark

THE FIRST DAY in Fairbanks was an introduction to a few peculiarities of life in the Interior. The first time I saw a water wagon I stopped and stared in amazement. It was a tank built of lumber mounted on a bobsled. It was as wide as an ordinary wagon bed, was about fifteen feet long and about two and one half feet deep, and at the rear were a couple of large faucets and a couple of five gallon oil cans converted into buckets. In the very center on top, a stove-pipe was sticking up and from it the smoke curled up lazily as the team of horses pulled it along. My curiosity got the better of me and when the team stopped and the driver got down and drew a couple of buckets of water and took them into one of the business houses, I went to the wagon and investigated. An airtight stove had been built into the tank and just the top of the stove extended above the top of the tank. An armful of wood was carried on top of the tank, and when the fire needed replenishing all the driver had to do was to lift the top off, put in more wood, open the draft on top, light his own pipe, and go merrily about his business. The water inside the tank had an opportunity to frolic around the hot stove and regardless of the temperature without, the water never froze.

The water stratum under a part of the town, especially the downtown part where the power plant was situated, is impregnated with vegetable matter and iron rust, and the water is absolutely unfit for drinking. Farther back from the river a number of wells had been dug to a depth of twenty feet and excellent water was secured. The water wagons were used to deliver the water to the business houses and to those of the residents who did not have wells of their own. The

216

charge then was and now is ten cents per five gallon can or twelve cans for a dollar. Placards were furnished by the water wagon drivers to their customers and after a few days I learned that when I saw a blue placard in a front window, reading "C 2" that meant that the driver of a wagon for the Crystal Wells was invited to leave two buckets of water that morning.

I went into one of the business houses and saw that the hinges on the door and all of the nail heads around the door and window casings were, as I thought, painted white, and that seemed rather odd until I touched one of them and found that it was frost. The temperature within the room was probably 75° above zero, but the frost was not thawed. In our home, whenever it gets real cold, every piece of metal near an opening would be covered with frost and would remain that way until the weather warmed up, regardless of the fact that the room was thoroughly heated.

And dogs! I never saw so many dogs in my life. They were everywhere; in teams scooting along the street; lying on the sidewalks, in the houses and saloons, in dog kennels behind the hotels. Huskies, malamutes, setters, and mongrels. Dogs that looked like wolves and were from a quarter to three quarters wolf. Dogs that looked like bewhiskered humans that I well knew in other climes. In fact a few months later, after the arrival of a young lady whom I had known in Stockton, California, and who, by the aid of a minister, some zealous friends, and a great waste of good rice, became related to me by marriage, we became quite well acquainted with several dogs in our neighborhood that reminded us so much of people we had both known in California that we identified them by the name of their prototype. People on the street who heard us address a dog with a "Good morning, Mr. L——" or "Good afternoon, Mrs. G——" probably thought us crazy or, as was most likely, passed it off as Cheechako ignorance. Whenever a newcomer did or said anything that outraged the Alaskan proprieties, it was excused by the half-contemptuous explanation, "Oh, he is a Cheechako and doesn't know any better." A splendid alibi and which like charity covered a multitude of sins of sheer asininity or stupidity.

If a dog was in a person's way on the street, the pedestrian walked around the dog. In any place outside of Alaska they would have kicked the dog out of the way. That changed attitude was a pretty good indication of how dogs were regarded in this country. They were useful and were respected. They performed tremendous labor. They were the sole means for traveling into the far places and without them the prospector would have been limited in his territorial peregrinations. At night they howled! And how they could make the night hideous! One dog would start "carolling softly," improvising as he went along. He perchance was telling of his experience on his last trip out of town or of his last rabbit chase. The dog next door would have a few words to say about his exciting chase of a fox, and the big malamute in the next block, not to be outdone in lying, would break in with his hoarse bass voice to lie a little about a fight that he had with a wolf early in the winter. The setter around the corner would chip in with a sonnet that he had improvised about one of his numerous love affairs, and when that started, every dog within half a mile would break in to tell the last singer what a liar he was and to threaten dire and bloody vengeance for his base slander of the perfectly "nice" lady dog that he referred to, or to tell him what he would do to the first singer for encroaching on his preserves. From clear across the river would come the howl of a huskie that wanted to sleep as he politely requested the dog that started the row to come over and have his throat cut. The lady dogs would start a conversation among themselves, telling what base, nasty brutes the other dogs were for discussing in public "us girls," and suggesting that they organize a society to snub their admirers when next they came around. It mattered not that none of the singers listened to the others, for like an afternoon tea party they were having a good time anyway, for were they not talking? The racket would keep up for half an hour or so, depending upon how interesting the topic then under individual discussion might be to those who had the floor, or rather the air, and then all at once it would die down. About that time some good-looking lady killer of a huskie would start broadcasting, trying to make a date with a lady friend for the next evening, and about that time the snubbing society would go out of business, and by the time the date was arranged forty other dogs would be on the air trying to persuade the lady that the malamute was not to be trusted and was a gay deceiver. Under cover of this racket, a measly huskie would get in touch with a number of his friends and make arrangements to meet them next day to lure a particular setter that they had in mind out into the woods where they proposed to kill him.

When matters had quieted down, some poor puppy that had been separated from its mother would commence to call aloud for comfort and companionship, and it would be answered by another class of dogs, the staid family dogs about town. Some would try to comfort the pup and others would express their opinion of the man who would break up a family before the puppy was able to take care of itself; while the mother would do her motherly best to soothe the lonesome little cuss over in the other part of town. Finally the puppy would cease his moaning and settle down for the night and all would be quiet until about the break of day, when with one accord all of the dogs within a mile would start their hymn of praise for the new day and rejoice that the night was past.

It was hard on the newcomers but after a time one became so accustomed to it that, like the sound of the street cars to the city dwellers, it was only noticeable when it had ceased.

And dog fights! They were for the most part free for all. There was nothing particularly private about any of them and like the fights on market day at Kilkenny they were open to any dog that had sufficient "intestinal stamina" to climb in. There was generally but one way to measure the size of the fight and that was by the acre. I have seen two, fifteen or twenty dog teams meet in the middle of the main street of the town and within the fraction of a second thirty or forty dogs would be one writhing mass of canine ferocity. When the row was once started, every dog within hearing would rush to the spot and jump in and start slashing right and left. Not that he had anything against any of the others, but just because it was a fight and it was free. The dog team drivers would jump into the midst of the row with their dog whips and commence trying to disentangle the dogs and harness. The overburden of volunteer fighters would first have to be eliminated by the use of loaded whips, clubs, boots, and the aid of the bystanders, and then the rest of the mess cleared up by pulling one dog at a time from the tangle. Just how it was done no one ever knew, but after a time the two teams would be pried apart, and about that time they would have decided that, as the day was still young, it would be well to go in and finish it, and they would tangle up again, and it would all have to be done over again. And what a sight it would be. Torn and broken harness, gashed bodies, split and shredded ears, and blood over everything. Sometimes under the heap would be found one or more dogs who had fought their last fight. They would be disentangled, carried to the river bank and dumped on the ice, where they would stay until the ice carried them away in the breakup in the spring. As the Vikings, the great sailors, hoped after death to start on their voyage to Valhalla in a burning ship, sailing away on their native element, so what could be more appropriate than that the dog whose services were most in demand in traveling the frozen rivers should start on his last journey with a shroud of snow and a great cake of ice as a vessel to carry him to the dogs' heaven?

Twenty years ago there were few if any house dogs in the camp and the work dogs were sufficiently furred to enable them to curl up in the snow and defy the coldest weather. With their noses covered by a thickly furred tail, they would calmly go to sleep even though the mercury was trying to crawl through the bottom of the tube. Some of the teams were as wild as wolves and many of them were almost pure wolf and as savage, so that they could not be allowed to run loose. There was but little danger to grown people, but if a child ever fell down near them, they would immediately pounce upon the child. I knew of two tragedies of that character where three children were involved.

The more I see of dogs, the more convinced I am that, take them as a whole, they fairly represent the types of the human race. There are the dignified dogs whose attitude is "no one but a gentleman could insult me and a gentleman wouldn't"; the bullies who glory in whipping the smaller dogs and who when once licked are the most arrant cowards; the gentlemanly dogs who attended to their own business and are perfectly willing that others should do the same, but who have evidently taken to heart Shakespeare's advice: "Beware of entrance into a quarrel, but being in so bear it that thy opponent may beware of thee." There are the natural-born cowards who slink through life with their tails between their legs and are ever fawning upon all with whom they come in contact, and if a quarrel is forced upon them, if they cannot escape, they lie upon their back with their legs in the air and beg for mercy. There are the dogs who grant that boon upon request and others in whom there is no pity and who would ruthlessly throttle the supplicating brute. There are the dogs, stout of heart, that look you straight in the eye and do not fawn upon anyone; who are good friends and who recognize no superiors, but are devoid of arrogance; the aristocrats of the dog world. There are the hypocrites who fawn and crouch and await but the chance to get a bite without getting caught. There are the vindictive dogs that are good haters and who never forgive another dog for a real or fancied injury; and then there are those who even though defeated will not admit that fact and keep on trying until they finally win out.

Illustrating the last two varieties, I recall a number of malamutes that belonged to a man over in the Kuskokwim district. There were six of them and for some reason they took a dislike to four other dogs that belonged to a neighbor. The malamutes realized that it would not do to go and jump the dogs they were after while with the others of the team, as they would probably get the worst of it, as there were about twenty belonging to the man who owned the four they were after. So the malamutes tried guile and diplomacy. They pretended to be friendly with the other dogs and gradually lured one that they were after out into the woods. As soon as they were out of hearing of the other dogs, they turned upon the poor deluded brute and tore him to pieces. The same tactics were used until they had lured away and killed the four they were after, and then they stopped.

A friend of mine a few weeks ago had occasion to drive to the little town of Ester, situated about three miles from the mine he was working. He took with him in his car a beautiful big malamute that he owned, and when he reached the town tied the dog to the front wheel while he went into the store. Soon he heard a great racket and ran out and found that the town bully, a dog almost twice the size of his dog, had attacked the malamute, which, being hampered by being tied, was getting the worst of it. When they were separated, the dog was put in the car and they went back to the mine. The next day the dog was missing and didn't show up until evening and he seemed rather tired. When next my friend had to go to Ester, he heard the end of the story. His dog came back the three miles from the mine the day after the first fight, lay around the store all day waiting for the big bully to show up, and when he did come the malamute gave him the first real licking he had ever received. After the fight was over and the bully had been chased all over town and finally into his own yard, the malamute came back to the store, where he begged for a drink, and then with his tail up started up the mountain to the mine. On subsequent visits to the town he was never molested.

In the town of Iditared the dogs of a certain class organized a minutemen's club and were always ready for business. One day a collie was accosted by a dog that seemed to be a cross between a St. Bernard and a railroad locomotive, and the latter took the collie by the neck and, after shaking him thoroughly, threw him under a sidewalk. When the collie came to, he ran home and in five minutes came back with five of his friends, and it took six men to save the life of the aggressor.

Within the last couple of weeks (January 1927) the intelligence and usefulness of the dog have been abundantly demonstrated. A quartz mine, in which ex-Governor Sulzer of New York is heavily interested, is situated in the Chandalar, more than a hundred miles north of the Yukon River. Until about a month ago there was no telegraph or wireless in that country and it took a letter all the way from three weeks to a month to reach Fairbanks. A small wireless station was finally installed by the government and within a week its usefulness was demonstrated. Two men had been down to the telegraph or wireless station on business and upon starting back to the mine borrowed a dog from the operator, presumably to pack some provisions. Upon the return to the mines, distant about thirty or forty miles from the wireless station, they tied up the dog and were experimenting with some fuse, not realizing that an open box of detonating caps was on the table. An explosion ensued, and the men were blinded by the explosion and their bodies from the waist up were riddled with pieces of the caps. There was no way of getting word to the station, as there was no telephone, and they were alone and no one was likely to come that way for months. They were badly wounded and there was no doctor available short of Fairbanks. One of them thought of the dog. He managed, blinded as he was, to scrawl some sort of a note to the wireless operator, fastened it to the dog's collar, and turned it loose and ordered it to go home. It was all they could do. He could not see, so did not know what the dog had done. The only thing they could do was to give themselves such care as was possible and then wait. The dog went straight home, the operator found the note, sent a dog team for the men, and wirelessed to Fairbanks for an airplane to come and get them. It was the time of the short days, only about four hours of daylight, and a flight of over three hundred miles to make. The weather was stormy and the plane had to wait a few days to catch a clear day. When he started he reached Beaver on the Yukon, was again delayed by storms, and finally was able to cross the range to the Chandalar station, where he again had to wait until the weather was favorable before starting home. It was 40° below zero. One of the men weighed almost 300 pounds and how both men were squeezed into the plane compartment no one knows. They returned to Beaver, were again delayed, but finally reached Fairbanks more than two weeks after they had been injured. One man had one eye removed and will probably be able to use the other. The second man does not know whether or not he will ever regain the sight of either eye. If the dog had not been there, it would have meant a slow death to both of them, for it would have been impossible for them to travel back to the station blinded as they were.

That country is infested with the great black timber wolf and if the dog had met one of them, it would have been the end of the story. This last summer four dogs belonging to the Alaska Road Commission left the road camp on the upper Chatanika River for a rabbit hunt. A number of the big grey wolves had been seen near the camp. The dogs never came back and no one has any question as to their fate.

When I was a boy in school in California, I was taught and firmly believed that the "sun rose in the east and set in the west." When I came to Alaska, I had to unlearn all of that hard-won knowledge and now, speaking from twenty-one years' observation, would state that the sun rises any place from due north to a point just a trifle east of south and that it sets at any place from the location of Mt. McKinley in the south clear around the western horizon to due north, and that sometimes it forgets to set at all. When Frank W. Carpenter was in Fairbanks about 1910 he stated that he would have to revise some of his geographies that he had written and had introduced in the schools all over the States. The sun having set a bad example of contradicting the geographies and common knowledge, the moon follows its example and performs in the same manner as the sun but at opposite seasons. In summer the sun gets up in the north, wanders clear around the whole horizon, and dips behind the hills to the north for a few minutes just before midnight, and a few minutes later comes up a short distance to the east and starts another pilgrimage. The moon on the contrary, during the summer months is not in evidence, but when it does put in an appearance, it is away down in the south and only shows for a few hours and even then is scarcely discernible. In wintertime the sun is in the south, on the shortest day being above the horizon only about three hours, and the moon then has her innings and "struts her stuff" through the same orbit traced by the sun in the summertime. Working opposite shifts, they do not get their wires crossed and as a consequence we never have any of the black darkness of southern climes. After the snow comes, either the stars or the moon with the great mass of snow keeps the nights from being very dark. In the summertime there is nothing but daylight and the clock tells us when to go to bed and the alarm portion of that mechanical pest terminates the time of rest.

The life of the chickens (the feathered, egg-laying variety) is a hard one. In summertime, unless cooped up in a darkened chicken house at the proper time, they would cluck around for twenty four hours per day until they died of weariness or lack of sleep. In winter they would sleep their fool heads off unless their houses were lighted with electric lights, so they would know when to get off of their roosts. All chicken houses are thoroughly heated and at stated hours the lights are turned on and off.

In the early days here fresh eggs were selling at $5.00 per dozen, and through the years as the number of chicken raisers has increased, the prices have come down so that now they are from $1.00 to $1.50 per dozen.

House cats are at a disadvantage in wintertime, as their ears are entirely unprotected by fur of any kind and if one of them gets shut out for a few minutes when the weather is 40° or 50° below zero, its ears are frozen stiff and as a consequence it loses those very useful appendages. There are several cats around town entirely devoid of ears.

For several years I marveled at the great numbers of chickadees that wintered here. Whenever the weather moderated they would be flying about in flocks of from fifty to several hundred, and I wondered where they went during the extremely cold weather. It seemed that their extremely frail legs would freeze. One spring I happened to pass a great clump of lambs quarters just as the snow was melting and I could see dozens of little trails around the stalks of the weeds and great quantities of feathers. The weeds grow in extremely close order and generally to a height of five and six feet, and on every stalk are thousands of seeds. When the snow comes they bend down with the weight of it and standing so close together they form a sort of roof. The birds find a way to get into this very effective shelter and there have their food and protection from the cold. When it warms up, they come out and feed on the tiny seeds on the birch trees. These tiny birds and the ravens and camp robbers are the only winter birds we see except for the grouse.

Even the grouse have to find shelter during the terribly cold spells. The snow when it falls is as fine as flour and doesn't crust. After a fresh fall of snow when an auto runs along the street, it leaves a small cloud of snow dust behind it just as a dust is kicked up on a dirt road in summer. When a cold spell is coming on, a grouse will start from some height and fly with great speed at a snow bank, and as a consequence will be completely buried a foot or two beneath the surface. When it warms up, it digs itself out some way and goes about its business. One spring there came a chinook wind and thaw right after a very cold spell, and then it froze solid. This formed a crust on the top of the snow and hundreds of grouse were trapped and starved to death, their fate not being known until the spring thaw when their frozen bodies were exposed.

The powdery nature of the snow is what has probably preserved the moose of the country and permitted them to multiply so fast. If the snow crusted, the wolves could overtake them, as they would break through the crust and the wolves stay on top. But in the loose snow the moose can outrun the wolves. In the summertime the moose can always reach a lake or other body of water where he can fight off the wolves, but in the late winter when he has lost his horns or when the snow is very deep is his time of danger. Hunters have frequently told me of finding the moose "yards" where they have, in times of extremely heavy snow, tramped down a great area of snow so as to be able to fight unhampered by snow if attacked. One man told me of stumbling into one of those "yards" while hunting grouse with a 22 caliber rifle. He was on snowshoes and the snow was six or eight feet deep. He found several trails leading to the "yard" and found seven moose there together ready for all comers. He took a good look and as they gave no evidence of intending to vacate he decided that he would not argue the matter but departed. They had evidently been driven in by wolves, as one of them had a gash on its hip, from which the blood was still dripping.

The Alaskan Bears and Other Interesting Characters

John A. Clark

HUMAN NATURE IS the same in Alaska as elsewhere, save and except that environment and circumstance, in some cases, cause men to do strange things. A hunter and prospector on the lower Yukon River developed certain queer traits, or rather I should say human nature caused these traits to be evidenced by rather peculiar actions. Two brothers were living together, and one day they went up on a high mountain, a few miles from camp, in search of sheep. They killed two, and the brother in question dressed his animal and started down the mountain with the sheep on his back. The going was bad and the trail practically nonexistent. As he rounded a great rock on the side of the mountain, his eyes were upon the trail rather than upon the lookout for danger. The first intimation that anything was amiss was when a large glacier bear sprang upon him, evidently taking him for a sheep by reason of his burden. He dropped the sheep and sprang back and brought his rifle into action with his right hand, the left shoulder having been crippled by the first blow of the bear's paw. One shot was all he could get, for the bear was again upon him, as his shot had not been fatal. Retreat was impossible and the issue was to be settled between the two, he having nothing but a hunting knife and the bear possessing the usual raiment and allotted supply of fangs and claws. The mountain was steep and very rocky, and the two of them, locked in an embrace that could only be broken by the death of one of them, went rolling and bumping down the mountain side, ending in a sheer fall of several score of feet onto the rocks at the bottom. The other brother, hearing the shot, dropped his burden and hurried forward, but was too late to be of any assistance. He fol-

227

lowed the bloody trail down the mountain to the rock heap at the bottom, where he found his brother on top of the bear, still clasped in its arms, and both a mass of blood. The bear was dead and he thought his brother was also, as it did not appear that any human being could be so terribly mutilated and still live. However, he packed his brother to their cabin a couple of miles away and there did what he could to revive the injured man when he found that he was still alive. Both arms were broken and almost stripped of all flesh. One shoulder had been crushed in the bear's jaws. The scalp was practically torn from the head and the breast bone was laid bare, and one leg was broken. In addition he was a mass of cuts and bruises, and his face was practically obliterated. They were hundreds of miles from a doctor, and his brother was in no condition to be carried, even in a boat, to where he could receive the necessary medical attention. Blood poisoning developed, and for many days it looked as if the injured man would die. Finally a steamboat came along, and the patient was taken aboard and taken to a hospital at St. Michael, where he hovered between life and death for almost a year. Later he was sent out to the States and remained in a hospital there for more than a year before he was able to travel about. Youth and an iron constitution pulled him through, and when he was discharged he headed back to the North, to the place where he was injured. Since that time he has devoted his life to the killing of bears, and the last that I heard of him, a couple of years ago, was to the effect that he had killed almost seventy up to that time and that he was still going strong.

A Russian trapper, living down on the flats below Nenana, was cooking his dinner one evening in the late fall, and as he had a small cabin of but one room he opened the door a trifle for ventilation. The door swung inward, and as it was pretty cold he opened it but a few inches. In a few minutes the door swung open several feet. He was standing at his stove right near the door and merely reached around with his left hand and partially closed the door, leaving an opening of but an inch or two in width. He had no sooner turned around to the stove than the door again opened, and he again reached around to close it. This time before he let go of the door he felt it pushed in again, and then he turned around to investigate and through the partially opened door he observed what appeared to him to be a mountain-sized brown bear. It was sitting on its haunches and was evidently desirous of further investigating the savory odors that emanated from a skillet full of moose steaks on the stove. Not having invited the bear to share the meal with him, the Russian was somewhat peeved and attempted to completely close the door. This evidently was not entirely satisfactory to the bear, so he exerted a trifle more force on the door, and it flew open and nearly upset the trapper. He retaliated by attempting to slam the door in the bear's face. The bear blocked this and with a growl attempted to put his good right arm clear through the door. This made the Russian mad, as he had put in a great deal of time in fashioning that particular door, and besides he could smell his moose steaks burning on the stove. He paused in the game of battledore and shuttlecock long enough to reach over to the stove where he espied the poker and abandoning his attempt to shut out the cold night air—and the bear—he went into action with the poker and his first blow landed on the bear's nose. The bear, for a moment diverted, forgot to push on the door, and the trapper slammed it shut and dropped the bar across the door and then had time to reach for his rifle. He had a lamp sitting on a table by the window just back of the stove, and almost immediately the bear's face appeared at the window. The bear's hide the next spring brought fifteen dollars—total cost to the trapper, one cartridge, one small hole in a window pane, and two burned moose steaks.

A friend of mine in the same neighborhood had a somewhat similar experience. During the night he heard a noise outside his door and got up to investigate. It was a bright moonlight night, and as he opened the door, there, entirely blocking the doorway, was a big brown bear that was so busily engaged in investigating the bottom of a three-gallon dog feed bucket that sat beside the door that he did not hear the door open. He had pushed the bucket so far ahead that his head was actually past the corner of the building and therefore was not available as a target. Knowing that a brown bear at close quarters is a rather disagreeable customer and that it takes a lot of lead to kill it with body shots, my friend decided that, before he did any shooting, he wanted to see that bear's head. He therefore did the most natural and obvious thing and that was to kick the bear in the ribs with his bare foot. His enthusiasm was better than his judgment, as he nearly cracked his toes, but the results so far as the bear was concerned were eminently satisfactory.

It is rather interesting to talk to the trappers and others who spend most of their time in the wilderness, for they become philosophers and also close students of animal life. They attribute almost human qualities to certain animals and treat them according to their judgment of the animal's temper and disposition. A few days ago I was talking to a trapper and he was telling about the different bears with which he was personally acquainted. It was as real to him as his acquaintance with human beings. He spoke quite affectionately of one black she-bear that for two or three seasons lived near his camp. He stated that, when he first saw her, he was hanging up a caribou that he had just brought into camp. He looked around and there, a couple of rods away, was Madam Bear with two small cubs. "I could tell from her face that she was friendly and naturally kind," he stated. So he gathered up the scraps, walked part way over to where she was and laid them down and then went on with his work while she and the cubs dined. Not having a dog with him at that time, it being in the summer, he thereafter saved all of his cooking scraps and put them out for his adopted family. He could go within a few feet of her and she didn't even growl, so his judgment of her disposition seems to have been good.

Not so with a big black bear that came to visit him one day. As he tells it, "The minute I set eyes on that bear I knew that he was a trouble maker and was mean, so I took my shot gun and blazed away at the end of his nose." As the bear was twenty or thirty yards away, the only result of the shot appeared to be that the bear got the impression that he was not wanted around there, so departed in haste.

A prospector over Kantishna way had considerable trouble by reason of the fact that the black bears always raided his caches and packed off the greater part of his provisions. He put his cache up on stilts, and still they raided it. One time he was going away for a couple of weeks and wanted something to eat available when he returned, so he decided to outwit the bears. He selected a good-sized birch tree, and after placing his provisions in a stout canvas bag, around which he wrapped a waterproof sheet, he tied a rope to the top of the bag and then climbed the tree until it bent over with him and the top almost reached the ground. He tied the rope securely to the top part of the tree and then let go. The tree jerked the sack of provisions off of the ground and left it suspended about fifteen feet from the ground and about five feet from the trunk of the tree. Thoroughly satisfied with his masterly strategy, he departed. He returned in due time. The tree was there, the rope was there, but the tree was upright, and on the end of the rope were the remnants of the canvas bag. On the ground was a part of the bag, the rubber sheet, and the tarred rope that had formerly graced one end of a slab of bacon. As for the provisions, they had disappeared, having in all probability departed within a safer container than they had theretofore occupied. A postmortem showed that the bear had climbed the tree until he was about even with the suspended bag and had then practised punching (and puncturing) the bag with his trusty right paw. When the bag was empty he descended, and he and the provisions departed in company.

Another friend of mine was coming down the White River on a raft, and a few miles before he reached the Yukon, as he was rounding a bend, he heard a great commotion on the right bank, so he ran the raft onto the edge of a bar, grabbed his rifle, and went ashore to investigate. A narrow gravel spit, backed by an abrupt cliff, ran down to the water. The spit at the widest place was not over fifty yards in width, and about half way between the water and the base of the cliff was an immense black bear, and between the bear and the cliff was a cow moose with her calf. When she tried to escape by water, the bear would head her off. The cliff was too steep for her to scale, with or without the calf. The fight had evidently been going on for a long time, for the calf was completely tired out and was lying down between its mother and the cliff, and the bear was keeping the mother going all of the time. She was panting and about ready to go down when my friend shot the bear. It was in the act of rushing her and fell within ten feet of her. The instant the bear fell, the moose lay down panting. The hunter proceeded to skin the bear, and the moose made no attempt to move. Once he turned and patted her on the head and then went on with his work. When the hide had been removed from the bear, he packed it down to the raft, put it aboard, and resumed his journey, leaving the mother and calf to rest up and hunt more peaceful surroundings.

One fall, while on a hunting trip to the Big Chena Hot

Springs, a party of us started for a camp in good moose country, where a tent had been pitched and a stove and cooking utensils installed early in the summer. It was snowing, and we were thankful that we had a tent for shelter that night. When we reached the tent about dark, we found that a bear had visited it during the summer. He had evidently entered by the front door, for the front of the tent was a mass of canvas ribbons as he had dispensed with the formality of untying the string that held the flaps together and with one swipe of his paw had created a new entrance. Once in he tried his prowess on the opposite end of the tent, with excellent results. Finding himself outside, he went around to the side and did some more experimenting, for that side of the tent looked as if it had been sent to the laundry, and it was quite evident from all signs that when he once found himself again inside the tent he kept right on going through the opposite wall. He was evidently not a French bear as he unquestionably believed in plenty of ventilation. In fact he had carried his fad to extremes. It was quite apparent that it was warm weather when he paid his visit, for he had evidently believed that a stove was superfluous and he had done his bear's best to put it out of commission by stepping on it. Fortunately he had overlooked the tent roof, for it was intact, and we spent the night blowing the snow off of our pillows as it drifted in through the walls.

The black bears are harmless unless cornered or unless they think their cubs are in danger, although they will rob a cache if they get the chance. The brown bears are much the same. The glacier bears have mean dispositions and a dirty-white-colored coat. The grizzly bears are the lords of creation and have practically no sense of humor. I haven't lost any and therefore do not hunt them.

They evidently consider themselves direct descendants of the F.F.A.'s, and when you meet one on a trail, if you are courteous you will concede their blue blood and right of preference; also their right of way, and in fact their right to an unobstructed view of the surrounding landscape. If you are an obstructionist or belong to some "independent bloc" and have the temerity to join issue with them, you should be sure you have a good gun, a good nerve, that you are a good shot, and that you have kept up the premiums on your insurance policies. They would make excellent Marines as they are "always ready" and are fighting fools. Bullets in their carcass act as a stimulus unless perchance the brain or backbone is punctured. I know of one case where twelve high power rifle bullets planted in the chest and sides failed to stop a charging bear. He traveled almost two hundred yards from the time he was first knocked down, and was only ready to stop when he received a brain shot at ten feet from the hunter.

I know of another instance where the hunter came upon the bear when it was asleep with its back to the hunter. At twenty feet he planted a bullet between the bear's shoulders from the back, and the bullet, having a soft nose, tore a tremendous hole through the bear, barely missing the backbone, tearing the liver to pieces, and spreading pieces all over the hillside. A second after this shot, the bear was on its feet charging up hill and was stopped virtually at the end of the rifle barrel by a shot in the mouth that blew off the top of his head.

As stated before, I haven't lost any grizzly bears.

Speaking of bears reminds me of one of the most succinct and damning analyses of character that I have ever heard. I was trying a case in court and brought in a witness to prove the character or lack of character of the principal actor on the other side of the case. This happened before the days of prohibition. My witness had been doing a little quiet celebrating the night before and had, to a well-developed extent, that feeling that has been so aptly described as "the morning after the night before," and he was rather ugly. When I asked him the usual conventional question as to whether or not he was acquainted with the general reputation of the man in question for truth and veracity, he asserted, in no uncertain manner, that he was. He was then asked, "Is it good or bad?", and his answer was: "Say, mister, he is the kind of a man that would sell a bear in its hole or moose on the hoof." The "dignity" of the Court was for a short time non-existent, and the witness was excused without cross-examination by my opponent. The jury, being men of intelligence, decided the case in favor of my client.

The same character witness referred to above was, and still is, one of the characters of the North. Without much education, but shrewd withal, he amassed a very considerable fortune running a road house and catering to the thirst of the miners, and from the sale of an interest he had in one of the claims on one of the best-producing creeks in the camp. When he had cleaned up, he came into my office to tell me that he was on his way to another new camp, a couple of hundred miles down the river, and explained that he was going into the mining game in earnest. He exhibited $52,000 that he expected to cause to grow in much the same manner as Jonah's gourd or a California pumpkin. Why it is that a man who knows nothing about mining is always convinced that he will be a great success in that line of endeavor is one of the unsolved mysteries of every mining camp. He was determined not to have his light hidden under a bushel or any other obstruction or receptacle. He was not going to be any gem "of purest ray serene" in the "unfathomed caves of ocean." In other words, he was going to "show 'em." He did. He showed his money, and in a few weeks he had a flock of mining claims, above and below discovery, on the main creek and its tributaries. He owned the ground, but the great distributor of gold had neglected to mix any of it in with the gravel, sand, silt, and other dense substances to make up the overburden above bedrock. He had acquired "water rights" which would enable him to extract the non-existent precious metal. He also acquired with the water rights a full-grown lawsuit, which had been thrown in by the vendor, who, being a modest and retiring individual, much given to good works, failed to mention it. Having reached the dangerous forties, he acquired a wife, and the danger overtook him. The lady saw him first, then his bank roll, and then the two of them saw the U. S. Commissioner, who possesses, among other powers, the right to consummate such romances. The happy pair repaired to the creek where the "claims" were located. He commenced to mine. He went broke with neatness and dispatch. His wife died, and he hired a hall for the funeral; he retained a minister to do it right, and the minister, not being able to find anything good to say of the deceased's past and being very fearful of the future, preached a sermon that lasted an hour and twenty minutes. I know, for I timed him.

A few years later he managed to get in on a lay that netted him about $20,000. He "married another," as they used to sing in *Two Little Girls in Blue*, so popular in my youth. The new stake and the wife came together and together departed; elapsed time, about seven months. He had in the meantime visited another new camp where he attempted to introduce some new ideas in mining and to infuse the "go get 'em" spirit into the populace. His infusion was successful and potent, and they sold him all of the worthless claims in the camp. He is now cutting wood on the river, where they use principally oil burners.

His case is but one of scores of like nature. When I first arrived in Fairbanks, one of the sights of the camp was a tall, rugged, but rather oldish, man who was never seen on the streets except accompanied by his mule. At one time, less than ten years before, he took more than a million dollars out of one claim in the Dawson country, and in 1906 his sole possession on earth, outside of the clothes he wore, was one lop-eared brown mule.

Another man I knew, a Russian I believe, had been "grub-staked" by twenty of his countrymen in New York or Pennsylvania. He was to receive something like twenty per cent of whatever he made, and the balance was to go to his backers, who were all poor laboring men like himself. Fortune or luck was with him, as is so often the case with those who know least how to spend money after they get it. He cleared up something like $400,000, and then conceived the idea that it would be an economic crime (he didn't call it that, however, as he would not have known what that meant) to give any part of that sum to his friends at home, as it might lead them into cultivating some bad habits or cause them to become extravagant, so he decided to keep it all. He was a great admirer of "wine, women, and song," but evidently there was something wrong somewhere, for the only song he knew was the Russian national anthem and no one here seemed to know how to sing it. His countrymen who knew of the conditions under which he came to the country gave him the cold shoulder, but other of his "friends" did not. On the contrary. Two years later a mine foreman took pity on the great hulking Russian, who was clothed in rags and looked hungry, and gave him a job using a shovel in the drift in one of the mines here. A few weeks previous one of the trinity mentioned above returned to Paris to spend her remaining days in luxury. One of our citizens, who, from patriotic motives, spent a considerable time in France a few years back, was spending a few days in Paris, and he met the former resident of Fairbanks, who took pride in a magnificent "house" she had in not the least known portion of the city. She was very hospitable. Who was it who said that "time is fleeting"? He meant money.

My wife has often remarked that the Lord is very careless in the distribution of wealth. That is well exemplified in any mining camp, for it generally happens that those who acquire the largest stakes are those upon whom money is wasted, as they have no capacity for the enjoyment of wealth and no knowledge as to how to spend it. Their conception of having a good time was to come to town and have a real good drunk and see how much they could spend in a single night. I once chanced to hear two Scandinavians who were "on the pay" discussing their last trip to town. One of them stated that he had dropped about eight hundred and fifty in one night in the saloons and elsewhere in the town. The other classed him as a piker.

I do not know whether or not the expression "gaudy and Swede-like" originated in Alaska, but it might well have done so. To those who may not be versed in the nomenclature of a northern mining camp, it refers to gaudy clothes, shiny shoes, and a great nugget chain, much resembling a log cabin, strung from east to west across the intermediate portion of the human frame. As a finishing touch, there is generally a very large diamond worn in a very conspicuous place on the bosom of a woolen shirt. As an accompaniment to this tasty outfit, there is generally in evidence a broad gold ring on one or both hands. The ring is generally surmounted by a miniature windlass with a gold pan and crossed pick and shovel in the middle, and, if the wearer is of the elite, a very large diamond is very noticeable among the emblems of toil and honest effort that adorn the ring.

Many years ago, the date not being at all important, there lived in a small town in Colorado a very large, aggressive young man of Irish parentage, who, for the purpose of this record, will be called Tim. About the time that the Klondike stampede was getting good, Tim, the lad in question, decided that the mining camps of the North offered a suitable field for the betterment of his fortunes. The distance was great, fares high, cash non-existent, but determination strong. In all of the books written for boys when I was a youth, the hero found a way or a miracle happened by which he was enabled to climb to the very top of the ladder without sanding his shoes and regardless of how greasy the ladder was. But truth in this case was stranger than fiction. One day young Tim hired a team of horses and a spring wagon to drive to some place in the neighborhood and blithely started on his journey, never, of course, for one moment realizing that that day he was to behold a miracle. When he got out on the road, which ran in a general westerly direction (the team was hired to drive easterly), much to his amazement he found that the team and wagon were also determined to go to the Klondike; this manifestation of the supernatural had such an over-powering effect upon his mind and will that he was unable to think coherently until the team, still attached to the faithful spring wagon, reached Seattle. He then discovered that the faithful, fortune hunting horses had worn out their shoes, and as he had no money to pay for having them re-shod and as he could not dream of driving back to Colorado in that condition, he sold the team and wagon and thus plucked the fruits of the miracle. A steamer being on the point of sailing for Skagway—what was more natural than that he should purchase a ticket to the gateway to the then best-known gold field, for who was he to scorn that which the Gods had sent?

The Royal Northwest Mounted Police were quite active in the new gold fields, and the Alaska line was but a couple of score miles down the Yukon from Dawson. Law in Alaska was at that time "sketchy"—the administration thereof more so—and one who pined not for the "new freedom" but a continuation of the old generally sought the great open spaces below the line. Tim was not only youthful but cautious, so he too crossed the line and determined to grow up with the country.

When Fairbanks was still in swaddling clothes, and the new arrivals were nursing its growth with ax, hammer, and spade, we find our hero comfortably domiciled in a well-built log cabin (not too far from a saloon), with an Alaskan aborigine for a wife and with several half-breed children as proof thereof. Gone was the slimness of adolescence and in place thereof adipose tissue made of his mighty frame a thing of curves of size if not of beauty.

His brawn and sense of humor made many friends for him, especially in the days when about every third place of business was a place where liquid refreshment might be had at 25¢ per, and in the course of time he was elected to the City Council, which office he held for many years. His cohorts, to use a political expression much in vogue then and not quite obsolete now, were well organized, and at election time, while there would be six others running for office, his friends, with a singleness of purpose that could not be excelled even in the politically pure states of Pennsylvania and Illinois, voted a "plunker" for Tim alone.

To a certain class he was a demigod—also a monthly visitor. About the first of each month he would make a trifling loan of five or fifteen dollars from each of the residents and habitués of a certain section of the town. The lily of the field had no advantage over him when it came to toiling and spinning, for with a docile wife to do the work and plenty of friends who were perfectly willing to relieve his financial embarrassment once a month, why should he perform work that might just as well be performed by a more friendless one? Besides that, what was the use of being on the town police committee if there was nothing to be made out of it? He was, as can readily be seen, a second Abou Ben Adhem, and like Abou Ben, at election time his name "led all the rest."

Tempus fugited, as it is wont to do, and Congress in its infinite wisdom gave to Alaska the power to elect a Legislature with power and authority to meet at Juneau and, as one applicant for citizenship expressed it while being examined in open court as to his qualifications, "try to make laws." Tim conceived the idea that he would like to sit in the seats of the mighty, even though the law had caught up with him by reason of a felonious slip made here in Fairbanks, and he had served a year in the Federal penitentiary before the Circuit Court discovered that some evidence of guilt had been admitted at the trial of the case that didn't properly belong and sent his case back for a new trial (resulting in acquittal). He was elected and served in one of the Legislatures and missed re-election by less than a score of votes.

In the early days of the camp a school house was erected in a hurry, and after a few years it was found to be too small to accommodate the increased number of children, and it was also a menace. The subject of a new school house was discussed, and someone interviewed Tim, who was then on the City Council, as to his attitude. He wasn't impressed with the need of a new building, and when he was urged to provide a safer building, as the old one was a firetrap, he stated that he had no fear on that score, as he would guarantee that, if the building caught fire, his "redskins would escape."

Years afterwards, when a new building had been erected, a high school established, and a principal in charge, some of his "redskins" were still in attendance in some of the grades.

It is quite evident that the natives of Alaska are not descendants of the Romans or kindred peoples whose flair was the erection and use of baths. In fact, they appear to be hereditary enemies of the idea itself. One of the teachers, under whose charge had been placed some of Tim's progeny, went to the principal and complained, as she was unable to get any of the other pupils to sit within olfactory range of young Tim. The principal, being very conscientious and very bashful, decided that his duty required that he call upon the parents of the noisome offense and request that some action be taken to abate the nuisance. He went at an hour when it was quite probable (purely a coincidence, however) that Tim would not be at home and the mother would be. When he reached the house and knocked, he heard a bellow that invited him in. Tim was at home. He stands about six feet two and weighs about two hundred seventy five, and to the principal looked bigger than a house. He asked for the mother and found that she was out, and Tim wanted to know what he wanted. The principal, being diffident and prudent, didn't care to state and stood on one foot and twisted the other around the one still on the floor until finally he was compelled to blurt out the truth; not, however, until he had outlined his line of retreat. No explosion occurred, however, and all Tim had to say was: "Huh! I *thought* the little son of a b- - - - had been stinking pretty bad lately."

Another of the residents of the town was married to a native, and his wife developed a very strong liking for a beverage that was very popular in pre-Volstead days, and as a consequence she neglected her household duties and otherwise made a nuisance of herself. Her lord and master, knowing Tim to be well versed in the management, control, and subjugation of the natives, consulted him to what he should do to break her of her habits of conviviality. Tim's advice was concise and to the point: "Whale hell out of her." His friend was shocked and remonstrated that "no gentleman would beat his wife." Tim's answer was: "Oh hell, no gentleman would marry a squaw."

While on the subject of wife beating, which pastime was not as prevalent as might appear from these tales, I am reminded of an incident in the city magistrate's court. About twenty years ago the city magistrate was a pompous individual, noted for his flowery language and his brutality to his wife, it being currently reported that he frequently treated her for imaginary offenses by the "laying on of hands." One day a prisoner was brought before him, charged with striking his wife with an ax. He explained that it was purely a disciplinary measure, etc. The justice was horrified and started to give him a lecture as to the heinousness of his offense, and declaimed in an oratorical manner that "no gentleman would beat his wife," when he chanced to catch the eye of a friend of his who was present and who, he knew, had knowledge of the methods used by the judge to maintain his supremacy under his own roof. The judge hastily amended his pronouncement by adding, "with an ax."

The "judge," as he was commonly called (being from Georgia, suh), furnished a perfect example of one who is able to strut sitting down. He dearly loved an opportunity to talk in public and while in action resembled a pouter pigeon. His conceit and admiration for himself were colossal, and he would rather have people condemning him in a most wholehearted manner than have nothing said about him. He established a custom, which, however, did not become universal, of making his afternoon New Year's calls dressed in evening clothes.

Hailing from the land where mint juleps flourished, he sought to bring into the cold of the North some of the brightness and warmth of the sunny South by patronizing the drink emporiums where the best juleps were concocted, and frequently when he went home at a late hour he was so filled with the julep spirit (perhaps it should be plural) that his wife remonstrated with him for living too much in the past. Perhaps these remonstrances were construed by the fiery Southerner as a reflection upon the land of his nativity and perhaps that was the reason for his working over of his wife. The night there was to be a ladies' night at the Tanana Club for some reason he was unable to go, but his wife was going. When she was ready to leave, she asked him how he would like it if she went out at night and came home drunk and his answer was: "Mah deah, I would show you how a gentleman should be treated."

Acknowledgments

The final manuscript was typed through the service of the Faculty Development Program of Baldwin-Wallace College, Berea, Ohio.

ABOUT THE AUTHOR

HERBERT L. HELLER is Associate Professor of Education at Baldwin-Wallace College in Berea, Ohio. He was born in Indiana but during his college years, and for many years thereafter, he lived in Alaska, and it made an indelible impression upon him. Through the vivid, first-hand knowledge of his uncle, Lynn Smith, and his own rich experiences, he came to know the country well. SOURDOUGH SAGAS is his first book on Alaska. Another is currently in preparation.

Among his other works are THE STORY OF INDIANA, and READINGS IN THE HISTORY OF NEW CASTLE, INDIANA.

GLACIER PILOT

Beth Day

The story of "Mr. Alaska," Bob Reeves, and of the rugged breed of bush-pilots who pioneered and conquered the Alaska skies in their single-engine planes.

$1.65

A COMSTOCK EDITION

TWO IN THE FAR NORTH

Margaret E. Murie

When Margaret Murie went to Alaska by sternwheel steamer in 1912, Fairbanks was a raw, new town, a fan-shape of rough buildings and low log cabins stretching into a cold and lonely wilderness. Later she explored that wilderness with her husband, biologist Olaus Murie, and the stark land became friend and ally in a lifetime of discovery. TWO IN THE FAR NORTH is a warm personal account of their adventures spanning four decades in the vast, rich northern frontier.

"Wilderness and grandeur captured in an unusually graphic, sensitive, interesting and enjoyable work."
—*The New Yorker*

$1.25

A COMSTOCK EDITION

To order by mail, send price of book plus 25¢ per order for handling to Ballantine Cash Sales, P.O. Box 505, Westminster, Maryland 21175. Please allow three weeks for delivery.